MORE PALEO RECIPES FOR PEOPLE WHO LOVE TO EAT

BY MELISSA JOULWAN
Photos by David Humphreys
Foreword by Melissa and Dallas Hartwig
Design by Braid Creative

WELL FED 2: MORE PALEO RECIPES FOR PEOPLE WHO LOVE TO EAT

WELL FED 2: MORE PALEO RECIPES FOR PEOPLE WHO LOVE TO EAT

Author: Melissa Joulwan
Foreword: Melissa and Dallas Hartwig
Copy Editing: Walker Fenz, Alison Finney
Proofreading: Walker Fenz
Photography: David Humphreys
Illustrations: David Humphreys
Design: Braid Creative

ISBN 10: 0989487504
ISBN 13: 978-0989487504

Published by:
Smudge Publishing, LLC
405 El Paso Street
Austin, TX 78704
www.smudgepublishing.com

1st printing, October 2013

TO MY PARENTS WHO TAUGHT ME THAT THE KITCHEN IS THE HEART OF THE HOUSE

AND TO MY HUSBAND DAVE, MY PARTNER IN COOKING UP DELICIOUS SCHEMES

THANK YOU

TO MY INTREPID AND HONEST TASTE-TESTERS
Stacey Doyle, Blake Howard, Weston Norton, Yoni Levin, Tannen Campbell, and Aimee Roberge for taking a bite and weighing in.

TO TANNEN CAMPBELL
for letting us raid your cabinets (again!) for plates, bowls, and linens that prove you have far better taste than we do.

TO STEFANIE DISTEFANO
for providing much-needed enthusiasm, beautiful pottery, photography locations, and on-demand taste-testing.

TO ALISON FINNEY AND WALKER FENZ
for unflagging enthusiasm and down-to-the-last-detail copyediting. You make us look much smarter than we are.

TO MICHELLE TAM AND HENRY FONG
for your unfailing generosity and friendship – and for helping us shut down just about every restaurant we visit.

TO MELISSA AND DALLAS HARTWIG
for continuing to show us how to live well and savor every bite on our plates.

TO ADDIE BROYLES
for breakfast tacos (*sans* tortillas, of course) and restorative conversation.

TO HILAH JOHNSON AND CHRISTOPHER SHARPE
for all the lively dinner conversation, big laughs, and willingness to test recipes on each other without judgment.

TO ROBIN "DHARAMPAL" BRUCE AND KIM SCHAEFER
yoga instructors of the highest caliber, for keeping us grounded through the book production process.

TO KATHLEEN SHANNON AND KRISTIN TATE OF BRAID CREATIVE
for proving that lightning can strike twice by making *Well Fed 2* sing just as loudly as the original.

TO EVERYONE AT SERVE GOURMET (BUT ESPECIALLY MAMIE!)
for letting us raid the store for props that made our food look so good.

TO BANG PRINTING AND GREENLEAF BOOK GROUP
for helping us get our books out in the world with first-rate customer service.

TO KRISTA CRAMER, MONA ALAUDHI, AND KRISTIN LUKOWSKI
for answering our frantic call for Arabic language newspapers.

TO MICKEY TRESCOTT
for scrutinizing the AIP-friendly recipe adaptations to ensure they're compliant as well as tasty.

TO STEVE WILLIAMS OF CHAMELEON COLD BREW
for damn fine coffee and the charming chameleon in the Lizard Sauce photo (p. 68).

AND TO ALL THE READERS OF THE CLOTHES MAKE THE GIRL
for reading the blog, testing the recipes, asking questions, and being super supportive of this book.

A LOT HAS HAPPENED SINCE THE DEBUT OF WELL FED IN 2011.

First, author Melissa Joulwan said, "*Sayonara!*" to her corporate overlords, and now spends her days writing articles for her blog, developing new recipes, and connecting with her loyal fans. We have upgraded our cooking skills to a solid B+, due in no small part to the tips and tricks we learned in *Well Fed.* Most importantly, tens of thousands of people have improved their lives thanks to the heart, soul, and passion that Melissa poured into the *Well Fed* series.

YES, WE SAID "IMPROVED THEIR LIVES," NOT "IMPROVED THEIR EATING HABITS."

What Melissa has created both in *Well Fed* and here in *Well Fed 2* isn't just about ingredients or recipes. It's about living a better life through cooking delicious, healthy food. Since we wrote the foreword for the original *Well Fed,* we've heard from thousands of people reporting incredible life changes after following Melissa's simple guidelines. They mention their weight loss and health improvements, sure, but then they invariably say...

"MY WHOLE LIFE IS BETTER NOW."

They tell us they are happier. They spend more time with their families and friends. They have less anxiety and stress. They love to cook, they started to exercise, and they have a new sense of self-confidence. They *glow.* Others look at them and say, "What have you been doing?" The answer: Through *Well Fed,* they have made themselves healthier from the inside-out – mind, body, and soul.

All of this from a cookbook, you ask? Ah, but this is no ordinary cookbook. What Melissa has magically woven into the recipes and stories here in *Well Fed 2* is the idea that changing your diet is not the end goal – it's just the first spark in a series of healthy chain-reactions.

By following her recommendations, you are spending more time with your food and with those you love. You feel good about your kitchen accomplishments, whether you're whipping up a batch of homemade mayo or grilling your first steak – and that translates to confidence in the rest of your life. Because you are consistently eating Good Food, you *feel* healthier, you *are* healthier – which gives you the momentum to start other healthy pursuits and unburdens you from the frustrations and self-doubts that have been holding you back from trying new things.

What you'll find in this book is *so much more* than just food (although the food is mouthwatering). As you read and cook, you'll also find yourself embracing a happier, healthier life, and reaping a myriad of benefits that follow the ignition of the Good Food spark.

For those of you who have already begun to live a better life thanks to the first *Well Fed,* welcome back. Here, you'll find enough recipe variations, inspiration, and excitement to propel you even further down your own individual path of health and happiness. For those who are starting with *Well Fed 2,* you are about to embark upon a journey. Trust us when we say these are not just recipes, and this is not just a cookbook. The information contained here will help you change your life the way it's helped so many others.

Are you as excited as we are? (With recipes like the SB&J Burger, Roasted Pizza Veggies, and Bacon-Pear Bites, of course you are.) So turn the page, immerse yourself in *Well Fed 2*'s world of Good Food, and get ready to embrace the best version of you.

We wish you the best in health.

MELISSA & DALLAS HARTWIG

Creators of the original Whole30® program

New York Times bestselling authors of *It Starts With Food*

TABLE OF CONTENTS

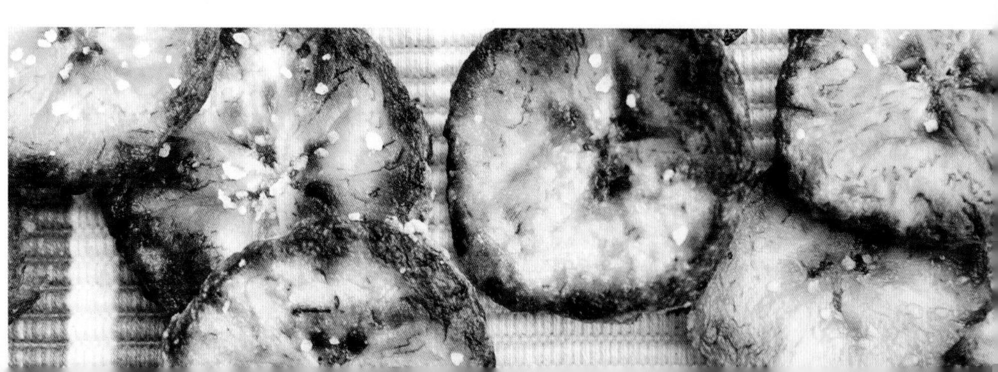

VEGGIES & SALADS

FRUITS

RESOURCES

WELCOME TO WELL FED 2

In case you're new to my writing and recipes, here are a few things you should know about me, my cookbooks, and my approach to food. (Spoiler: I really love to eat.)

THIS IS THE FOOD I EAT EVERY DAY.

When I wrote the original *Well Fed* in 2011, it was based on the way I'd been running my kitchen for the previous two years. Since then, I've been cooking up new, paleo-approved recipes... stuff I was craving, like favorite dishes from my college days, gyros and Italian food, take-out Indian and Chinese, and – thanks to an experiment with the autoimmune protocol (AIP) of the paleo diet – a handful of AIP-approved dishes.

Well Fed 2 is the result of my recent kitchen adventures, and the recipes in this book are the things I cook regularly in my kitchen in Austin, Texas.

I GREW UP IN THE KITCHEN.

I'm from a melting pot family: Lebanese on Dad's side, Italian and Slovak on Mom's. That means as soon as I could reach the stove, I was learning how to make Lebanese Stuffed Grape Leaves (p. 148) and Italian Meat Sauce (p. 94). But my parents also knew how to find the best restaurants, so I fell hard for dishes like Moo Shu Pork (p. 144) and Shrimp Scampi (p. 114).

My grandfather owned a diner, and my dad ran The Country Squire Restaurant, a combination coffee shop, formal dining room, and motel. I learned my way around a spice rack at the same time I learned the alphabet. My family ate stuff, like plantains (p. 184), that none of my friends had ever tried, and "international cuisine" was our home cooking.

Which is a long way to say that I love food, and I know the best way to enjoy it is to share it with others.

PALEO DOESN'T HAVE TO BE COMPLICATED AND TIME-CONSUMING.

It can be overwhelming to adopt new eating habits and to realize, suddenly, that you're going to be cooking at home. A lot. I've kept these recipes as simple as possible, without sacrificing flavor, and for those times you just really need to eat *right now,* I've included quick meal ideas that fancy up basic ingredients, no recipe required. There are also 15 varieties of sausage-inspired meatballs that come together in less than an hour and can be made in bulk. (Make friends with your freezer!) And because that time between work and dinner can be a dark valley frought with danger, I've included plenty of meals you can throw together in less than an hour on a weeknight. For lazy weekends when you want to putter in the kitchen, there are satisfying "project" recipes that take more time, but reward you with deliciousness that lasts for days.

My goal with this book is to teach you what I know about how to run a paleo kitchen and how to combine ingredients to make food that's truly nourishing.

LET'S HAVE FUN WHILE WE COOK.

Some of the times I've laughed the longest and smiled the hardest have been when I was in the kitchen, cooking and eating something delicious – or even something disastrous – with my family and friends. I take my good health (and your good health) very seriously, but I also think that chopping and mixing and stirring up something you'll want to eat can be a rip-roaring good time. You might not have spent as much time in the kitchen as I have, but that doesn't mean you need to be intimidated by food prep. Here's a secret that should give you confidence: You really can't mess it up. The worst that will happen is that you might burn the bottom of a stew or learn that you don't like a particular spice. How awesome is it to learn new things about yourself?!

I hope my recipes will help you find playfulness in the kitchen – a way to celebrate real food without feeling like you're stuck in "good health jail." To help you along your way, I've included lots of ideas for how you can make my recipes *your* recipes – and sprinkled throughout the book, you'll find silly trivia that makes me laugh. I hope it will remind you that a light-hearted approach might be the best one of all.

PREPARING QUALITY FOOD IS AMONG THE MOST CARING THINGS WE CAN DO FOR OURSELVES AND THE PEOPLE WE LOVE.

FAVORITE RECIPES

I'm often asked to name my favorite recipes – which feels next to impossible because if I don't love a recipe, it's not included in the book. There are no B-sides here, my friends! They're all keepers. But there are some recipes that I rely on almost every week. If you're not sure where to start, you might give these a go.

And for ultimate comfort food that lasts:

I should also mention something else: You won't find paleo-ized desserts in my cookbooks. I'm more interested in helping you eat well every day (which is why you ***will*** *find a few fruit recipes that are great for dessert – or breakfast or a snack).*

HEADS UP! NEW CONTENT

The next few pages cover the basics of paleo and other information that will be helpful for navigating this book. If you're one of the people who bought my first book **Well Fed** *(thank you!), you might think you know all of this info already. But heads up! It's been updated a bit, so you might not want to skip it. Or... you might want to skip it now to jump ahead to the recipes because you're excited – and I'm glad! – but then come back here to read the fine print.*

LET'S JUST CALL IT THE BEST FOOD YOU CAN EAT

YOU'VE PROBABLY HEARD THE PALEO DIET CALLED A LOT OF THINGS.

Just eat real food (#JERF). The Caveman Diet. Going primal. Living the paleo lifestyle. Around our house we call it "dino-chow." All of these terms refer to roughly the same way of eating. They're based on the idea that we are healthier – both mentally and physically – when we remove inflammatory foods from our diet.

What's an inflammatory food? The inflamers are foods that were not part of our hunter-gatherer ancestors' daily meals but appeared later in history, after agriculture took root. Edibles like grains, dairy, added sugars, and processed foods are the big bullies of the food world, and they're linked to the "diseases of civilization," nasty stuff including heart disease, diabetes, and cancers.

When we stop eating those problematic ingredients, we not only fight disease, everything in our lives improves. I know that's a bold claim, but it's true! What we put in our bodies forms the foundation for our moods, our energy, our creativity, and our vitality. When we nourish our bodies with paleo-approved foods, our energy levels are better, we look years younger, and we enjoy life more.

THE "NO" LIST

YOU WON'T FIND THESE FOODS IN WELL FED RECIPES

Let's get the bad news out of the way immediately: Eating paleo is probably going to mean eliminating many foods that may top your list of favorites. Different paleo practitioners promote varying guidelines. I follow the standards outlined by Melissa and Dallas Hartwig in their *New York Times* bestselling book *It Starts With Food* and their Whole30® program. The guidelines are fairly stringent but extremely practical, and they're based on the idea that we should eat the foods that make us the healthiest.

Each of the "No" foods has its own unique properties that ensure its place on this infamous list. Generally, these foods are excluded because they either negatively affect your metabolism, cause systemic inflammation, or both. Some are so bad that they both wreak havoc on your metabolism and fire up your immune system. We eschew them. (We're looking at you, grains. We eschew you!)

FOR AN OVERVIEW OF THE WHOLE30 AND 30 REASONS WHY IT'S A GREAT IDEA, SEE PAGE 10.

PROCESSED FOODS

As a former Doritos diehard, I know it can be hard to give up junk food. But anything found in the middle of the grocery store and sold to you inside brightly colored plastic or cardboard is not a healthy choice.

ADDED SUGAR

All forms of added sugar – even "natural" sugars, like brown sugar, maple syrup, agave nectar, stevia, evaporated cane juice, and honey – are out. Also out are artificial sweeteners like Splenda, Equal, Nutrasweet, and aspartame.

ALCOHOL

Alcohol has no redeeming nutritional qualities. It's essentially sugar with a flirtatious attitude. Plus, you have a drink, then your drink has a drink, and soon, you're face first in a pile of french fries with cheese sauce.

GRAINS

Despite conventional wisdom, even whole grains are not a good idea. Grains include wheat, rye, bulgur, buckwheat, amaranth, sprouted grains, corn, oats, rice, quinoa, barley, and millet. Avoid them in all their devilish forms: bread, tortillas, pasta, breading on fried foods, and "healthy" cereals, including oatmeal and granola.

LEGUMES

Beans – including black, kidney, pinto, white, and chickpeas – fall into this category, along with lentils, peas, and peanuts, including peanut butter. Legumes like green beans, snap peas, and snow peas are given a green light because they're more pod than bean.

SOY

Soy is a legume, but I've called it out separately because it's insidious and can be found in unexpected places, like cans of tuna. Avoid soy in all its forms: edamame, soy milk, tofu, meat substitutes, and food additives like soy lecithin. Read your labels!

DAIRY

The source doesn't matter – cow, sheep, or goat – milk and the creamy things made from it are off our plates, including cream, butter, cheese, yogurt, and sour cream. Some primal people eat grass-fed, full-fat dairy; for me, the negatives, like bloating and blood sugar spikes, outweigh the pleasure. One exception is organic, grass-fed butter, but it must be clarified before you eat it. See page 60 for instructions.

WHITE POTATOES

Some paleo people eat potatoes; I'm not one of them. White potatoes are carb-dense, and they can be a trigger food for some people – especially when you consider that they're so often eaten in the form of french fries. The good news is that we've got two fantastic, nutrient-dense replacements in sweet potatoes and yams.

VEGETABLE OILS

Basic vegetable oil isn't made from vegetables at all! It's off the eating list, along with peanut, canola, sunflower, safflower, soybean, and corn oils. These oils are thugs that beat up on your immune system and promote inflammation.

THE "YES" LIST

WE EAT REAL FOOD.

When I tell people I don't eat grains, sugar, or dairy, they invariably look at me like I've got a jailhouse tattoo of Barry Manilow over my heart. Then they ask The Question: "What do you eat?!"

ANIMALS AND PLANTS.

Generally speaking, the paleo diet is made up of nutrient-dense foods that began with dirt, rain, and sunshine. They come from the earth, and a person from any time in history would recognize them as food.

It's just real food: animal-based protein, vegetables, fruits, and natural fat sources.

If all you remember about paleo eating is the "Yes" and "No" lists, you'll have all you need to eat well for the rest of your life. To understand the science behind these nutritional guidelines, I recommend you turn to the experts who educated me.

WHOLE9

To learn both the theoretical and practical information you need to develop healthy, happy eating habits, my number one recommendation is Melissa and Dallas Hartwig. Begin with their book *It Starts With Food: Discover the Whole30 and Change Your Life in Unexpected Ways* – or you can commit to their life-changing Whole30 program by visiting their web site. Melissa and Dallas consume and digest all the new paleo and nutrition research so that foodies like us can simply learn how to eat. Thanks to their guidance, I can enjoy my food without measuring every meal or recording every bite in a food journal. The Whole9 site is an excellent resource for knowledge and community support. If you've never experienced a full 30 days without a "cheat or treat," I recommend that you participate in a complete Whole30 at least once to see how your body and attitudes respond.
www.whole9life.com

ROBB WOLF

The author of *The Paleo Solution* goes deep into the geeky science with a sense of humor that makes the information easy to understand and relevant to daily life. Wolf's book broadened my understanding of the "why" behind a paleo lifestyle, so it's easier to make the best food choices on a daily basis. His podcast addresses reader questions with charm and solid information.
www.robbwolf.com

MARK SISSON

The author of *The Primal Blueprint* presents the case for more primal living in every aspect of life: nutrition, exercise, sleep, socializing, and sex (!). I like what he has to say about finding time to play. His eating guidelines allow some foods on my "No" list, but he is worth reading for new ideas. His most recent book *The Primal Connection: Follow Your Genetic Blueprint to Health and Happiness*, goes beyond the food to examine the other lifestyle factors that affect our well-being.
www.marksdailyapple.com

CHRIS KRESSER

As an acupuncturist and practitioner of integrative medicine, Chris Kresser's perspective is very helpful for anyone who follows the paleo diet to manage serious health issues like hypothyroidism, heart disease, diabetes, and depression. His web site offers a deep archive of information and recommendations that can help you educate yourself for conversations with your own doctor.
www.chriskresser.com

The Resources section (p. 229) includes more details about these mentors, as well as a comprehensive list of the other sources I turn to for inspiration and information.

MY PALEO STORY

I have excellent habits 95 percent of the time. I sleep eight to nine hours per night to recover from and prepare for lifting heavy barbells, occasional sprints, and plenty of yoga and walking. I keep the house stocked with paleo ingredients and cook nutrient-dense meals so my husband Dave and I can eat real food every day.

Then on rare occasions, I indulge. I become a temporary slug and give in to the temptation of corn-based chip products, buttered popcorn, an icy-cold glass of Prosecco, or a shot of Ouzo. I should mention that I have a known whipped cream problem.

These minor transgressions are possible because I make deposits in the good health bank the rest of the time. Every workout, every good night's sleep, every paleo meal is a deposit, so that every once in a while, I can make withdrawals for a food treat.

This way of living started about five years ago when I made the switch to the paleo diet. Before then, I didn't have such excellent habits.

FROM GRADE SCHOOL TO THE DAY I GRADUATED FROM COLLEGE, I WAS A CHUBBY NERD.

My parents are both exceptionally good cooks – my dad brought his restaurant training home and my mom won almost every cooking contest that she entered. By the time I was about eight, I was wearing Sears "Pretty Plus" jeans, mostly because I really liked food, but also because I really didn't like to sweat. After a broken ankle and vicious playground taunts, I stuck with reading, practicing the piano, and roller-skating to the library. I don't know how many gym classes I missed because I was "sick" or "forgot" my gym clothes. I do know that my P.E. attendance put my otherwise stellar grade point average in jeopardy.

Even though I avoided sports, I secretly admired the athletic kids; they walked taller than the rest of us. When I was in tenth grade, my dad took me to Annapolis to see the Navy band play a concert, and for about three weeks, I was determined to get in shape so that I could apply to the Naval Academy. I abandoned that dream because I was incapable of doing pushups and situps – and I was too embarrassed and overwhelmed to ask for help.

For most of my life, I was haunted by a deep desire to be different than I was. To be thin. To feel confident. To break the cycle of thinking of food – and my behavior – as "good" and "bad."

I joined Weight Watchers and eventually became a Lifetime Member with a weight loss of more than 50 pounds. I joined a CrossFit gym and learned to love being scared by my workouts. I developed a deep affection for lifting barbells. But despite my successes, it was still my habit to celebrate and to grieve and to stress out and to relax with food. Although I worked out regularly, I didn't feel as strong – inside or out – as I wanted to. I had insomnia, allergies, and stomach aches. My body didn't feel like it belonged to me.

IN 2008, I LEARNED I HAD A NODULE ON MY THYROID.

The risk of cancer was high, so I had the nodule surgically removed, and the doctor hoped that the remaining half of my thyroid would continue to function. It held on for a few months, but then stopped working. That was a very difficult time. It was

like constantly having a case of the blues. I was sluggish, foggy-headed, and desperately worried about re-gaining all the weight that I'd worked so hard to lose.

Then I found Whole9 and the Whole30.

It was surprisingly easy for me to give up grains, despite my deep affection for toast, but saying goodbye to my standard breakfast of blueberries with milk almost pushed me to the edge. I did not approach the paleo rules with an open heart. But I committed. I followed the eating guidelines. I made it a project to get eight hours of sleep every night. I worked with my doctor to try to find the right doses for my thyroid hormones. I was on track with my nutrition, but my training was all wrong for a girl with no thyroid. The constant physical stress of my sometimes twice-a-day workouts and beat-the-clock CrossFit – without restorative activities like yoga, meditation, and walking to balance it out – took its toll. I was diagnosed with adrenal fatigue.

SO I STARTED OVER... AGAIN.

My new routine now includes daily meditation, gentle yoga classes, walking, strength training, and occasional sprints and high-intensity workouts of short (but killer) duration. What's never wavered is my commitment to and affection for my paleo diet. I've been through a lot of self-experimentation in the last half decade to get back to optimal health. The solid foundation provided by the paleo diet makes it possible to measure other health and quality-of-life markers and to tinker with them. After five years, I'm more convinced than ever that this is the healthiest way for me to feed my body and mind – and it is sustainable in a way that no other "diet" has ever been.

I spent the first 30 years of my life at war with my body – with my short legs and stocky frame, with junk food cravings and emotional eating. Banishing grains and dairy, in comparison to three decades of negative self-talk and shame, has been easy. And in return for giving up grains, dairy, and sugar, I've gained a partnership with my body that uses good food as fuel.

Now I know when and how often I can indulge in non-paleo foods, and I enjoy those "once in a while" treats like never before. The food tastes a lot better when it's savored and is not followed by a chaser of self-recrimination. I finally know how to truly celebrate on special occasions, while I live healthfully and happily.

My husband Dave and I have been eating paleo since 2009. It's helped us sleep more soundly. weather some ailments, and recover from life's curveballs with grace. It's also given us the opportunity to eat lots and lots of great food and to meet many wonderful people in the paleo club.

THE BEST VERSION OF YOU

I've had a weight loss goal since I was 13 years old.

That's more than 30 years of living with a number hanging over my head. From Weight Watchers summer camp to the rice diet to Kathy Smith's Fat Burning Plan to Weight Watchers to the Zone to Paleo… with aerobics videos and step aerobics and triathlons and boxing and Roller Derby and half marathons and CrossFit along the way.

MY MOTIVATIONS HAVE BEEN MANY.

Fear of being fat. Health concerns. Peer pressure to conquer the 200-pound deadlift. A personal sense of pride. Unadulterated vanity.

Those motivations shaped my behavior. I ate "right" so I would reach my Weight Watchers goal weight. I set my alarm for 5:00 a.m. so I would some day see my name on the RX or PR board at my CrossFit gym. I was driven by a sometimes-debilitating fear that I would never be "better."

Then a thought began to flicker in my subconscious. It started on holiday in Prague when I realized I liked exploring narrow, winding stairways. I was starting to loosen my grip on "destination" and reveling in "getting there." That idea tickled me again when I was upside down during a handstand at the gym and during a fun, stopwatch-free run around the lake: What if I've been looking at this from the wrong direction?

My underlying motivation for all of it – the weight loss, the physical challenges, the healthy eating – has always been that I wanted to be the best version of myself. Happy, healthy, fit, strong, attractive. But that pure motivation was poorly translated into external measures that separated **what I wanted** from **what I did**.

So I got the notion to try something different. For the first time in more than three decades, what if I didn't set a physical goal? No weight loss, no "leaning out," no target time on the clock or weight on the bar.

Instead, what if I simply behaved like the best version of myself?

Then I would become her.

The best me eats clean and sleeps well and trains hard and smiles a lot. She's free of worrying about what number might appear on a scale or a measuring tape. Instead of being intimidated or threatened by stronger, faster, leaner athletes at the gym, she delights in their capabilities. And she remembers to encourage the people around her to be their best versions.

Finally, the best version of me knows that she's not *required* to eat clean or meditate or practice yoga or lift heavy or get solid sleep. There is no accounting ledger keeping track of exemplary behavior for a reward later. There is no opportunity to earn a metaphorical gold star.

The clean eating and training, meditation and lifting, the sound sleeping are the reward. They are the thing.

So I've banished my "concrete" fitness goals. I know that "Be the best version of me" doesn't follow the traditional goal format. I don't care. I've done it the conventional way; now I do it my way.

THE BEST VERSION OF ME REFUSES TO BE MEASURED BY SOME EXTERNAL YARDSTICK.

The best version of me happily goes to bed early, wakes up refreshed, eats paleo, trains wisely, lifts heavy things, remembers to take a fun run and to play a little every day, spreads love, looks up, leads with the chin, makes up new recipes, and sings out loud.

Not because I must.

Because I want to. Because that's me. The best me.

WHAT IS THE BEST VERSION OF YOU?

Not the one you think other people want to see, or the one the media tells you to be. The one you desire to be, deep down. Can you work toward being the best version of you? Without judgment? Without punishment? Without reward? Can you revel in being you?

I'm going to make a plug right here: If you haven't experienced a Whole30, I encourage you to seriously consider committing to the 30-day program (even if you've been following the paleo diet for some time). It will change your life.

I know that's a bold claim, but following the Whole30 guidelines for one month teaches you things about food you didn't even know you didn't know.

The Whole30 is a program developed by Melissa and Dallas Hartwig, founders of Whole9 and authors of the book *It Starts With Food*. I urge you to read their wonderful book. It clearly explains the science behind eating paleo, without getting bogged down in evolutionary details or inexplicable jargon. The heart of the book – and the program – is the fact that some foods make us healthier and some foods do not. Eat more healthy food; eat less unhealthy food.

What could be more simple or make more sense than that?!

As you saw on pages 4-5, the "No" and "Yes" lists outline the foods that are approved for eating during the Whole30. But there's more to the program than just eating from the approved food list. If you're serious about a "real" Whole30, you can find all the details you need at *whole9life.com/whole30* or in *It Starts With Food*.

Now let's talk a bit about what you can expect if you clean up your act for 30 days (and beyond).

By eating only the foods on the "Yes" list for 30 days, you can heal existing inflammation inside your body, learn invaluable information about your own personal eating habits and overeating triggers, break the grip the Sugar Demon might have on you, and potentially learn how to eat some of the "No" foods once in a while so you can enjoy a treat without doing harm to yourself.

Over the last four years, I've done a handful of Whole30 resets myself, and every one of them has been different from the others and incredibly eye-opening and helpful in some way. Sometimes I take on the Whole30 because I desperately need to clean up my act (after a European vacation fueled by schnitzel and beer, for example). Sometimes I go after it because I want to feel reinvigorated or push a little harder at the gym.

If you've never tried giving up your evening glass of wine or your Saturday morning pancakes – or you live in a household where other people don't eat paleo or aren't taking on the Whole30 – I know it probably seems daunting. And I'm not going to lie: It can be very uncomfortable at first. But change is always uncomfortable – and we can't evolve if we don't ride out the discomfort.

If you're a runner or CrossFitter or Zumba-er or workout DVD aficionado, you've endured the discomfort of pushups or burpees or a run or [insert your least favorite move here] that went on too long. But you did it because you wanted to get better. If you practice yoga or meditation, you've surely felt the discomfort of a pose that went on too long, or a meditation that woke up feelings you didn't know you had. But you rode it out because you wanted to learn from it.

Giving up some of your favorite foods – and having to explain to others over and over again why you're doing it – might very well be uncomfortable. But I encourage you to do it because you will heal your body; you will learn new things about how and why and what you eat; and, ultimately, you will feel so much better than you do right now.

30 REASONS TO WHOLE30

IN NO PARTICULAR ORDER

These are the things that I've encountered and loved about the Whole30. Not everyone's experiences are the same, and you might not enjoy all of these things during your month (and I can pretty much guarantee you won't experience them every day of the month. Some days are just hard). But I can promise you that if you tackle a Whole30 – and really commit to the spirit of the endeavor – it will change you and your perceptions of yourself and the world for the better. That's a tall order, I know! But it's also drenched in truthiness.

---

1. YOU'LL SLEEP LONGER & MORE SOUNDLY.

When sugar is out and protein/fat is in, you sleep the sleep of the righteous.

2. YOU'LL ENJOY CONSISTENT ENERGY.

Forget energy that peaks and drops like a roller coaster, you'll become a bullet train.

3. YOU'LL WAKE UP FEELING OPTIMISTIC & ALERT.

There is nothing, and I mean *nothing*, better than waking up with a smile and open heart.

4. YOU'LL SAY GOODBYE TO DIGESTIVE DISTRESS.

Forget about farts and tummy rumbling and... let's call them "uncomfortable bathroom experiences." You might have a little discomfort at first if you're not used to eating lots of veggies, but after that, it's smooth sailing.

5. YOU'LL BE HAPPIER.

No joke. When blood sugar is stable, life is happier. Period.

6. YOU'LL BE MORE PEACEFUL.

The swirly thoughts and anxiety that can be brought on by the sugar joyride vaporize and leave calm in their wake.

7. YOU'LL BE MORE CLEAR-HEADED.

Goodbye, brain fog and tip-of-the-tongue syndrome! Hello, Mensa!

8. YOU'LL DRINK MORE WATER.

Sugary drinks are out, so you'll naturally find yourself drinking more water – which is a brilliant thing for making your body function at optimal capacity.

9. YOU'LL EAT MORE VEGETABLES.

Get ready to eat like a bunny! You'll be eating about two to three cups of veggies per meal. Per. Meal. Think of all the nutrients!

10. YOU'LL SAVOR YOUR FOOD MORE.

For me, shining the spotlight on quality food makes me appreciate its nutritive power and flavor more than usual. I slow down, enjoy every bite, and think about how it's making me strong while it tastes so damn good.

11. YOU'LL FEEL THE DIFFERENCE BETWEEN EMOTIONAL APPETITE AND REAL HUNGER.

You know that mindless eating that happens when you're stressed or distracted? That's emotional appetite, and it's junky. During the Whole30, as your body gets off the sugar high and settles into better insulin management, your appetite starts to diminish, but real hunger – the need for quality food that signals when it's time to eat – kicks in. It feels so good.

12. YOU'LL FIND NEW FAVORITE FOODS.

Who knows which vegetables, spices, and meat preparations will become your favorites?! It's exciting to think about, no? There's so much room in your kitchen and on your plate for new taste sensations when you banish the grains, beans, and dairy.

13. YOU'LL HAVE FUN EXPERIMENTING IN THE KITCHEN.

The Whole30 is essentially what got me into the kitchen and playing with recipes. I was inspired to see what I could do with veg+meat+fat, and I encourage you to do the same. Let the Whole30 and *Well Fed 2* help you play with your food!

14. YOU'LL BECOME MORE ORGANIZED.

To some degree, the Whole30 requires you to embrace planning to ensure your success, and that level of organization can trickle into other areas of your life, too.

15. YOU'LL KNOW TRUE "WILLPOWER."

Most of us tend to blame ourselves for "lack of willpower," but the truth is that much of our mindless eating is driven by our hormones. When we manage our hormonal response by eating the right foods, the correct messages about hunger are delivered through our bodies. No superhuman, self-control required!

16. YOU'LL LEARN ABOUT YOURSELF.

By focusing on your habits for 30 days, you'll learn all kinds of things, including what triggers your appetite, who's part of your support system, what you need for self care, what time of day you go to the bathroom, and more!

17. YOU'LL SLAY THE SUGAR DEMON.

Vanquish that bad guy! And then, later, if you tangle with the Sugar Demon again, you'll know that it's within your power to take a sword to his carotid when the time comes.

18. YOU'LL MAKE NEW FRIENDS.

There's a huge community of Whole30 participants online and offline, and during your Whole30, you can tap into their support, knowledge, sense of humor, successes, and challenges.

19. YOU'LL POSITIVELY INFLUENCE OTHERS.

Yes, you'll inevitably get the "You need to eat whole grains." argument from some well-meaning acquaintances, and that will be annoying. But if you quietly stick to your program, you'll also have a positive impact on the people around you when they see your results. I can't tell you how many people were envious of my Whole30 packed lunches in my office, and that's a non-combative way to open the door to a great conversation.

20. YOU'LL LEARN MORE ABOUT HOW YOUR BODY WORKS.

This is a two-fold win. First, by understanding the principles of the science behind the Whole30, you'll learn a bit about how human bodies function, and second, you'll learn how you – a special, special snowflake – work in particular.

21. YOUR SKIN WILL BE BRIGHTER.

Sleep + water + vegetables + fat + protein + no sugar = clear, younger-looking skin.

22. YOUR HAIR WILL BE SHINIER.

Sleep + water + vegetables + fat + protein + no sugar = glossy hair. (And stronger nails, too.)

23. YOUR TUMMY WILL BE FLATTER.

The end-of-day bloat from dairy and legumes is gone, baby, gone!

24. YOUR WORKOUTS WILL FEEL INVIGORATING.

Workouts fueled by real food are the best.

25. YOU MIGHT GET A PR.

PR stands for "Personal Record," and it's cause for celebration. Sleep + water + vegetables + fat + protein + no sugar = a physically stronger, faster you.

26. YOU'LL FEEL ACCOMPLISHED (OR MAYBE EVEN SMUG).

I've stopped pursuing discipline for discipline's sake, but I wholeheartedly believe that committing to a short-term program like the Whole30 helps develop mental toughness that is valuable in all aspects of our lives. And yes, I do enjoy feeling smug about that once in a while.

30 REASONS TO WHOLE30

CONTINUED... YOU CONVINCED YET?

27. YOU MIGHT LOSE WEIGHT. OR GAIN MUSCLE. OR BOTH.

If losing body fat is your goal, a Whole30 can be a great way to start that process. Just don't cheat yourself out of a lot of joy by making that your *only* focus. Look for the fresh glow on your skin, the smile on your face in the morning, the disappearance of afternoon headaches – as well as looser jeans and the return of cheekbones.

28. YOUR BODY IMAGE WILL IMPROVE.

There is an undeniable connection between treating ourselves well and how we feel about our bodies. If you look at the Whole30 as an act of self care, then affection, love, acceptance, and celebration of your body – how it feels, what it can do, the amazing things it carries you through every day – will surely follow.

29. FOOD WILL BECOME BOTH MORE IMPORTANT AND LESS IMPORTANT.

I used to be very attached to food. I was sad at the end of the day when eating was over until tomorrow, and when faced with my favorite foods, I wanted to eat them until I was stuffed, just in case I never saw them again. But when I got my blood sugar under control with the Whole30, that changed. Food is both more sacred: It nourishes and sustains us. And less sacred: We get to eat again in a few hours! The emotional triggers attached to the food on my plate are gone. Don't get me wrong: I still feel deep affection for favorite foods, and I love to eat, but now I feel that there's a world of abundance out there. Fear of food – and fear of not having favorite foods – is gone.

30. YOU'LL STOP DIETING AND JUST EAT.

This might be the best reason of all. When you take out the non-food food and replace it with real food, you can stop over-analyzing how much you eat, when you eat, and where you eat. Yes, quantities still matter to some degree, but you can throw off the shackles of calorie counting and denial, and just eat. Peacefully. Healthfully. Robustly. With joy and pleasure and laughter. And cumin.

WHOLE30, NOT WHOLE 365

It's important to note that the Whole30 is not meant to be the Whole365. The idea is not to keep ourselves in good food jail every day of our lives, with no opportunity for parole to eat a piece of birthday cake. After the 30 days, you'll have learned enough about yourself and your body to know when and how you might indulge in non-paleo foods once in a while.

I eat paleo 90 percent of the time. What that means in practical terms is that I eat according to the "Yes/No" list of foods, except for one or two exceptions per week. If you figure I eat 21 meals per week (3 times a day X 7 days), I have a treat – a non-paleo food – at one or two meals per week. Sometimes it's a few corn tortilla chips at Saturday morning brunch or an ice cream from Lick, a shop that makes homemade flavors like Caramel Salt Lick from local, grass-fed milk and ingredients from nearby organic farms.

You might notice that both of those examples are foods outside my house. That's because my kitchen is 100 percent paleo. I keep my cabinets and refrigerator stocked with only "Yes" foods, and this helps me in two major ways:

1. When I eat a non-paleo food, it's a conscious decision. It's impossible to "fall off the wagon" and overeat "No" foods when they're not in the house. The vast majority of the time, any craving I have for non-paleo food will pass long before I feel motivated enough to get in the car and drive to the grocery store for junk food.

2. As much as I enjoy playing in the kitchen, I also like to eat in restaurants, but the first priority for most restaurant chefs is not to make us healthier, it's to cook food that tastes good. That means that restaurant food often contains hidden soy, sugar, and gluten – and most restaurants use canola oil, factory-farmed eggs, and other commercially produced frankenfoods. I don't expect my neighborhood Tex-Mex joint to use grass-fed beef in my Saturday morning machacado con huevo, so I eat squeaky clean at home to allow wiggle room for the less-healthy options at restaurants.

Once you get over the shock of not eating old favorites like pasta and bread and wine – and *Darn it! I can't have cereal or yogurt for breakfast anymore!* – another challenge of paleo begins to emerge: socializing. Many of my friends are at least paleo-aware and some of them are as committed as I am to this lifestyle. But I also know and love a bunch of people who fall into the "eat whatever they want" category, as well as the "stay up late" and "enjoy adult beverages every evening" groups.

I've learned a few tricks that take most out of the sting out of remaining true to my convictions without becoming the weirdo who never wants to have any fun.

1. BRING YOUR OWN FOOD OR EAT BEFORE YOU GO.

If your priority is socializing, rather than the food itself, your pre-meal doesn't have to be the world's greatest. It just needs to be nutritional duct tape to help you navigate the experience. Every meal need not be a sit-down feast that feeds your soul and all your senses. Sometimes you just gotta eat.

If you're going to a restaurant, investigate the menu and plan your strategy. Unless your friends are completely cold-hearted, you can probably convince them not to choose, say, a pizza joint for dinner. (If they refuse to bend, you may have a bigger problem than "eating weird.") At most restaurants, you can find *something*. It might not be the best meal ever, but you do get to hang with your friends and enjoy some very important-to-your-psyche social time. I also usually eat a snack before I go, that way if the food that lands in front of me is sub-par, I'm not starved into making poor choices.

At a restaurant or social occasion like a party or wedding – anywhere your friends will be drinking cocktails – head directly to the bar as soon as you arrive and...

2. ORDER CLUB SODA.

Immediately get a glass into your hand. Strut up to the bartender and request a large club soda with two slices of lime and a few olives; I like to call this a **Mediterranean Fizz**! Now you (a) look like everyone else in the room with a glass in your hand; (b) have a drink that appears to be a cocktail to stave off inquisitive friends who want to know why you're not drinking; and (c) can enjoy a refreshing drink that's not just a boring glass of water. This mocktail also allows you to dance your ass off, pose for silly photos, and remain in control of your vocabulary while the people around you potentially devolve into drunken idiots.

3. ENLIST HELPERS AND ENJOY YOURSELF.

A few years ago, I was in the midst of a strict Whole30 when it was time to attend a friend's wedding. I told all my close friends that I was sticking to my Whole30 and not drinking booze. They heckled me a little, but they also encouraged me. Don't be shy about creating an army of support. Unless the occasion is a dinner party thrown in your honor and prepared by a kickass chef, a social situation is not necessarily about the food and booze – it's about enjoying yourself and the company of your friends. WARNING: Sometimes, when the pleasure of food and the lubrication of booze is subtracted from a social situation, it becomes dull. This is a natural step in your evolution; do not despair! Other good and healthy and valuable and fun things will emerge. Believe it.

4. USE YOUR TRUE VOICE.

Mostly, no one notices what you're doing, and if they do, they don't care. If someone is antagonizing you – the waiter, a co-worker, a "friend" – look them in the eye and say, "I'm choosing to make my health a priority right now." It's not a bad idea to practice saying that phrase. Also, in the right circumstances, "Mind your own f*cking business." works like a charm.

5. EAT WHEN YOU GET HOME.

Congratulations! You stuck to your guns. Now celebrate a little. I always make sure I have one of my favorite paleo snacks waiting in the kitchen after a night out: an egg or two scrambled with some chives, or hard-boiled eggs topped with homemade mayo, or a handful of Magic Dust (p. 76). Then I put on my PJs, snuggle with my husband Dave and our cat Smudge, and sleep the sleep of the righteous, knowing I'm going to wake up feeling healthy and strong. (Sometimes I think of those poor suckers with hangovers, and I allow myself to gloat for just a second.)

EMOTIONAL APPETITE VS. TRUE HUNGER

We humans are complicated creatures, and we eat for all kinds of reasons not associated with hunger: happiness, sadness, boredom, excitement, stress, exhaustion, dehydration. Some people are very focused on eating fuel for their workouts. Others (like me!) might simply enjoy the pleasurable taste of their favorite foods.

One of the great gifts of eating paleo is that it's easier to identify when I'm eating from true hunger or when I'm eating because of an emotional trigger. It's important for all of us to learn to listen to our bodies' true hunger signals, so we can say "no" when our brains want us to pander to an emotion-induced craving.

It's important to remember that food cannot permanently change our emotional state. Sure, eating something might provide a momentary distraction and fleeting pleasure.

But whatever emotion we're facing – happiness, frustration, anger, fear, worry, excitement, boredom – will continue to exist after we've eaten. In many cases, depending on what and how much we eat, we could actually worsen our emotional state. **Food itself cannot be a permanent balm for our feelings.**

The exception to this rule, of course, is if we're eating because of true hunger.

So the trick is to learn the difference between emotional appetite and true hunger, and to feed real hunger with paleo foods. Our emotions want our attention, too, so it's also essential to feed our emotional appetite with something other than food to deal with those tricky feelings.

This kind of mindful eating can be challenging at first. The key is to be as present as possible. Take a breath, consciously slow down, and be honest with yourself about the physical and mental signals your body is sending.

Here are some tips to help you learn how to manage emotional eating and true hunger.

BAN ALL NON-PALEO FOODS FROM YOUR KITCHEN.

Eventually, it would be wonderful if you learned to circumvent emotional eating. But the first approach is a practical one: Don't keep non-paleo foods in the house. That way, if your emotions *do* overwhelm you and trigger a bout of overeating, you'll only have paleo-friendly foods on hand to consume, thus minimizing the damage (if not the calorie consumption).

DRINK A GLASS OF WATER.

Sometimes our bodies confuse thirst with hunger, and sometimes, we just need a distraction to physically slow us down. Simply drinking a glass of water can help you become present and consciously think about what you're doing. This short breather can help you determine if you need to eat because you're truly hungry, or if you just want to eat.

BE STUBBORN.

This is my specialty! I've been described as dedicated and determined, but who are we kidding? I am stubborn. I challenge you to be the same. Remember that you've deliberately decided to make your physical and mental health a priority. Be relentless in that commitment. (And then later, you can revel in the accomplishment!)

SET A 20-MINUTE TIMER.

Twenty minutes is kind of a magic number. When cravings strike, set a timer for 20 minutes and challenge yourself to avoid eating anything until the timer rings. In that 20 minutes, explore your physical and mental state. If you're truly hungry at the end of the 20 minutes, eat a paleo meal or snack. If you're not physically hungry, odds are good that by the end of that 20 minutes, your craving will most likely have passed. (The 20-minute rule is also a good one for determining if you really need seconds during a meal, too. Before hitting the kitchen to refill your plate, wait 20 minutes. That's how long it takes for the "I'm full" message to reach your brain. If you wait and you're still unsatisfied, add another small serving to your plate and dig in.)

SET KITCHEN HOURS AND STICK TO THEM.

This mental trick has prevented me from eating an entire jar of coconut butter with a spoon on many occasions. My kitchen hours are 7:00 a.m. to 8:00 p.m. Sometimes, if I'm feeling particularly snacky, I even say out loud, "It's 8:00. Kitchen's closed." You really can outwit your emotional appetite with this simple declaration.

ENLIST AN ALLY.

Misery loves company. Wait! That's not what I mean! There's strength in numbers. Make a deal with a family member, neighbor, online friend, or another comrade to commiserate with you. The simple act of talking about your cravings with another human can help you analyze if you're hungry or trying to eat your feelings.

If you determine that you really are hungry, and you're ready to load up your plate with paleo goodness, here are a few healthy habits to ensure that you feel satisfied at the end of your meal.

EAT AT THE TABLE.

There is something celebratory and decadent about grabbing a snack straight out of the cabinet or eating a bite of leftovers while your hip props open the refrigerator door. But that's not the most beneficial approach to feeding your body. One of the best tools you have in your arsenal is your brain. Use it to approach your meals with mindfulness. That means you eat your food from a plate or bowl. At a table. With utensils. (Unless you're eating Plantain Nachos, p. 146 or Vietnamese Chicken Salad, p. 162.) You don't need a formal dining room or heirloom china, but the act of slowing down to eat in a place dedicated to meals puts you in the right mindset to consciously enjoy your food. The simple act of sitting down to a meal sends a message that says, "We're eating now," so that all of your senses can play along in the act of nourishing your body.

ELIMINATE ELECTRONICS.

Sure, you can type and flip channels with one hand, while shoveling food into your mouth with the other, but that's a terrible idea. Studies prove that we eat far more when we're distracted by the television or computer while eating – and afterward, we feel less satisfied. The entertainment on those insidious blue screens doesn't permit you to turn your full attention to the food you're eating, and you mindlessly consume extra calories that leave you feeling unsatisfied. Eat first, watch later.

EAT SLOWLY, CHEW WELL.

My parents were sticklers for good table manners, so my brother and I were frequently instructed to put our forks down between bites and to chew our food very well – with our mouths closed, naturally. As it turns out, that's not just good manners, it's good health, too. Research shows that digestion and satiation are improved when food is well-chewed before being swallowed. And the act of placing your fork on the rim of your plate between bites ensures that you won't shovel it in too quickly – all the better to savor every bite.

ABOUT THIS BOOK

THIS ISN'T A DIET BOOK OR A HEALTH BOOK.

I know the word "paleo" in the title is probably what compelled you to choose this cookbook over others, which means you probably care about your health. Good for you! But my mission isn't to clobber you with the healthfulness of the recipes in this book. My mission is to inspire you with stories and tempt you with recipes that will make you want to smash in your face with joy.

I also want you to be healthy, so all of the recipes are free of gluten, grains, legumes, dairy, added sugars, and alcohol – and I've paid attention to things like Omega-6 and Omega-3 fatty acid ratios. I've worried about the somewhat annoying nutritional details so that you can just eat.

I want you to savor flavorful foods every time you eat, every single day. The majority of these recipes rely on meats, vegetables, fats, and spices to make your taste buds sing. When I've used calorie-dense foods like nuts or dried fruit, they act as condiments rather than primary ingredients.

JUST EAT.

There's no nutritional information included with the recipes. If we eat real food, in quantities that are satiating, there's really no need to niggle over how many calories we ate and what percentage of them came from fat or carbohydrates. The recipes, however, don't go overboard, either. Fat is an essential nutrient for health and an important component for flavor, so my recipes include just enough fat to make them work, without being overindulgent. My approach to the paleo framework is to eat protein, fat, and carbohydrates in fairly equal proportions. I'm not high fat, high protein, or low carb; I'm moderate (although I am kind of a veggie-holic). My recipes reflect this balance and don't require over-analysis of macronutrients to keep you healthy.

WHOLE30 APPROVED.

Every recipe in this book is Whole30 approved except for the Banana-Pecan Ice Cream (p. 224) and Sweet Potato "Waffle" (p. 116). While the ingredients in those recipes are paleo, the way they come together undermines the spirit of the Whole30. (If you're unfamiliar with the Whole30, see page 10.)

AUTOIMMUNE PROTOCOL (AIP) COMPLIANCE.

Some of my recipes are compliant with the Autoimmune Protocol of paleo. In addition, you'll find AIP adaptations of recipes, where possible, on page 231.

HOW TO USE THIS BOOK.

If you're new to paleo and aren't familiar with my recipes and style of cooking, you'll probably want to start with The Recipe Pages (p. 19) and the details in The Paleo Kitchen (p. 23). These sections explain how my recipes are put together, as well as ingredients, tools, and techniques that come up a lot.

When you're ready to dig into the recipes, you'll find they're divided by their primary ingredient, rather than meal type.

QUICK MEALS

This section is packed with ideas for satisfying paleo foods you can eat without following a detailed recipe, including ways to make basics like burgers, broccoli, and eggs more exciting.

SAUCES & SEASONINGS

This section features flavor boosters that transform simple, cooked ingredients, like protein and veggies, into luscious meals. From easy-to-make spice blends to sauces that can be whipped up in just a few minutes, these recipes add pizzazz.

PROTEIN

Many of these recipes, like stews and main-dish salads, also include vegetables, but the recipes in this section are primarily protein, which should form the basis of your paleo meals.

VEGGIES & SALADS

Savory side dishes can make even something as simple as a grilled chicken breast seem like a feast. The veggie recipes in this section range from simple to unexpected and include paleo basics like cauliflower rice and veggie noodles.

FRUIT

You can call them desserts, but why not enjoy these fruit recipes anytime? Snack, appetizer, dessert, side dish – they're welcome at any paleo meal.

THE CLOTHES MAKE THE GIRL

Some of the recipes in **Well Fed 2** *debuted on my blog The Clothes Make The Girl. I started my blog in 2008 to write about my triumphs and failures in the gym, in the kitchen, and in life. In addition to recipes for new dishes I'm working into our menus at home, you'll find stories about the wacky things I do in kundalini yoga, photos of my ridiculously cute cat Smudge, bragging about how much weight I put on the barbell at the gym, and, potentially, whining about how my workout didn't go as planned. I also write occasionally about other things that inspire me like books, music, art, and other bloggers.*

I've made a special page on my blog with goodies to supplement the recipes in this book, including how-to videos, menu suggestions, photos, links to my favorite blog posts, and other tasty stuff that I think you'll find helpful.

VISIT WWW.THECLOTHESMAKETHEGIRL.COM/WELLFED2

Some of my favorite and most popular posts include:

NOTHING MATTERS. EVERYTHING MATTERS.
An essay on what I've learned on my travels.

THE EGG FOO YONG STORY
The surprising history of this American-Chinese dish.

BEING COMFORTABLE WITH BEING UNCOMFORTABLE
Kind of about front squats but really about life.

ZOMBIE ATTACK PREPAREDNESS (ZAP) WORKOUT
A fun workout to prepare you for the zombie apocalypse.

WHY I LIFT HEAVY THINGS
A love note to strength training and its positive impact on my life.

YOU NEVER KNOW IF TODAY IS THE DAY
The true story of the day I learned to do a handstand.

WALKING YOUR PATH
A reminder that sometimes we just need to follow our feet.

KUNDALINI CONTINUES TO BE WEIRD
A silly recap of my adventures in yoga.

WELL FED: PALEO RECIPES FOR PEOPLE WHO LOVE TO EAT

*My first cookbook is packed with Whole30-approved recipes for dishes that you can eat every day, along with easy tips to make sure it takes as little time as possible to get you from "What the *$&^@ am I going to eat?" to stuffing healthy, irresistible food into your well-deserving mouth. In addition to 100+ paleo recipes, it includes detailed instructions for a Weekly Cookup and Hot Plates that show you how you can spend a few hours cooking on the weekend, then get dinner on the table in under 20 minutes during the week. You can download a free, 30-page preview of* **Well Fed** *at www.theclothesmakethegirl.com/wellfed2.*

PAGE 108

SUNRISE SCRAMBLE

LIKE A DANISH, MINUS THE PASTRY

1. SERVES 2 to 4

2. PREP 1[illegible] MI[illegible] COOK 10 MIN.

4. *It's kind of stunning to me that there are still places in the world where an apple Danish is considered an ideal breakfast. Don't get me wrong: I agree that apples and cinnamon taste great in the morning (and any time of day, really), but I'm happy to trade the gluten-filled dough for nutrient-dense sweet potatoes and the power of a solid protein infusion. This scramble cooks up quick, which mak[illegible] perfect for busy breakfast time, but the flavors are also savory enough to satisfy after a long, [illegible]* **Heads up! This recipe requires you to do something in advance; plan prep time acco[illegible]gly.**

INGREDIENTS

3.

- 1 tablespoon coconut oil or ghee
- 8 ounces ground turkey or pork
- 1 apple, diced (about 1 cup)
- 2 teaspoons S[illegible]rise Spice (p. ##)
- 1 cup cook[illegible]d sweet potato
- salt and grou[illegible] black pepper, to taste
- 8 large eggs, beaten
- 6-8 scallions, green tops only, thinly sliced

DIRECTIONS

5.

Heat a large, non-stick skillet over medium-high heat, about 3 minutes. Add coconut oil and allow it to melt. Add the turkey and apple, stirring with a wooden spoon to break up chunks of meat. Cook [illegible] no longer pink, about 5-7 minutes. When the mea[illegible] some of its fat, add the Sunrise Spice, sweet potato, [illegible] and pepper. Stir to mix and cook until sweet potatoes get little brown spots.

Pour the eggs into the pan and stir to combine. Continue to scramble until desired doneness. Top with scallions and eat immediately. Good morning!

YOU KNOW HOW YOU COULD DO THAT?

6.

Make the turkey/apple/sweet potato hash and top with fried or poached eggs, instead of scrambling.

TASTES GREAT WITH

7.

SPRING CHOPPED SALAD, P. ##

ROAST[illegible]AGE ROSES, P. ##

NOTES

8.

If this isn't a strong argument for B[illegible]ast For Dinner, I don't know what is[illegible]

The recipe pages are packed with lots of details and descriptions so it feels like we're in your kitchen, cooking together – probably gossiping about somebody and drinking a Mediteranean Fizz (p. 14).

It's always a good idea to read through the entire recipe before you start cooking, and although I might seem bossy in my instructions, I encourage you to experiment and make these recipes your own.

1. SERVES / MAKES

Serving sizes are based on an estimate of about 4-6 ounces of protein per person and/or 1 cup of vegetables per person. Keep this in mind if you're cooking for a giant, muscle-bound man or wee ones and adjust your quantity accordingly.

2. PREP / COOK TIME

Prep time is based on how long it takes me to prepare the ingredients, with a little padding added because I'm fast in the kitchen. Cooking time is an estimation of total time that heat is involved. Note that prep and cook time do not include the time necessary to make recipes within recipes; see #4 below.

3. INGREDIENTS

The ingredients are listed in the order they're used in the recipe and include as many details as possible to make sure you know exactly what you need. When substitutions can be made, they're usually listed at the end of the recipe. Keep an eye out for listings like "1 tablespoon plus 1 tablespoon coconut oil." This means you need 2 tablespoons of coconut oil, but you'll need them separate from each other, to use at different times in the cooking process.

4. RECIPE WITHIN RECIPE

Some of my recipes require you to make another recipe in advance, especially where spice blends or condiments like ketchup and mayo are in the ingredients list. Look for the note that says, "**Heads up! This recipe requires you to do something in advance; plan prep time accordingly**." Note that the prep time for the recipes does not include the time needed to prepare those ingredients.

5. DIRECTIONS

I've cooked all of the recipes in this book at least a half dozen times, so the directions I recommend are based on plenty of trial and error. Where I used tricks my dad taught me, I erred on the side of over explanation so you can learn from my dad, too.

6. YOU KNOW HOW YOU COULD DO THAT?

This is a game I play with my family. We eat a chef's restaurant creation or read a recipe, mull it over for a moment, then say, "You know how you could do that?" and come up with variations. Now you can play, too!

7. TASTY IDEAS / TASTES GREAT WITH

"Tasty Ideas" is found in the "Sauces & Seasonings" section. It tells you how to use the sauce or spice blend in your cooking. "Tastes Great With" lists other recipes in the book that turn a single dish into a complete meal.

8. CALLOUTS

These are usually fun facts and tips that aren't essential to the recipe but make kitchen time more fun and allow you to drop some boss trivia on your dining companions.

ABOUT THE RECIPES

I've tried to keep ingredients lists and instructions as simple as possible, without sacrificing big, bold, satisfying flavor. Here are some things to keep in mind as you read the recipes. (And, really, read the whole recipe before you start cooking; you'll be so much happier.)

HAPPY MEAT.

If you have a kind heart, it's both a blessing and a curse to be at the top of the food chain. We are blessed with access to a wide variety of animal proteins, and I honor and respect those animals for making us stronger and healthier. Factory farming damages the environment and produces animals that are not optimally healthy, which means they also make us less healthy. Remember: You are what you eat eats. Finances can be a concern, so I don't specify organic, grass-fed, pastured, or wild-caught protein in my recipes, but I do encourage you to buy the highest-quality protein you can afford. If you can't invest in grass-fed, buy the leanest cuts you can find, remove excess fat before cooking, and drain the fat after cooking.

ORGANIC PRODUCE.

It's best to eat local produce that's in season, both for the health of your body and your wallet. But sometimes I want eggplant in winter, even though it's not grown here that time of year. My recommendation is to buy local, organic versions of the produce identified by the Environmental Working Group as having the most pesticide residue. The "dirty dozen" includes apples, bell peppers, blueberries, celery, cherries, grapes, kale (and other leafy greens), lettuce, nectarines, peaches, potatoes, and strawberries. For the rest of your produce needs, buy local, conventionally grown produce, and wash it well under running water to remove dirt and pesticides.

COOKING FATS.

Fat is an essential part of good health, and it's *so* tasty. Double win! There's no reason, however, to go overboard either. I'm not afraid of fat, but I'm also not on the team that thinks paleo requires diving face-first into a vat of lard. My recipes include enough fat to appropriately cook and flavor the food. Feel free to increase the amount of fat if you'd like, but keep in mind that you will probably be disappointed in the taste if you *reduce* the fat.

I use three primary sources of fat in my recipes: olive oil, coconut oil, and ghee (organic, grass-fed, butter that's been clarified; see page 60). For higher temperature cooking – like sautéing and baking – I recommend coconut oil or ghee. They can be used interchangeably in my recipes, but if I specify, it's because I think that fat tastes best in that recipe. (All fats can be swapped with each other in a 1:1 ratio.) I do not recommend using olive oil for cooking at high heat. Hot temperatures cause olive oil to oxidize, which has some health ramifications. I usually reserve olive oil for drizzling on already-cooked foods, salads, and homemade mayo, but I've also included a few recipes that use olive oil at very low heat.

SEASONING WITH SALT.

American table salt is devoid of trace minerals; sea salt is a slightly superior option. Most sea salt, however, doesn't include the iodine found in table salt. I don't specify the type of salt to be used in these recipes, but I recommend iodized sea salt. All measurements refer to fine (not coarse) salt.

It's important to taste food for salt levels throughout the cooking process. Some of my recipes, where I think a particular amount makes it sing, specify the amount of salt, others simply say "salt and ground black pepper, to taste." I recommend that you season with salt during cooking and adjust seasonings again just before the end of cooking to get the best flavor. And with all spice quantities, feel free to adjust down or up according to taste.

OMITTING INGREDIENTS.

In many of these recipes, garnish ingredients and some seasonings are listed as optional. Keep in mind that in *all* recipes, flavoring ingredients are *always* optional. Rather than skip an entire recipe if it includes something that's not on your list of favorites, just omit the element you don't like. For example, none of these recipes will fail if you omit hot peppers or leave out the cumin.

WORKING WITH HOT PEPPERS.

Some of these recipes include fresh jalapeños, which add a kick, but can be a hazard to chop. When working with fresh jalapeños or other hot peppers, it's a good idea to either wear gloves or rub a little oil on the hand that's holding the pepper (but not the one holding the knife!) to protect yourself from the seeds and ribs. You can also burn a candle next to your cutting board to burn off the offending vapors or rub your hands with oil AFTER chopping a hot pepper to remove the capsaicin residue. Absolutely, positively do not touch any part of your face while working with fresh hot peppers. (Gentlemen, be careful in the restroom. *Ahem.*)

MIXING TOOLS.

For stovetop cooking, I usually recommend a wooden spoon because it's versatile, durable, the handle doesn't (usually) get hot, and it won't scratch non-stick cookware.

MISE EN PLACE.

(Chef-talk for "everything in place.") Prior to starting a recipe, set yourself up like a cooking show: Measure and prep the ingredients you need to make the recipe, organize the equipment you need within easy reach, and preheat the oven or stove so you don't suddenly realize you need a diced onion when you've got your hands buried in a bowl of ground meat.

NUTS AND DRIED FRUIT.

When a recipe includes nuts, seeds, or dried fruit, those ingredients are included as a flavoring components, rather than primary ingredients. All nuts, seeds, and dried fruit included in these recipes are optional. If you're trying to minimize your Omega-6 fatty acids or fruit/sugar intake, you can omit the nuts and fruit without damaging the recipe.

COOKING TEMPERATURES.

If you're using grass-fed meats, you'll get the best results if you use medium-high (or even medium) heat. High heat can make leaner, high-quality meats taste tough. You'll also notice that most of my recipes instruct you to preheat the pan before cooking; you'll be happiest if you heed this advice.

AUTOIMMUNE PROTOCOL (AIP) COMPLIANCE.

Some of my recipes are compliant with the Autoimmune Protocol of paleo and most of them can be adapted to be AIP-friendly. On page 231, I've listed specific instructions for how to modify each recipe to be safe for those of you following the AIP.

YOU'RE GONNA NEED A BIGGER BOWL.

A few words of advice from my dad that I included in the original *Well Fed* that warrant repeating here: *Always*, ***always*** use a bowl that's bigger than you think you need. (Thanks, Daddy!)

THE PALE

KITCHEN

ESSENTIAL KITCHEN TOOLS

With these gadgets, you should be able to make everything in this cookbook. For my recommendations on specific pieces of equipment, along with buying information, visit www.theclothesmakethegirl.com/wellfed2.

LARGE CUTTING BOARD

Almost every recipe begins with chopping. A hefty cutting board protects the knife, your countertop, and you.

A REALLY GOOD KNIFE

In the kitchen, your knife is an extension of you. Choose a knife that feels comfortable in your hand. I like an 8-inch blade; it works well on both meat and produce. Don't forget a good knife sharpener, too!

FOOD PROCESSOR OR BLENDER

Helpful for the sauces and seasonings that make paleo food more enticing, a food processor is a solid investment in your healthy, happy taste buds. You can get away with either a processor or blender, but I have both, and I'm glad.

SOUP/CHILI POT

Get a pot larger than you think you need, preferably with a non-stick interior and heavy bottom.

LARGE SAUTÉ PAN

Essential for everyday cooking, invest in a non-stick, 12-inch skillet. I like one that's fairly deep with curved sides.

CAST-IRON SKILLET

Non-stick and ideal for cooking at high heat, cast-iron adds a lovely crust to meats (see Perfect Steak, p. 134) and is ideal for making the perfect omelet (Scheherazade Omelet, p. 154).

COLANDER OR WIRE SIEVE

For washing produce, draining steamed foods or fatty meats, and sweating raw vegetables.

LARGE, RIMMED BAKING SHEETS

Insulated sheets help prevent burning and a rim prevents smoke-inducing drips inside the oven. Ideally, you should have at least two of these.

STURDY MIXING BOWLS

Graduated sizes ensure you have a bowl for larger projects – like meatballs, p. 87 or Moo Shu Pork. p. 144 – and spice-sized bowls to keep your workspace tidy.

STANDING OR HAND MIXER

You can get by with just a food processor, but a mixer can handle more volume and gets meatballs ready in a snap (p. 87).

MANDOLINE SLICER

Not required, but super helpful for making paper-thin slices of veggies and fruits – handy for Plantain Nachos (p. 146) and Cucumber Relish (p. 156).

MEASURING CUPS & SPOONS

For measuring cups, you'll have everything you need if you invest in a 2-cup liquid measuring cup and a set of dry measuring cups that range in size from 1/4 cup to 1 cup. For spoons, look for a set that includes 1 tablespoon, 1/2 tablespoon, 1 teaspoon, 1/2 teaspoon, and 1/4 teaspoon. Bonus points if you also get an 1/8 teaspoon.

RUBBER SCRAPER

I don't like to leave even one drop of Olive Oil Mayo (p. 53) inside the blender! Look for a scraper that's both sturdy and flexible, so it bends into corners.

PARCHMENT PAPER AND/OR ALUMINUM FOIL

Invaluable for minimizing clean-up time. I prefer having both on hand, but if you must choose one, go with aluminum foil.

BPA-FREE STORAGE CONTAINERS

Critical for stocking up on paleo ingredients. You'll need more than you think, and there is acute satisfaction in a fridge filled with ingredients and homemade food.

WOODEN SPOONS

My preferred tool for sautéing, mixing, and tossing.

GARLIC PRESS

Not required, but a real time saver unless you're adept at mincing with a knife.

PASTRY OR BARBECUE BRUSH

Cheap to buy and priceless in the kitchen for adding the finishing touch to your homemade dishes.

KITCHEN SHEARS

A huge time saver for prepping raw meat, cleaning produce, and mincing fresh herbs.

TONGS

Useful for grilling and browning meat for stews – or flipping Crispy Chicken Livers (p. 106).

GRATER/ZESTER

You're not grating cheese anymore, but citrus zest is a transformative ingredient on veggies, salads, meats, and stews.

JULIENNE PEELER

This $10 gadget is handy for turning vegetables like zucchini (p. 168) and cucumbers (p. 192) into noodles.

WAFFLE IRON

Do you have a waffle iron gathering dust in the back of a cabinet? It turns sweet potatoes into "waffles" (p. 116), and it's a fun way to transform an omelet into something new.

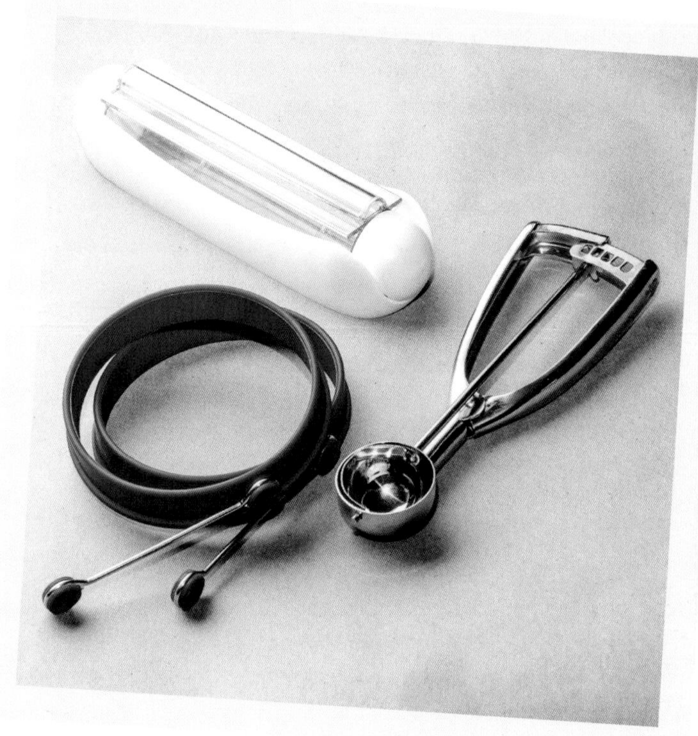

HAM DOGGER

It's that crazy-looking white thing in the photo above. This sorta silly tool turns ground beef into sausage shapes in seconds (p. 87).

PANCAKE RINGS

No, I don't use them for pancakes, but they're super handy for making burger patties (p. 87).

MINI SCOOP

A 1-tablespoon scoop, intended for cookies but repurposed for meatballs, is just the right size for shaping meatballs quickly (p. 87).

YOUR PALEO PANTRY

Paleo eating is basically about animal protein, piles of fresh produce, and quality fat sources. But there's more to it than that. Those ingredients are the foundation, but with a well-stocked pantry, you can turn raw materials into meals, every day of the week.

The ingredients listed below show up in the recipes in *Well Fed 2*. You don't need to stock up on all of them at once, but the ones with checkboxes ☑ are staples in my pantry that I never let run out.

☑ ARROWROOT POWDER

Made from tropical roots, this starchy powder is a good stand-in for wheat flour or cornstarch in "breading" meats and thickening sauces. Check the ingredients to be sure it hasn't been cut with potato starch. The substitution ratio in recipes is 2 teaspoons of arrowroot per 1 tablespoon of cornstarch or wheat flour.

ALMOND FLOUR (ALMOND MEAL)

Another substitute for flour, this one is made from ground, blanched almonds. Its consistency is more like corn meal than powdery wheat flour. It adds structure to baked foods and is a good substitute for "breading" on meats.

ANCHOVY PASTE

Salty, rich, and loaded with umami flavor (that "something" that adds depth to food), anchovy paste is made from anchovy fillets, salt, and olive oil – check the label for added sugar! If you don't have fish sauce on hand, 1 tablespoon coconut aminos mashed with 1 teaspoon anchovy paste (or 1 anchovy) is a good substitute.

☑ BROTH

Look for organic chicken, beef, and vegetable broth that doesn't contain any added sugar, starches, or soy. (Or make your own!)

☑ COCONUT AMINOS

Almost identical to soy sauce in taste, coconut aminos are a healthy replacement for Asian-inspired recipes. You can find them online or in stores like Whole Foods.

☑ COCONUT OIL

Use organic, unrefined coconut oil for optimal health benefits. It lends a somewhat buttery flavor to dishes and can be used at higher temperatures without oxidizing (which means it remains good for you, even if you turn up the heat). Because it's saturated, it's solid at cooler temperatures, so it's a good stand-in for butter in baked treats.

COCONUT FLAKES, UNSWEETENED

Eaten on their own or sprinkled into and on top of dishes, coconut flakes add another dimension of flavor and texture.

COCONUT FLOUR

Another gluten-free alternative to wheat flour, coconut flour is made from dried, ground coconut. Check labels to make sure it's unsweetened.

☑ COCONUT MILK

Equally at home in sweet and savory dishes, it's an excellent replacement for heavy cream or yogurt in curries and sauces. According to my friends at Whole9, it's okay if the ingredient list includes guar gum, but avoid brands that include sulfites or added sugars. Always use the type found in a can; the coconut milk packaged in a carton includes undesirable ingredients.

☑ DIJON MUSTARD

Tangy and smooth, Dijon mustard adds zing to salad dressings and sauces. Read the ingredients list to make sure it doesn't include sugar, wine, or unrecognizable chemical ingredients.

DRIED FRUIT

Because it's naturally high in sugar, I don't snack on dried fruit, but a few dates, figs, raisins, or dried cranberries can add just the right touch of sweetness to savory foods. I keep a small amount in the cabinet (just enough to flavor my food but not to feed the sugar demon). Be sure to look for varieties without added sugars or oils.

☑ EXTRA-VIRGIN OLIVE OIL

Fruity with a peppery kick at the end, EVOO is best for salads and finishing cooked dishes. For higher cooking temps, use coconut oil.

☑ FISH SAUCE

Fish sauce is a key ingredient that gives many Asian dishes their singular taste. Most brands include sugar, but Red Boat Fish Sauce is 100 percent paleo and Whole30 approved. It's available online and at stores like Whole Foods. If you don't have fish sauce handy, you can substitute 1 tablespoon coconut aminos mashed with 1 teaspoon anchovy paste (or 1 anchovy).

☑ GHEE

Ghee is clarified butter, which means it's butter that's been melted and drained of protein solids so only the fat remains. It's rich and creamy and when it comes from an organic, grass-fed cow, it's paleo and Whole30 approved. See instructions page 60.

☑ HOT SAUCE

Most hot sauces are good to go, just read the label to make sure there's no added sugar or weird chemicals. The ingredients should be simply hot peppers, vinegar, and spices.

☑ LIGHT-FLAVORED OLIVE OIL

Less expensive and less flavorful, use this type of olive oil for Olive Oil Mayo (p. 53).

OLIVES

A salty, chewy addition to salads, snacks, and garnishes, olives also add a dose of healthy fats. Again, check ingredient labels for added junk; you want only water, olives, and salt.

NUTS

I try not to snack on nuts, but instead save them for adding crunchy flavor to cooked foods. I keep a small amount of pine nuts, dry-roasted unsalted almonds, pistachios, pecans, macadamias, walnuts, and cashews on hand.

PICKLES, BANANA PEPPERS, JALAPEÑOS

These crispy, vinegary nibbles transform salads and sautés from yawn to yum. Jalapeños are my husband Dave's favorite addition to eggs.

SUNFLOWER SEED BUTTER

A healthier alternative to peanut butter, get the sugar-free variety that includes only seeds and salt. (Prepare for lusciousness!) In most recipes, you can substitute almond or cashew butter for sunflower seed butter, if you prefer.

TAHINI SAUCE

Made from ground, hulled sesame seeds. It's creamy, nutty, and adds lusciousness to Asian and Middle Eastern food.

☑ THAI CURRY PASTE

These flavorful pastes – available in red, green, and other varieties – quickly transform coconut milk, veggies, and protein into a luxurious meal. Look for brands that are sugar free and have no preservatives or colorants. My favorite is Mae Ploy, but Thai Kitchen is also good and paleo approved. Both brands can be found online or in a well-stocked grocery store.

☑ TOMATOES & TOMATO PASTE

For quick sauces and to add depth to soups, stews, and sautés, tomatoes are like a secret weapon. Look for brands that contain only tomatoes and salt. I recommend all of the Muir Glen varieties because the cans are BPA free; I especially like the fire-roasted options.

UNSWEETENED APPLE SAUCE

This fruit purée is a paleo-approved way to add a light sweetness to savory dishes instead of honey or other sweeteners that are pure sugar.

☑ VINEGARS (BALSAMIC, CIDER, RICE, WHITE & RED WINE)

Tangy and sharp, vinegar is an easy way to perk up food and complement oils. For balsamic vinegar, look for varieties with no added sulfites (naturally-occurring sulfites are okay). In many cases, you can swap around vinegar varieties, so feel free to experiment to find your favorites.

ALWAYS IN MY KITCHEN

After years of paleo eating, my husband Dave and I have drilled down our grocery shopping list to the essentials we need to stay, um... well fed. When our local grocery store rearranged all of its aisles, Dave used the map of the new layout to develop a spreadsheet that cross-referenced the stuff we buy most often against its new location in the store. So smart! (And nerdy!)

We keep a printout of that list on the front of the fridge and check off the food we need throughout the week, then one of us hits the store, list in hand, and follows the path around the perimeter – from produce to meat, across the back of the store from eggs to canned tuna and pickles and vinegar, to a swoop across the front for frozen veggies and bulk nuts, which conveniently drops us right at the checkout. We supplement our grocery store haul with a monthly delivery of grass-fed beef from a local farm, with an occasional side trip to a natural foods store for other goodies like sunflower seed butter, coconut aminos, and pastured pork.

The foods listed below fall into a special category all their own; they're the foods we never let run out. They're always checked on our list, and we have backups for the backups in our cabinets.

ORGANIC, UNSWEETENED COCONUT FLAKES

Eaten on their own as a snack or sprinkled into and on top of cooked dishes, coconut flakes add another dimension of flavor and texture. They're lovely, little wisps of good-for-you fat that can go savory or sweet. I like to toss a few on top of Thai curries or sprinkle them on a bowl of fruit and coconut milk for dessert.

ORGANIC, GRASS-FED GROUND BEEF

If I have a few pounds of grass-fed ground beef in the fridge, I know I'm only about 10 minutes away from a delicious dinner. Browned and seasoned with garlic and spices, ground beef is like a blank canvas that can be turned into just about any ethnic-inspired meal. Stir-fried with veggies and Chinese five-spice powder, it's instantly Asian. Formed into a burger and piled on top of a big salad, it's all-American. Wrapped in a lettuce leaf with cucumbers, jalapeño, lime, and garlic, it's a Thai wrap.

And don't even get me started on the meatball possibilities – just head on over to page 87. Our favorite application of ground beef right now is the Deconstructed Hamburger Salad: browned ground beef on a bed of lettuce with onion, cucumber, and red bell pepper, dressed with extra-virgin olive oil and vinegar, then topped with a dollop of Olive Oil Mayo (p. 53).

BONELESS, SKINLESS SARDINES PACKED IN OLIVE OIL

These little fish are perfect on-the-go food. My super-secret lunch weapon is a can of sardines, a red bell pepper cut into strips, a cucumber cut into coins, and a small handful of fresh blueberries or cherries. Just a little oily and not too fishy, the sardines are power food – and the leftover oil is perfect for dipping raw veggies. I like the brand Crown Prince (boneless, skinless) the most.

COLLARD GREENS

Kale seems to be the superstar of the paleo world, but I'm here to make a case for collard greens. They're a little sturdier and tenderize during steaming and sautéeing without disintegrating into mushy territory. They can be braised in a coconut milk curry, wrapped around meat fillings and baked in tomato sauce, or sautéed in oil with seasonings to make a vitamin-packed side dish. They're also mild enough to taste great at breakfast with eggs and leftover protein. I like to cut them into 1-inch strips, steam until tender-ish, then sauté them with coconut oil until they get a little dry and crispy. (Or be lazy: Just defrost frozen, chopped collard greens and sauté in coconut oil or ghee.)

ZUCCHINI

I always have a big batch of Silky Gingered Zucchini Soup (p. 206) in the refrigerator so I can start my day with a warm blast of veggies at breakfast. I also make sure I have a big pile of zucchini noodles (p. 168) in the fridge, so I can quickly toss them into an Asian stir-fry or nestle them under Old School Italian Meat Sauce (p. 94) or Shrimp Scampi (p. 114). But whole zucchini are great to have around, too, for last-minute inspiration, like throwing them on the grill or into the oven for roasting.

CAULIFLOWER

Cauliflower might be the most versatile vegetable in the kitchen, so I always have two heads in the fridge at all times. Grated in a food processor and sautéed with fat and spices, it's instant Cauliflower Rice (p. 167). Or boiled in broth and mashed with coconut milk (or a dollop of homemade mayo), it transforms into mashed "potatoes" (p. 167). It also adds a big crunch when chopped raw in salads, and becomes crisp-tender when roasted in the oven.

FROZEN, UNSWEETENED BLACKBERRIES

Low in fructose and high in anti-oxidants, blackberries are loaded with nutrition and flavor. I like to eat them frozen with coconut milk drizzled over the top as a go-along with eggs for breakfast, or as dessert after a paleo dinner. Because they're not too sweet, they don't trigger the sugar demon, but they're sweet enough to feel like a treat.

JICAMA

To be fair, jicama isn't a nutrition powerhouse, but it's not doing any harm either. I love its crisp texture and almost-sweet taste. Peeled, cut into matchsticks, and kept in the fridge, jicama is a cool addition to a crudité platter. Julienned, it makes a lovely salad mixed with lime juice, diced avocado, and slivers of red bell pepper. Its mild taste makes it great at breakfast, too! (Don't miss it as a transport vehicle for Vietnamese Chicken Salad, p. 162.)

FREE-RANGE, ORGANIC EGGS

Any time of day, eggs are a quality source of fast protein. I like to keep a dozen hard-boiled on hand for egg salad or deviled eggs made with Olive Oil Mayo (p. 53). When my day has been long, and I want something comforting, an omelet (like Scheherazade, p. 154) does the trick, and gently scrambled eggs with Zucchini Noodles (p. 168) are amazing comfort food in a flash.

Is this not a photo of the most emo cauliflower ever? It's so moody! Here's a playfully angst-ridden song list to make your time in the kitchen really deep and meaningful. Dancing wholeheartedly encouraged.

THIS CORROSION / Sisters of Mercy (Get the 10-minute version!)
FRIDAY I'M IN LOVE / The Cure
PEEK-A-BOO / Siouxsie and The Banshees
UNDER THE MILKY WAY / The Church
BRING ME TO LIFE / Evanescence (Get the Kevin Roen remix!)
I'M NOT OKAY (I PROMISE) / My Chemical Romance
LIPS LIKE SUGAR / Echo and the Bunnymen
EIGHTIES / Killing Joke
DESIRE (COME AND GET IT) / Gene Loves Jezebel
SHE SELLS SANCTUARY / The Cult
BIZARRE LOVE TRIANGLE / New Order
HEARTBREAK BEAT / The Psychedelic Furs

SPICE IT UP!

One of the things I love about spices and other seasonings is that much like a good book, they can take you just about anywhere in the world. These are the spices and dried herbs you'll need to make the recipes in this book. You don't need to stock up on all of them at once, but I do encourage you to slowly build your collection as you explore new recipes. An unfamiliar spice or herb can open up a whole new world of flavor.

ALEPPO PEPPER

Used in Middle Eastern food to add a fruity kick of moderate heat. Named after the city of Aleppo, located along the Silk Road in northern Syria.

ALLSPICE

Prevalent in Caribbean cuisine, it combines the flavor of cinnamon, nutmeg, and cloves. Also known as Jamaican pepper.

BAY LEAF

Adds depth to soups, stews, and braises, especially in Mediterranean cuisine. According to legend, the oracle at Delphi chewed bay leaves to promote her visions.

CAYENNE PEPPER

Adds a little heat to just about anything. Named for the city of Cayenne in French Guiana.

CHILI POWDER

Used in Tex-Mex, Indian, Chinese, and Thai cuisines. A blend of chili peppers, cumin, oregano, garlic, and salt. Heat varies based on the type of chilies used.

CHINESE FIVE-SPICE POWDER

Balances the yin and yang in Chinese food with star anise, Szechuan peppercorns, cinnamon, cloves, and fennel seeds. In Hawaii, it's used as a condiment in a table-top shaker.

CHIVES, DRIED

Used in French and Swedish cooking, these are the smallest species of edible onion with a mild flavor. Ideal for scrambled eggs, steamed veggies, and creamy salad dressings, I throw them into everything!

CINNAMON

A must-have basic for sweet and savory foods in just about every ethnic cuisine. In ancient times, it was prized as a gift fit for the gods.

CLOVES

Used in sweets, as well as Indian, Vietnamese, Mexican, and Dutch cooking. Eaten on their own, cloves will numb your tongue!

CORIANDER, GROUND

Common in Middle Eastern, Asian, Mediterranean, Indian, Mexican, Latin American, African, and Scandinavian foods. Coriander is the seed of the cilantro plant.

CRUSHED RED PEPPER FLAKES

Made from a combination of dried red peppers including ancho, bell, cayenne, and others. Add a gentle kick to Italian and Asian dishes.

CUMIN, GROUND & WHOLE

Key in North African, Middle Eastern, Mexican, and some Chinese dishes. The Greeks used cumin at the table as a seasoning and that habit continues in modern Morocco. My favorite spice!

CURRY POWDER

Essential for curries, egg or tuna salad, and vegetable dishes. My favorite is Penzeys salt-free Maharajah Style Curry Powder.

GARLIC POWDER, GRANULATED

For just about everything. Fresh is best for cooking, but homemade spice blends require dried garlic. I'm not going to lie to you: Sometimes I just reach for the powder when I don't feel like dealing with mincing the fresh cloves. I'm a culinary pragmatist.

GINGER, POWDERED & FRESH

A necessity for Indian curries and Asian dishes. Scrambled with eggs, it's a paleo home remedy for a cough.

ITALIAN HERB MIX

Enormously helpful for providing a taste of Italy to vegetables, soups, stews, and sautés.

MARJORAM

Slightly sweeter than oregano, but related. Used in the cuisine of the Middle East, Mediterranean, and Eastern Europe.

MINT, DRIED & FRESH

A powerful flavor in Middle Eastern and Mediterranean cooking.

MUSTARD, GROUND & WHOLE

Used in homemade mayo, salad dressings, and piquant spice blends. Jewish texts compare the knowable universe to the size of a mustard seed to teach humility.

NUTMEG

Ground from seed, it's sweet and earthy. Used in many cuisines from around the world. It gives eggnog its holiday taste.

OLD BAY SEASONING

A blend of herbs and spices from the Chesapeake Bay area. Perfect for seafood and chicken.

OREGANO

The "pizza herb" for everything Italian, also good in Turkish, Syrian, Greek, and Latin American foods.

PAPRIKA

Adds a peppery bite and rich color to Moroccan, Middle Eastern, and Eastern European dishes.

PEPPER, BLACK

Important for just about everything. Buy it whole and crush just before using for optimal flavor.

SEA SALT

Salt brings out the best in everything we eat. I like fine sea salt for cooking, preferably iodized.

THYME, DRIED

Used in Middle Eastern, Indian, Italian, French, Spanish, Greek, Caribbean, and Turkish cuisines. The ancient Greeks believe thyme was a source of courage.

TURMERIC

Brilliant yellow, it adds the tang and immediately identifiable color to curry powder.

VANILLA EXTRACT

So sweet! Be sure to read ingredient labels to get pure extract with no added sugar.

ZA'ATAR

A classic Middle Eastern finishing seasoning – made from sesame seeds, dried sumac, salt, and thyme – to sprinkle on salads and cooked vegetables.

A NOTE ON USING DRIED HERBS

When you cook with dried herb leaves like oregano, thyme, or mint, measure the amount you need, then crush the leaves between your fingers before adding to the recipe to unleash the flavor of the herbs.

TASTY TERMINOLOGY

I generally don't use complicated cooking techniques, and I've done my best to explain the directions so that when you make one of my recipes, it comes out just like it would if we were cooking together in your kitchen. I've been told, however, that I have a very aggressive simmer... *hmmph.* I thought it might be useful to explain what I mean when I use generally-accepted cooking terms.

COOK

BOIL

Crank it up! When I say "boil," I mean bring that liquid to a roiling frenzy. ***Fun fact!*** Despite what you might have learned in your cooking education, adding salt to water does not make it boil faster. But salt does make it *hotter.* The boiling point of water is 212F; adding salt increases its boiling point to about 216F. (Nerd alert! The boiling increase is calculated by using the ebullioscopic constant of water. Drop that little tidbit into your dinner conversation.)

BRAISE

When meat and vegetables are braised, they're cooked first in fat, to caramelize and heighten the flavor, then simmered, slow and low, in a small quantity of liquid, usually while covered. This process locks in flavor and juices, while gently cooking the ingredients to fall-apart tenderness. Braising is my favorite technique for pastured meats because even the fattier cuts of grass-fed meat are still leaner than factory-farmed. Grass-fed varieties require TLC to stay tender.

SIMMER

Liquid is said to be simmering when its temperature is 180F to 205F. But who wants to plunge a thermometer in the pot every day? When I say simmer, I mean that the liquid in a pot should have a few small- to medium-sized bubbles that disrupt the surface. This is in contrast to a full boil, in which the surface of the liquid is rockin' and rollin', with large bubbles rising fast and furious to the surface.

SAUTÉ

In French, sauté means "to jump," in reference to the way food is tossed while being sautéed. The trick to a good sauté is to use medium-high heat and a smallish amount of fat to brown the food fairly quickly. This is different from pan frying which, traditionally, uses more fat so the food is immersed, more like deep frying. In my recipes, the terms "sauté" and "pan-fry" can usually be used interchangeably.

MEASURE

PINCH

This is a very tiny amount of seasoning, generally, the amount you can grab between your thumb and index finger. Here's the thing: we all have different-sized hands (and mine are kinda big!). When I say a pinch, I usually mean about 1/8 teaspoon. If you want to be precise about it, you can buy a 1/8 teaspoon measuring spoon – or live dangerously and pinch away!

WHOLE VS. CUT

In many of my recipes, I list the quantity for a whole ingredient (for example, 1/2 cup fresh parley leaves) and the amount you'll have after prepping it (about 2 tablespoons minced). This extra info is provided to help guide your kitchen technique, but don't let it stress you out. It's just another way to explain the recipe. When you chop your 1/2 cup parsley, if it doesn't equal exactly 2 tablespoons, it's just fine; the recipe will still work.

LEVEL VS. HEAPING

Like my simmer, I tend to measure aggressively, too. The ingredients in my measuring cups and spoons aren't exactly *heaping* when I measure, but I'm not super attentive about leveling them off like a construction engineer either. Because the recipes in *Well Fed 2* are not for baked goods (which require a lot of precision), you have flexibility in your measuring. Feel free to make the recipes your own.

TO TASTE

Many of the recipes call for "salt and ground black pepper, to taste." That's so you can season things they way you like them. If you're not sure where to start, 1/2 teaspoon salt and 1/4 teaspoon ground black pepper per 1 pound of meat or vegetables is a good beginning. Be sure to taste your food frequently throughout cooking and season along the way.

CUT

CHOP

When an ingredient is chopped, I mean it should be cut into small, bite-sized pieces that do not need to be uniform in size. I mostly use this term in reference to coarsely chopping fresh herbs or vegetables that will later be puréed.

DICE

In contrast to "chop," food that's diced is cut into pieces that are as uniform in size and shape as possible. Dicing vegetables into an even 1/2-inch or 1/4-inch cube serves two purposes: (1) They cook evenly, and (2) they look pretty in salads and garnishes.

MINCE

This is the smallest cut I can make with a knife. The idea is to create confetti-sized pieces. **Note:** "1 teaspoon minced parsley" means that after mincing, the parsley equals 1 teaspoon. In contrast, "1/4 cup parsley, minced (about 1 tablespoon)" means you measure 1/4 cup leaves, then mince until it equals about 1 tablespoon.

GRATE OR SHRED

To grate or shred an ingredient, you'll probably need a box grater or food processor. This is not the kind of thing most of us can do by hand, no matter how impressive our knife skills.

JULIENNE

Julienne is just about impossible to do with a knife, so I recommend a julienne peeler to make long skinny noodles from vegetables like zucchini, summer squash, carrots, and cucumbers. Many mandoline slicers and food processors have julienne attachments so now might be a good time to read the manual.

MATCHSTICKS

It's pretty easy to cut veggies into thin, stick-like shapes. First, cut lengthwise into thin slices, then stack the slices and cut into narrow sticks. For roly-poly veggies like carrots or cucumbers, cut a thin slice off one side first to create a flat edge. A rolling vegetable is a dangerous vegetable.

0
5
10
15
20
25
30
35
40
45
50
55
Polder

QUICK MEALS

KEEP IT SIMPLE, SWEETIE*

*THAT MAKES 'KISS'

It may seem overwhelming to transition from whatever your "normal" way of eating is to the paleo diet. It's not easy to give up some of your favorite foods, and even though paleo can be very straight-forward – animal protein, vegetables, fruits, and high-quality fats – putting together meals can be confusing when you're just getting started.

I encourage you to keep it as simple as possible for the first week or two. Instead of diving right into the recipes in this book, you might want to simply prepare a bunch of protein and vegetables in advance. That way, you can mix and match throughout the week to make your meals.

PROTEIN

You can grill some chicken, brown a few pounds of ground beef with salt and garlic, and roast a pork shoulder (try Italian Pork Roast, p. 132).

VEGETABLES

Stuff your refrigerator with a rainbow of vegetables and eat them raw, in salads, or steam-sautéed (p. 166) and tossed with melted ghee. The taste-tastic trick? Dust them with aromatic spice blends or drizzle them with luscious sauces. That's it! That's all it takes to "go paleo" without going crazy in the kitchen.

Here are some protein+veggie combinations to get you started:

- **ground beef + broccoli, slivered carrots, mushrooms + coconut aminos**
- **ground pork + red cabbage, roasted spaghetti squash + Sunrise Spice (p. 78)**
- **ground lamb + carrot coins, zucchini coins + Merguez Sausage Seasoning (p. 80)**
- **ground beef + bell peppers, onions + Lizard Sauce (p. 68)**
- **pork roast + zucchini noodles + Romesco Sauce (p. 70)**

For more meal ideas like this, you might want to check out the original *Well Fed* which includes detailed instructions for 47 meat+veggie+spice combos.

NO RECIPE REQUIRED

Here are more ideas for satisfying, paleo-approved meals that you can make without the need to buy specific ingredients at the store or to measure attentively.

BUNLESS BURGERS

You'll never miss the bun! Thick, juicy burgers made from beef, turkey, pork, lamb, bison, or a combination taste great when you top them with all the traditional fixings and serve them alongside a big tossed salad or your favorite cooked vegetables. For 11 fast-and-easy ideas, see page 43.

ANTIPASTO PLATE

Pile some pretty lettuce leaves on a plate, then top them with tuna or skinless, boneless sardines. Arrange a few hard-boiled eggs, green pepper strips, cucumber slices, diced tomatoes, artichoke hearts, and olives alongside the fish. Drizzle with extra-virgin olive oil and red wine vinegar – or with one of the dressings or sauces in the Sauces and Seasonings section (p. 51).

STUFFED AVOCADO

Cut an avocado in half and fill that creamy green shell with tuna, shrimp, crab, or shredded chicken mixed with homemade Olive Oil Mayo or a luscious variation (p. 53). Place it on a plate with carrot sticks, red pepper strips, and cucumber slices on the side, and you've got a beautiful, colorful meal in no time.

ROTISSERIE CHICKEN

Take advantage of pre-made foods at the grocery store! Load up a dinner plate with rotisserie-roasted chicken on top of a salad made from pre-washed greens and broccoli slaw. It's not exactly homemade, but it's a better option than pizza delivery.

STUFFED BAKED SWEET POTATO

Warm, satisfying, and loaded with nutrition! Just brown ground beef, lamb, or turkey with salt, pepper, garlic powder, and a pinch each of cinnamon and chili powder, then spoon the meat into a baked sweet potato and top with chopped fresh herbs and a drizzle of melted ghee (p. 60).

SNACKS IN SECONDS

As much as I like to sit down at a well-set table to eat a leisurely meal, modern life doesn't always allow for that good habit.

Sometimes, you just gotta eat. Here are some grab-and-go snack ideas that balance protein, carbs, and fat so you're fueled up and ready to go at a moment's notice.

Canned kipper snacks with red and green bell pepper strips

Boneless, skinless sardines (packed in olive oil) with cucumber and apple slices

Hard-boiled eggs with a dollop of Olive Oil Mayo (p. 53) and red bell pepper strips

Smoked salmon wrapped around cucumber spears

Cooked chicken spears dipped in guacamole and salsa

Cooked, diced chicken with diced cucumber, sliced black olives, extra-virgin olive oil, salt, and pepper

Diced cooked shrimp tossed with diced tomato, avocado, and lime juice

Cooked chicken piled on half of a baked sweet potato and drizzled with sunflower seed butter

Fresh berries drizzled with a few tablespoons of coconut milk

Paleo-approved lunch meats (Applegate Farms brand is great!) with raw veggies

Sliced roast beef wrapped around pickle spears

Tuna salad with Olive Oil Mayo (p. 53) stuffed in a cucumber boat.

Egg salad made with Olive Oil Mayo (p. 53) spooned in a half bell pepper.

Boneless, skinless sardines wrapped in a nori sheet and dipped in coconut aminos.

Smoked salmon slices and avocado rolled in nori sheets

WEEKLY COOKUPS & HOT PLATES

In my first cookbook Well Fed, *I outlined a plan for a Weekly Cookup and dishes called Hot Plates that make it easy to eat satifsying, paleo meals every day, without spending all of your free time in the kitchen. If you're new to paleo or are a veteran looking for new ways to put together meat+veg+fat, you might want to check it out.*

You can download a free, 30-page preview of Well Fed *at www.theclothesmakethegirl.com/wellfed2.*

So here's an unexpected consequence of switching to paleo: Breakfast might get confusing.

Once you stop thinking of breakfast as toast and oatmeal or a muffin and a glass of milk, you might be stymied by how to start your day. Let me make it a little easier for you. Instead of thinking about breakfast as special – a time when you eat foods that you *only* eat in the morning – think of it as awesome. You can eat whatever you want from the "Yes" list! Anytime!

Grilled chicken and vegetables make an excellent breakfast, and eggs with zucchini can be a comforting dinner after a tough day making your way in the world. Why would you deny yourself the fun of breakfast at 7:00 p.m. or steak after your morning workout by adhering to the conventional notions of breakfast, lunch, and dinner?

Why?

Rather than retrofitting old meal ideas into your new paleo life, just eat whatever combo of protein, vegetables, and fat pleases you at the time. Wake up hungry for steak and sweet potatoes in the morning? Crank up the heat under your cast-iron skillet! Craving the comfort of an omelet after a long day? Scramble it up!

My typical breakfast is usually something like this:

- a small bowl of Silky Gingered Zucchini Soup (p. 206). If I'm really hungry, I might eat it while I'm making the rest of my breakfast.

- a sauté made from grilled chicken thigh cut into cubes, a cup of chopped collard greens (usually frozen greens that have been defrosted in the fridge), a 1/2 cup of roasted sweet potatoes (roasted in advance and cut into cubes), and a dollop of ghee. (We always have a jar of homemade ghee in the cabinet.)

Sometimes I replace the chicken with browned ground beef or leftover meatballs (p. 87) cut into quarters or bits of pulled pork (p. 132) – and instead of collard greens, I might eat steam-sautéed broccoli or cabbage or green beans (p. 166) – but my breakfast looks a lot like my lunches and dinners.

It might seem unusual to eat piles of vegetables for breakfast, but that's what millions of people do all over the world. Here are a few more suggestions to get you started.

LEFTOVERS

Why not eat leftover stew or chili for breakfast?! You can make just about any casserole or curry take on a decidedly breakfast-y vibe when you top it with a fried or poached egg. Or just enjoy it again, as is.

SOUP

Warm and comforting, a mug of soup is a gentle way to start the day – and it's especially nice in colder months. A simple slurp of beef or chicken broth can take the place of coffee, and a smooth, veggie based soup – like Silky Gingered Zucchini (p. 206), Golden Cauliflower (p. 180), or Sweet Potato (p. 210) – is a sneaky way to get more veggies into your day. You can make it a full meal by adding cooked protein or poached/fried eggs.

VEGGIES

I understand that it might be challenging to stare down a plate of Brussels sprouts at 7:00 a.m., but milder veggies like broccoli, zucchini, asparagus, tomatoes, green beans, and spinach are benign enough to face in the morning – and they all pair beautifully with eggs in a scramble or an omelet.

FRY UP!

Let's all thank the Brits right now for a proper cuppa tea and the traditional British fry up, which includes grilled tomatoes and mushrooms with fried eggs, sausage, and bacon. It's a protein-packed way to start (or end!) the day, and it comes with built-in veggies.

SALAD

I admit this might be advanced paleo eating, but one of my favorite breakfasts is a brunch-inspired salad plate: cold smoked salmon, a few hard-boiled eggs, a cucumber cut into thin slices – all drizzled with a little extra-virgin olive oil – and a handful of grapes or berries.

BURGER TOPPERS

WHO NEEDS A BUN?!

Oh, the bunless burger! It's the safe refuge of the paleo eater in a non-paleo world. From low-rent burger joints to high-end restaurants, you can almost always find a variation of meat-and-veg in the shape of a burger without a bun.

A humble meat patty can save you from a meal-related meltdown at home, too. (And all of these ideas taste pretty darned great on a grilled boneless, skinless chicken breast, too.)

As you can see in the Burgers, Balls & Bangers section (p. 87), there are all kinds of ways to flavor the meat itself to make the burgers special, but this list isn't about that. This list is about the simplest, fastest, easiest way to make a plain burger taste good: piling interesting stuff on top of it.

For all of these ideas, you can either load up the rest of the plate with cooked veggies (steam-sauté (p. 166) them then toss with crushed garlic, crushed red pepper flakes, salt, pepper, and olive oil) or piles of fresh, raw veggies for what we always called, "sporty supper" when I was a kid. Done and delicious!

1. ALL-AMERICAN

This one is a "no duh" but it must be included because it's the classic. Pile the following on top of the burger: a thick slice of red onion, a slab of organic tomato, a bunch of your favorite pickles, and a healthy dollop of Awesome Sauce or Russian Dressing (p. 54). If you're a bacon person – and who isn't? – add a slice and revel in the smokiness.

2. PESTO

I love classic basil pesto, but you can experiment with other herbs, too: parsley, mint, and oregano are all fun. Or go big! Spinach, kale, and collards all mellow in a lovely way when whirled with olive oil, nuts, and garlic. Just purée the following in a food processor or blender: 2 cups of herb leaves, a clove of garlic, 1/4 cup extra-virgin olive oil, 1/4 cup walnuts, and a few shakes of salt and pepper. Spread on a hot burger and be transported.

3. AN EGG

Eggs rule. Put a fried egg on top of a burger and both are transformed from their ho-hum natural state to humdinger! Then turn the yum up to the nth power and top the egg with ideas from Stuff To Put On Eggs (p. 47).

4. GO-TO VINAIGRETTE (P. 66)

The sweet, tangy taste of this dressing adds panache to the burger, but you can also play around with your own take on vinaigrette. This simple equation is all you need: extra-virgin olive oil + acid + herbs = lip-licking flavor. Whisk a few tablespoons of citrus juice or vinegar with an equal amount of olive oil, then add crushed, dried herbs or minced, fresh herbs, salt, and pepper. If you want to put in another minute of work, you can add a crushed garlic clove. Good combos include: lemon + oregano, orange + rosemary, lime + cilantro, vinegar + parsley.

5. VEGETABLE RELISH

You cannot go wrong here. Pick out some raw veggies you like – cucumbers, zucchini, carrots, tomatoes, radishes, scallions, bell peppers – and dice them very fine. Throw them in a bowl with a little acid (citrus juice or vinegar), extra-virgin olive oil, salt, and pepper. Let sit for ten minutes, then pile on top of the burger. Bonus points if you add a small dollop of Olive Oil Mayo (p. 53) on top of that.

6. SEASONED FATS

Even a small amount of fat is a major flavor booster. Top your burger with a little seasoned fat and you will be so happy. (By "a little," I really mean a little. Even just 1/2 teaspoon makes all the difference.) Try Better Butter (p. 60), coconut oil, or extra-virgin olive oil – plain or mixed with a favorite spice or blend like Lebanese Seven-Spice Blend (p. 84) or Jerk Seasoning (p. 82). Sesame oil is particularly nice with a crushed garlic clove and instantly makes any meat burger (pork, turkey, beef, chicken) taste Asian. And don't forget all the Mayo Variations (p. 54).

7. FRUIT SALSA

Summer is a great time to mix the sweetness of fresh fruit with some savory goodness; berries, cherries, and stone fruits are all good choices. (In colder months, use defrosted frozen fruit.) You can eat fruit salsa hot or cold. Just mince the fruit, toss with a little lemon juice or vinegar (wine, pomegranate, raspberry, and cider are all nice), and a pinch each of ginger and salt. Let flavors meld at room temp or cook for 3-5 minutes over medium-high heat, then spoon onto a hot burger.

8. GRAVY

Bet you thought paleo meant no gravy! Think again. Mix 1 teaspoon arrowroot powder with a little cool water until smooth. Heat 1 cup of beef broth in a saucepan over medium-high heat until boiling. Drizzle in the arrowroot and whisk until smooth. Season with salt, pepper, and 1/2 teaspoon dried thyme. Simmer until thickened to a consistency you like and drizzle over your burger. Make it a diner dinner with Mashed Cauliflower (p. 167) on the side.

9. QUICK WARM ASIAN SLAW

Julienne these veggies: cabbage, red bell pepper, zucchini, carrots, and scallions. Quickly stir-fry in coconut oil until tender, then toss with a dash of coconut aminos, a pinch of ginger, and a crushed garlic clove. Pile on the burger. Earn bonus points if you serve the slaw-topped burger on a bed of Basic Cauliflower Rice (p. 167).

10. THAI CURRY SAUCE

Stir-fry a tablespoon of green or red curry paste in a teaspoon of coconut oil over medium-high heat for 30 seconds. Add 1/2 cup coconut milk, bring to a boil, and simmer 5 minutes. Drizzle over burger and top with minced cilantro.

TURN IT UP TO 11: MORE PROTEIN

I once ate a "sushi" burger in Venice Beach, California, that just about blew my mind. Top a hot burger with shredded lettuce, avocado slices, and a salad made of shredded crab, scallions, celery, and parsley tossed with Wasabi Mayo (p. 54).

BEYOND BEEF

If you're American, a "burger" usually means 100% beef, but ground lamb, pork, and poultry are also worth grilling. Here are some guidelines to help you choose meat for your burgers; see the Resources section (p. 227) for shopping recommendations.

BEEF: *Your best bet is grass-fed beef, preferably organic.*
PORK: *Look for pastured pork or wild boar to avoid the hazards of the omega-6 fatty acids found in factory-farmed pork.*
LAMB: *Pastured lamb is the healthiest choice.*
POULTRY: *Look for organic, pastured chicken and turkey that's also free of antibiotics.*
GAME MEATS: *Look for pastured, organic, antibiotic-free elk, bison, rabbit, and more.*

If your budget doesn't allow you to buy grass-fed, do not despair! Choose leaner cuts of conventionally-grown protein, then remove excess fat before cooking and drain excess fat after cooking.

DRESS UP YOUR BROCCOLI

BANISH BORING BROCCOLI

I feel like I need to apologize to broccoli.

Whenever I talk about the painful dieting experiences of the past, the example I use for my soul-sucking, pre-paleo food is always, "chicken breast with steamed broccoli."

When I was a "dieter," I ate a lot of chicken breast and broccoli. A lot. Truckloads full. I distinctly remember asking a sales clerk once if a Teflon pan was really, really non-stick because, "I need to be able to put a plain chicken breast in there without any oil to cook it."

And the broccoli didn't fare much better. It was insulted by being steamed, garlic-salted, and tossed with Smart Balance fat-free margarine. Now, of course, I know better. I know that the right amount of healthy fats goes a long way toward making everything taste ever-so-much better, while keeping me fit, healthy, happy, and not feeling deprived.

Sorry, broccoli. Please forgive me!

To atone for my previous bullying of naturally sweet, friendly, nutritious broccoli, here are fun ways you can dress it up.

Let me be clear on one thing: Steamed broccoli is a wonderful way to get it started. It's the food equivalent of perfectly broken-in jeans – not paparazzi-worthy on their own, but a comfortable start to an outfit that gives you the confidence to strut across the room. Put on your broccoli swagger, people!

For all of these ideas, start with broccoli that's steamed or blanched until it's just tender. If you need some guidance on that, read all about how to steam-sauté veggies on page 166. (You might want to try these ideas on green beans and cauliflower, too.)

1. ASIAN FLAIR

Toast some sesame seeds in a dry skillet, then drizzle steamed broccoli with a little sesame oil, sprinkle with sesame seeds, and top with thinly-sliced green tops from scallions. You could also swap in Hoisin Sauce (p. 62) for the sesame oil.

2. ITALIAN SUNSHINE

Thinly slice a few sundried tomatoes and olives, toss with the steamed broccoli, then drizzle the whole shebang with olive oil. Season with salt and pepper, to taste. Add a crushed garlic clove if you're feeling sassy.

3. INDIAN CURRY

Heat some ghee (or Better Butter, p. 60) in a skillet, then fry a little curry powder and raisins in it for a few seconds. Toss with the steamed broccoli. You might also top with sliced, toasted almonds if you really want to treat yourself right.

4. BUTTER & HERBS

Heat some ghee (or Better Butter, p. 60) in a skillet, toss in the broccoli, then sprinkle in dried or fresh chives. Season with salt and pepper. Simple, scrumptious!

5. GO GREEN

Imagine broccoli tossed with a creamy, garlic-herb sauce – either Garlic Mayo or Green Goddess Dressing (p. 54) – then eat that very thing. (And really, let's be honest: Any of the Mayo Variations on page 54 will work wonders on steamed veggies.)

6. ABRACADABRA!

Heat the coconut oil in a skillet, then some cumin and fresh, crushed garlic. Cook over medium heat until the spices are fragrant, then toss with steamed broccoli and sprinkle with Magic Dust (p. 76).

7. LEMON, GARLIC & PEPPER

Place extra-virgin olive oil, red pepper flakes, and crushed, fresh garlic in a skillet to warm over very low heat. Toss with steamed broccoli, then finish with a spritz of fresh lemon juice.

8. THANKSGIVING ANYTIME

Heat coconut oil in a skillet, then add dried cranberries, chopped walnuts, and a pinch of dried thyme. Cook over medium heat until the nuts are toasty, then toss with steamed broccoli and finish with a dusting of orange zest.

9. ZING!

Toss steamed broccoli with Zingy Ginger Dressing (p. 72) and top with thinly sliced scallions.

10. OPEN SESAME

Plate a pile of steamed broccoli, then drizzle with Tahini Dressing (p. 74), plus a light sprinkle of salt and ground black pepper. Bonus points if you add a few toasted sesame seeds and/or sliced black olives.

TURN IT UP TO 11: GRATEFUL FOR GRATIN

Make "bread crumbs:" Mix 1 tablespoon almond flour with 1/2 teaspoon ghee (or Better Butter, p. 60), then sprinkle it with a smidgen of salt. Sauté in a pan over medium-high heat, stirring often with a wooden spoon, until it forms toasty brown crumbs, about 1 minute. Toss steamed broccoli with a little olive oil, then sprinkle with the bread crumbs, salt, and pepper.

BROCCOLI 101

Here are some tips for how to choose, store, and prepare fresh broccoli for maximum nutrition and flavor. Broccoli isn't one of the Dirty Dozen, so you don't have to fret about finding organic; it usually doesn't end up with a pesticide residue.

GO GREEN: *Choose broccoli that's dark green or purplish-green, but pass on yellow. The greener color indicates higher antioxidants.*

FIERCE FLORETS: *Look for florets that are compact and evenly colored. The leaves should be fresh and alert, not wilted, and stalks should not be overly thick or rubbery.*

JUST CHILLIN': *Store broccoli unwashed in the refrigerator. At room temperature, its natural sugars are converted into a fiber called lignin, making your broccoli tough and woody.*

WRAP IT UP: *Keep fresh broccoli in a plastic bag or container in the crisper drawer to maintain proper moisture.*

DIRT IS GOOD: *Don't wash broccoli until just before you're ready to use it. The stems are less nutritious than the florets, so feel free to trim away the tougher ends.*

THE NOSE KNOWS: *Overcooking causes odor. To avoid that distinct broccoli smell, don't cook it in an aluminum pan and steam the broccoli just until it's crisp-tender and bright green.*

STUFF TO PUT ON EGGS

NOT JUST FOR BREAKFAST ANYMORE

Oh, how I love an egg fried in sizzling hot coconut oil! The edges crinkle and brown like ruffles, and in just three to four minutes, the yolk reaches the ideal consistency: no longer liquid, but not quite solid. It's tender and flavorful and luscious.

But you know what makes something good even better?
Good stuff on top.

In no particular order, here are suggestions for stuff you can put on top of eggs. Whether you like 'em fried, scrambled, poached, or folded into an omelet, these toppings will ensure that your humble eggs become something special.

1. CHOPPED CHIVES

A generous sprinkle of dried or fresh chives, along with salt and pepper, adds a light, oniony kick without being overpowering.

2. VIVA ITALIA!

Drizzle with extra-virgin olive oil, then sprinkle with minced parsley and crushed red pepper flakes. The bright, grassiness of the parsley is mellowed by the olive oil and gets a *zing!* from the red pepper.

3. COOL & CREAMY

Try basic Olive Oil Mayo (p. 53) or go gourmet with one of the Mayo Variations (p. 54). The contrast of the cool homemade mayo with the warm egg is irresistible.

4. ROMESCO SAUCE (P. 70) OR LIZARD SAUCE (P. 68)

Say good morning to your taste buds! Just dollop a few spoonfuls of sauce on top of hot eggs and luxuriate in the flavor and texture. You might also add a slinky slice of avocado.

5. TRUFFLE SALT

Truffle salt feels indulgent and tastes like decadence. It's a little pricey, but you use just a pinch at a time, and you're worth it. Rich, mellow, earthy…

6. HOISIN SAUCE (P. 62)

The creamy-sweet-spiciness of the hoisin shines against the backdrop of a simple egg.

7. HEAD EAST, FAR EAST

Dig into the umami of a few drops of coconut aminos and a pinch of spicy-sweet Chinese five-spice powder. Bonus if you add sliced scallion greens.

8. BACON & TOMATO

Slice a strip of raw bacon into 1/4-inch pieces and cook until crisp, then toss with a little finely-minced tomato to make a relish that's even better than traditional bacon-and-eggs.

9. BETTER BUTTER (P. 60)

Warm a teaspoon or two of Better Butter in a saucepan, then spoon over hot eggs and sprinkle with salt and pepper. Prepare to have your mind blown by the taste sensation.

10. SUN SALUTATION

Finely mince a piece of apple, then sauté it in coconut oil or ghee until it's tender, about 5 minutes. Sprinkle with a pinch of Sunrise Spice (p. 78), then spoon on top of hot eggs. You would not be remiss if you added crumbled bacon to this one, too.

TURN IT UP TO 11: MORE SPICES

A pinch of spices along with a touch of ghee is heavenly.
Try Jerk Seasoning (p. 82), Lebanese Seven-Spice Blend (p. 84), or Magic Dust (p. 76).

EGG SAFETY TIPS

- *Inspect eggs in the carton for dirty or broken shells.*
- *Store eggs in their carton to protect shells and maintain moisture.*
- *Keep eggs on a low shelf in the fridge where it's coldest – not on the door.*
- *Wash your hands and work area after handling raw eggs.*
- *Serve hot egg dishes within 2 hours of cooking.*

PALEO FLAVOR BOOSTERS

YOU DESERVE BETTER THAN DULL

Anyone with a dark history of dieting knows all too well that keeping our food simple can sometimes wander dangerously close to boring – and boring leads to binging. That's why it's essential to amp up the flavor of your food whenever possible. A first step to that is understanding how our tasting mechanism works.

Humans can recognize five basic tastes: sweet, bitter, sour, salty, and umami. *Oooooh, umami!*

That's a Japanese word, defined by scientist Dr. Kikunae Ikeda, who discovered this unique taste. It's based on the words *uami* (delicious or savory but not meaty) and *mi* (taste). In practical terms, it's that almost undefinable thing that makes certain foods so luscious. Think about a Thai coconut curry and that little something extra underlying it all. That's the umami of the fish sauce. (Is it a coincidence that umami and yummy kinda sound the same? I think not.)

Here are fast, easy ideas for adding a Super Flavor Power Boost™ to ordinary ingredients. By satisfying your desire for different flavors, you can eat healthful food that's never bland or boring.

1. GOOD FINISHING SALT

When I'm playing in the kitchen, I usually use iodized sea salt during the cooking process, but at the end, when it's time to "taste and adjust," I like to finish with fancy salt: truffle salt, smoked salt, Jane's Crazy Mixed Up Salt (which I used to eat on popcorn all the time, but now enjoy on steamed veg with coconut oil), or the Savory Spice Shop's Ornate Onion Salt. Try a pinch of flavorful salt on browned ground meat, grilled chicken or chops, and cooked veggies to instantly amp up the flavor.

2. TOMATO PASTE

That humble little can is packed with umami flavor. Try this: Sauté onion in a little coconut oil. When the onion is tender and translucent, add a crushed clove of garlic and cook for 30 seconds, then add a tablespoon or two of tomato paste, frying it in the oniony, garlicky oil for a minute. Then add whatever seasonings you like – chili powder + cumin or ginger + Chinese five-spice powder, or Lebanese Seven-Spice Blend (p. 84) – and crumble in ground meat. Cook 'til browned, place on top of a pile of veggies, and chow down.

3. CITRUS JUICE

No matter what you're eating, I bet it can be improved with a spritz of citrus. Try it! You'll see! Grilled chicken and broccoli? Lame. Grilled chicken and broccoli and a spritz of lemon juice? YUM! But don't put yourself in lemon jail! Limes and oranges are brilliant flavor boosters, too. Lime is particularly good with Mexican flavors: cilantro, chili powder, and cumin. Orange is nice with Asian (five-spice powder, ginger) and Middle Eastern (orange + cumin + parsley = profound deliciousness). Want to be even bolder? Sure you do! Grate a little of the zest over your plate for instant wow.

4. OILS OR HOMEMADE MAYO

Sometimes it's not about spicing things up so much as making them luscious. Even half a teaspoon of flavorful oil like high-quality extra-virgin olive oil, drizzled over a plate of meat and veggies, transforms them from "ingredients" to "meal." Rather than cooking with a lot of fat in my food, I reserve my fats for flavoring on top where I can enjoy the taste the most. A tiny drizzle of toasted sesame oil instantly makes Chinese food taste more like the eat-it-from-the-takeout-carton restaurant food I don't enjoy any more. A dollop of Olive Oil Mayo or any of the Mayo Variations (p. 53-54) on top of a hot-from-the-grill chicken breast tastes decadent. TRICK! It's really healthy.

5. CRUSHED GARLIC

Here's a move I learned from *Cook's Illustrated*: place a little of your favorite cooking fat – coconut oil, ghee, extra-virgin olive oil – in a non-stick pan, along with 1-2 crushed garlic cloves. Turn the heat to low. Very low. Let the garlic and fat hang out together for 10 minutes or so, 'til the garlic is tender and mellow, then spoon over whatever meat and veggies are making a guest appearance on your plate.

6. CHOPPED CHIVES

When my plate looks like it might be boring, my secret weapon is dried, chopped chives. I put them on everything from fried eggs to hard-boiled eggs to broccoli to cucumber salad. I have never eaten a vegetable or meat that was not improved by the application of chives. (For Asian food, I usually use the thinly-sliced, green tops of scallions instead because they're bolder.)

7. FRESH HERBS

Forget the sad sprig of parsley used as garnish on the side of the plate. Grab a handful of fresh parsley, mince it, and throw it with abandon over the top of whatever you're eating. It's an instant picker-upper, kind of like the right red lipstick (You know what I mean, ladies.) or a fresh shave (I'm looking at you, gentlemen!). Suddenly, everything is brighter, fresher, and more attractive.

8. COCONUT AMINOS

If you use the recipes from *Well Fed*, you're familiar with coconut aminos in Asian-influenced dishes, but they're also a good stand-in for Worcestershire sauce in other recipes – anytime you need a dark, salty, underlying flavor. Don't be afraid to splash a little into soups and egg or tomato dishes to deepen the flavor.

9. TOASTED COCONUT

It's so easy and instantly makes a plate feel exotic and tropical. Heat a non-stick pan over medium-high, then throw in a handful of unsweetened coconut shreds or flakes. Stir, stir, stir until toasted, then season generously with salt. Sprinkle the coconut over curries, grilled meat, cooked veggies, or whatever.

10. TOASTED, CHOPPED NUTS

Same instructions as #9. Toast the nuts, chop with a sharp knife, and toss onto your plate at will. Sliced almonds and green beans are a winning combo. Broccoli and pecans. Macadamia nuts and… anything. If you like this idea, you will love Magic Dust (p. 76).

TURN IT UP TO 11: COMBOS

This probably goes without saying, but just in case: Holy shmoly! You will be so happy if you combine these tricks. For example:

3. Citrus Juice + 5. Crushed Garlic
3. Citrus Juice + 7. Fresh Herbs
4. Oils or Homemade Mayo + 6. Chopped Chives
5. Crushed Garlic + 6. Chopped Chives
5. Crushed Garlic + 7. Fresh Herbs
5. Crushed Garlic + 10. Toasted, Chopped Nuts
9. Toasted Coconut + 10. Toasted, Chopped Nuts

1 TEASPOON
1 tbsp = 15ml

SAUCES

& SEASONINGS

OLIVE OIL MAYO

AND LOTS OF VARIATIONS!

Lemony, light, silky, and luxurious, homemade mayo makes just about everything better. I recommend that you mix up a batch of the basic Olive Oil Mayo every week so you can use it as a base for lots of creamy variations, depending on your mood.

A FEW THINGS TO KEEP IN MIND:

The blender version is fluffier and thicker; the food processor version is thinner, but still creamy. Both versions will get thicker as they chill in the fridge and both work well as a base for all of the sauce variations.

Cheapo, light-tasting olive oil is best for mayo; the flavor of extra-virgin olive oil is too strong – and bottled lemon juice is better than fresh because of its reliable acid content.

For a video demo of the perfect oil drizzle, visit ***www.theclothesmakethegirl.com/wellfed2.***

Go ahead! Lick the spatula! No one but you needs to know what you do in the kitchen.

OLIVE OIL MAYO

MAKES 1 1/2 *cups* | PREP 10 *min*

INGREDIENTS

1 large egg
2 tablespoons lemon juice
1/4 cup plus 1 cup light-tasting olive oil (not extra-virgin!)
1/2 teaspoon dry mustard
1/2 teaspoon salt

DIRECTIONS

Science! The magic of mayo is that it's an emulsion: The oil and egg plus lemon create a colloid. You don't need to understand all the chemistry, but you do need to bring all of your ingredients to room temperature.

In a blender or food processor, place the egg and the lemon juice. Put the lid on your appliance and allow the liquids to come to room temperature, at least 30 minutes and up to 2 hours.

Add 1/4 cup oil, dry mustard, and salt to the canister and blend on medium until the ingredients are combined. Now the exciting part begins. Your mission is to incorporate the remaining 1 cup oil by pouring very, very slowly. You want the skinniest drizzle you can manage; this takes about 2 to 3 minutes. Breathe. Relax. Sing to yourself.

If you're using a blender, you'll hear the pitch change as the liquid begins to form the emulsion. Eventually, the substance inside the blender will resemble traditional mayonnaise, only far more beautiful. Do not lose your nerve and consider dumping! Continue to drizzle. Slowly.

When all of the oil is incorporated, revel in your triumph and transfer the mayo to a container with a lid. The mayo and whatever sauces you make with it are good for 7-10 days in the fridge.

HEADS UP! *A few of these recipes require you to make a batch of Kickass Ketchup (p. 64) first; plan your prep time accordingly.*

Place all the ingredients in a bowl and mix gently with a spatula until blended. Allow the flavors to meld for 10 minutes before serving. Store covered in the refrigerator.

AWESOME SAUCE

THE NAME SAYS IT ALL

1/3 cup Olive Oil Mayo (p. 53)
1 tablespoon Kickass Ketchup (p. 64)
1 clove garlic, minced (about 1 teaspoon)
1 teaspoon white wine vinegar
1/2 teaspoon coconut aminos
1/2 teaspoon paprika
1/4 teaspoon ground cumin
dash cayenne pepper
salt and ground black pepper, to taste

TARTAR SAUCE

CREAMY AND KICKY —
IDEAL FOR SEAFOOD AND FISH

1/3 cup Olive Oil Mayo (p. 53)
1 tablespoon finely minced dill pickle
2 teaspoons minced fresh parsley leaves
2 teaspoons minced chives (fresh or dried)
1 teaspoon lemon juice
1 teaspoon pickle juice
dash cayenne pepper
salt and ground black pepper, to taste

RUSSIAN DRESSING

THE CLASSIC... GREAT ON A SALAD
OR SCHMEARED ON MEAT AND VEG

1/3 cup Olive Oil Mayo (p. 53)
1 1/2 tablespoons Kickass Ketchup (p. 64)
1/2 tablespoon prepared horseradish
1/2 teaspoon coconut aminos
salt and ground black pepper, to taste

GARLIC MAYO

A LUSCIOUS REPLACEMENT FOR PLAIN MAYO

1/3 cup Olive Oil Mayo (p. 53)
1 clove garlic, minced (about 1 teaspoon)
1/4 cup fresh parsley leaves, minced (about 1 tablespoon)
1/2 tablespoon minced chives (fresh or dried)
salt and ground black pepper, to taste

GREEN GODDESS DRESSING

LUSH WITH HERBS

2/3 cup Olive Oil Mayo (p. 53)
2 tablespoons lemon juice
1/2 cup (packed) fresh parsley leaves
3 tablespoons minced chives (fresh or dried)
1 tablespoon dried tarragon leaves
2 teaspoons anchovy paste (or 2 anchovies)
1 clove garlic, smashed
salt and ground black pepper, to taste

*Blend all ingredients in a food processor or blender.

SPICY COCONUT MAYO

TASTE OF THE TROPICS

1/2 cup Olive Oil Mayo (p. 53)
1/2 small jalapeño, ribs & seeds removed, finely minced
1 clove garlic, minced (about 1 teaspoon)
1/2 tablespoon lime juice
1 tablespoon unsweetened, shredded coconut, toasted
1/4 teaspoon Jerk Seasoning (p. 82)
salt and ground black pepper, to taste

WASABI MAYO

WHAMMO! MAYO WITH A KICK

1/3 cup Olive Oil Mayo (p. 53)
2 teaspoons wasabi paste
2 teaspoons coconut aminos
2 teaspoons rice vinegar
1/2 teaspoon lemon juice
1/4 teaspoon powdered ginger
salt and ground black pepper, to taste

REMOULADE

CAJUN CLASSIC TO AMP UP YOUR SEAFOOD

1/2 cup Olive Oil Mayo (p. 53)
1 scallion, finely minced
1 tablespoon Dijon mustard
1/4 cup fresh parsley leaves, minced (about 1 tablespoon)
1/2 tablespoon white wine vinegar
1/2 tablespoon Louisiana-style hot sauce
1 teaspoon coconut aminos
1 small shallot, minced
1/2 teaspoon lemon juice
1/2 teaspoon mild paprika
1/8 teaspoon salt
1/8 teaspoon cayenne pepper

GYRO/KEBAB SAUCE

LIGHT, LEMONY, MINTY

1/3 cup Olive Oil Mayo (p. 53)
1/4 cup fresh parsley leaves, minced (about 1 tablespoon)
2 tablespoons lemon juice
1 teaspoon dried mint leaves
1 teaspoon za'atar
1 teaspoon Aleppo pepper
1 clove garlic, minced (about 1 teaspoon)
salt and ground black pepper, to taste

This is stick-to-your-ribs thick, but can be thinned with a little warm water if you prefer.

BBQ SAUCE

NATURALLY SWEET AND SPICY

MAKES *2 cups*

PREP 15 MIN. | COOK 25 MIN.

Any respectable BBQ sauce balances sweetness and spice with a touch of sour, all the better to enhance the meatiness of hunks of slow-smoked beef, pork, or chicken. The problem is that most recipes rely on various forms of sugar as their base: commercial ketchup (a.k.a., corn syrup), molasses, brown sugar, honey, and in one classic version, three cups of cola! In this sauce, a humbly-sweet, dried date, sugar-free apple sauce, and the natural sugars in tomato paste do the trick.

INGREDIENTS

- 1 cup water
- 1 (6 ounce) can tomato paste
- 1/3 cup unsweetened apple sauce
- 1/4 cup cider vinegar
- 2 tablespoons coconut aminos
- 1 tablespoon Dijon mustard
- 1 tablespoon sunflower seed butter (no sugar added)
- 1 teaspoon hot pepper sauce
- 1 date, pit removed
- 1 tablespoon coconut oil
- 2 cloves garlic, minced (about 2 teaspoons)
- 1 teaspoon chili powder
- 1/4 teaspoon cayenne pepper
- 1/4 teaspoon dry mustard powder
- 1/4 teaspoon ground cinnamon
- 1/4 teaspoon ground black pepper
- pinch ground cloves
- pinch ground allspice

DIRECTIONS

In a blender or food processor, combine the water, tomato paste, applesauce, vinegar, coconut aminos, mustard, sunflower seed butter, hot pepper sauce, and date. Purée until smooth.

Heat the coconut oil in a medium saucepan over medium heat, about 2 minutes. Add the garlic, chili powder, cayenne, dry mustard, cinnamon, black pepper, cloves, and allspice. Cook until fragrant, about 30 seconds.

Pour the tomato mixture into the saucepan, and whisk to combine. Bring to a boil, then reduce the heat to medium-low and simmer gently, uncovered, until the sauce thickens, about 20 minutes.

Enjoy warm or at room temperature. Store covered in the refrigerator for 1-2 weeks.

YOU KNOW HOW YOU COULD DO THAT?

LIKE IT HOT? *Amp up the amount of cayenne.*

WANT IT SMOKY? *Add 1/2 teaspoon chipotle powder or 1/2 teaspoon liquid smoke.*

TASTY IDEAS

BBQ BEEF "WAFFLE" SANDWICH, P. 116

ALMOST AMBA

TANGY MANGO SAUCE FROM IRAQ

MAKES *2 cups*

PREP	COOK
10 MIN.	1 HR.

Traditional amba is a sort of pickle condiment made from mango and spices. It originated in Iraq, but is also found in Israel and India, where it shows up in street food like falafel, shawarma, and Sabich (p. 136). I'm not ashamed to admit it: After reading about sabich and amba sauce, I became a little obsessed. I'd never eaten either of these things, and I needed to know how they tasted. But it's not like I can just fly off to Israel to eat a snack from a street vendor, so I experimented in my kitchen and made my own version of each. Authentic? Doubtful. Delicious? Definitely.

INGREDIENTS

- 1/2 tablespoon ghee (or coconut oil)
- 1 teaspoon salt
- 2 teaspoons whole mustard seeds
- 2 teaspoons whole cumin seeds
- 2 dried red chile peppers
- 1 teaspoon paprika
- 1/2 teaspoon ground turmeric
- 3 cloves garlic, minced (about 1 tablespoon)
- 1 green mango, peeled, cored, and cut into thin slices
- juice of 1/2 medium orange (about 3 tablespoons)
- 2/3 cup water

DIRECTIONS

Heat a large saucepan over medium-high heat, about 3 minutes. Add ghee and allow it to melt. Add the salt, mustard seeds, cumin seeds, chile peppers, paprika, and turmeric to the pan and toast, about 2 minutes. (You might hear the mustard seeds "pop." That means they're happy!) Add the garlic and stir constantly until fragrant, another 30 seconds.

Add the mango to the pan and stir to combine. Pour in the orange juice and water, and bring to a boil. Reduce heat to low and simmer, covered, until mango is very tender and sauce is beginning to thicken, about 45-60 minutes.

Working in batches, carefully transfer to blender or food processor and purée until smooth. (Hold a dish towel over the lid of the blender to avoid splatters.) Pour into a heat-proof jar and refrigerate. Allow flavors to meld for about a day before eating. Store covered in the refrigerator for up 3 months.

NOTES

This sauce is tangy and addictive. Traditional amba is chunkier, more like chutney in texture, but I like it smooth.

TASTY IDEAS

SEMI SABICH, P. 136

Use as a dipper for raw veggies and grilled meats – it's especially good combined with Tahini Dressing (p. 74) or mixed into mayo for tuna and chicken salad with personality. You can also use it as a simmer sauce for chicken, fish, or shrimp: Lightly sauté your protein of choice, then add Almost Amba, cover, and simmer until cooked through. For bonus points, drizzle with Tahini Dressing before eating.

I ♥
grass

BETTER BUTTER

WHAT'S BETTER THAN BUTTER?

MAKES 1 *cup*

PREP: 10 MIN.

COOK: 1 HR.

It was a celebratory day when I learned that by clarifying pastured, organic butter, I could switch it from the paleo "No" list to the "Yes" list. Then I found this recipe in an out-of-print, 1970s, hippy-dippy cookbook, and the world blew up and was re-formed even better. Despite all the spices in this butter, the end result is subtle, with toasty, warm undertones that heighten the natural butteriness of the butter. And it's even better because turmeric, chiles, ginger, cinnamon, and garlic all have healthy, medicinal qualities.

INGREDIENTS

- 1/2 pound organic, pastured butter
- 1/4 small onion, coarsely chopped
- 6 cloves garlic, peeled and smashed
- 3-inch piece fresh ginger, peeled and smashed
- 2 whole cloves
- 1 cinnamon stick
- 1 or 2 small dried chiles
- 1/4 teaspoon ground turmeric
- 1/4 teaspoon ground cardamom
- pinch ground nutmeg

NOTES *Ginger aids digestion and relieves migraines. Cinnamon helps manage blood sugar and lowers cholesterol. Turmeric fights inflammation. Garlic is anti-viral. And chiles provide flavorful pain relief and heart health.*

DIRECTIONS

Place the butter in a saucepan over medium-high heat and bring to a bubble. When the surface of the butter is foamy, add all the other ingredients. Reduce heat and simmer uncovered on very low heat until the surface is transparent and the solids are on the bottom, about 45-60 minutes.

Place 4 layers of cheese cloth over the mouth of a jar and carefully strain the butter through the cloth. Discard the spices and milk solids. You can store your Better Butter at room temperature for 2-3 months (but I betcha it won't last that long).

YOU KNOW HOW YOU COULD DO THAT?

Plain clarified butter, known as ghee, is another must-have kitchen staple. To make plain ghee, just melt the butter as directed above, simmer for 10-15 minutes, then strain to remove milk solids. OMGhee!

TASTY IDEAS

Use Better Butter in savory dishes: Melt it on top of steamed vegetables, toss with veggies for roasting, drop a small dollop on top of grilled meat, or use it to fry eggs.

GET FANCY! *Pour melted Better Butter into differently shaped dishes and chill in the refrigerator to make shapes like sticks, cubes, or rounds.*

How can you have a
beautiful ending without
making beautiful mistake

HOISIN SAUCE

THE GOOD FORTUNE OF DIPPING SAUCE FROM BEIJING

MAKES 1 *cup*

PREP	COOK
5 MIN.	N/A

Hoisin sauce is traditionally made with toasted, mashed soy beans, sugar, vinegar, and spices. When it's made in a commercial kitchen, preservatives and artificial colors are usually thrown in, too. We can do so much better! This homemade hoisin sauce is the perfect drizzle over Moo Shu Pork (p. 144) and while it lacks the dark brown color of store-bought hoisin, its kick of flavor more than makes up for it.

INGREDIENTS

- 1/2 cup coconut aminos
- 1/4 cup sunflower seed butter (no sugar added)
- 4 teaspoons rice vinegar
- 2 cloves garlic, peeled and smashed
- 1 dried date or dried fig (pit and/or stem removed)
- 1 tablespoon toasted sesame oil
- 1 teaspoon hot sauce
- 1/4 teaspoon ground black pepper

DIRECTIONS

Place all the ingredients in a blender or food processor and purée until smooth.

Allow the flavors to meld about 10 minutes before using. Store covered in the refrigerator for up to 2 weeks.

TASTY IDEAS

MOO SHU PORK, P. 144

TAKE A DIP! *Use as a dipping sauce for steamed shrimp and grilled strips of chicken, steak, or pork – or drizzle onto a beef or pork burger.*

STIR IT UP! *Throw into the pan to flavor a stir-fry. (Lamb and scallions are particularly nice.)*

ROAST IT! *Toss with halved Brussels sprouts or cubed sweet potatoes, then roast (400F, 35-40 minutes).*

NOTES

ketchup

KICKASS KETCHUP

FORGET THE SQUEEZABLE PACKET

MAKES 1 1/2 *cups*

PREP	COOK
10 MIN.	10 MIN.

More than 650 million bottles of Heinz Ketchup are sold around the world each year. But not to you and me, my friends, because most big-name ketchup brands include the always-suspect "natural flavoring," along with xantham gum, corn syrup, and high fructose corn syrup. Bet you didn't know that 25 percent of ketchup is sugar – unless you make it yourself with this recipe. It really couldn't be easier, and it tastes even better than the bottled stuff on burgers, sweet potato fries, your favorite paleo meatloaf, sauces made with Olive Oil Mayo (p. 53), and more.

INGREDIENTS

- 1 (6 ounce) can tomato paste
- 1/3 cup plus 1/2 cup water
- 2 tablespoons cider vinegar
- 2 dried figs, stems removed and coarsely chopped
- 1/2 tablespoon coconut oil
- 1/4 teaspoon dry mustard powder
- 1/4 teaspoon ground cinnamon
- pinch ground cloves
- pinch ground allspice

YOU KNOW HOW YOU COULD DO THAT?

Make it spicy with 1 teaspoon cayenne pepper, or smoky with 1 teaspoon chipotle chili powder, or exotic with 1 tablespoon curry powder.

TASTY IDEAS

GO-TO VINAIGRETTE, P. 66
CHICKEN NANKING, P. 124
RUSSIAN DRESSING, P. 54
AWESOME SAUCE, P. 54

DIRECTIONS

Place tomato paste, 1/3 cup water, vinegar, and figs in a blender or food processor and purée until smooth, scraping down the sides a few times to make sure the figs are incorporated. Set aside.

Heat a small saucepan over medium-high heat. Add coconut oil and allow it to melt, about 2 minutes. Add dry mustard, cinnamon, cloves, and allspice to pan and stir until fragrant, about 30 seconds.

Remove from heat, then add tomato purée to the pan and stir until combined. Return to heat and cook 2-3 minutes, then add remaining 1/2 cup water, stirring to combine. Bring to a boil, then reduce heat to low and simmer gently, uncovered, for 5 minutes. (The ketchup will thicken as it cools, but if you like it thicker, allow it to cook slightly longer. Want it thinner? Add a bit of water.)

Cool the ketchup to room temperature before you eat it. Transfer to a container with a lid and store in the refrigerator for 2 to 3 weeks.

NOTES ***Outside the United States, ketchup doesn't always mean tomatoes. Other flavors include lobster, anchovy, walnut, mushroom, cucumber, cranberry, lemon, and banana.***

GO-TO VINAIGRETTE

TURNS SALAD INTO SOMETHING SPECIAL

MAKES 1 1/2 *cups*

PREP	COOK
10 MIN.	N/A

Every cook needs a signature salad dressing, and I encourage you to make this one yours. It combines elements of a sweet French dressing and a standard oil-and-vinegar to become its own thing. It's a little tangy, with the light taste of chives and the sweetness of homemade ketchup to balance the slight acidity of the lemon.

Heads up! This recipe requires you to do something in advance; plan prep time accordingly.

INGREDIENTS

- 1 shallot, finely minced
- 1/3 cup lemon juice
- 2 tablespoons Kickass Ketchup (p. 64)
- 2 tablespoons water
- 1 teaspoon salt
- 2 tablespoons dried (or fresh) chives
- 1/2 teaspoon dry mustard
- 1/2 teaspoon dried oregano leaves
- 1/2 teaspoon paprika
- 1/4 teaspoon hot sauce
- 2/3 cup extra-virgin olive oil

DIRECTIONS

In a medium bowl, whisk all ingredients except olive oil.

While whisking continuously, drizzle the olive oil into the bowl in a slow, steady stream until combined.

Allow the flavors to meld about 10 minutes before eating. Store covered in the refrigerator for up to a week.

YOU KNOW HOW YOU COULD DO THAT?

Adding 1-2 tablespoons of poppy seeds is not a bad idea.

TASTY IDEAS

DRIZZLE WITH ABANDON! *Salads, steamed veggies, or cooked meats – it's your go-to, your wing-man, your bestie in the kitchen.*

NOTES

LIZARD SAUCE

THE TASTE OF COSTA RICA

MAKES 2 cups

PREP	COOK
10 MIN.	30 MIN.

Once upon a time, we took a spur-of-the-moment trip to Costa Rica, thinking it would be a big adventure. For a variety of reasons, it wasn't a dream vacation. But there were two bright spots: I loved the lizards that ran rampant over the landscape, and at every meal, a bottle of Salsa Lizano was on the table. Kind of like Costa Rican ketchup, it's poured on everything from eggs to tacos to burgers to plantains. Made from vegetables, it's lightly sweet with a hint of cumin and smokiness from guajillo peppers. Don't be put off by the guajillos; they're easy to work with and can be found in most grocery stores or online.

INGREDIENTS

- 4 dried guajillo peppers
- 2 cups water
- 1 tablespoon coconut oil
- 1/2 medium yellow onion, diced (about 1/2 cup)
- 1 medium carrot, peeled and diced (about 1/2 cup)
- 1/2 rib celery, diced (about 1/4 cup)
- 1/4 red bell pepper, diced (about 1/4 cup)
- 4 cloves garlic, peeled and smashed
- 1 tablespoon ground cumin
- 2 teaspoons salt
- 1 teaspoon cayenne pepper
- 2 tablespoons lemon juice
- 1 tablespoon cider vinegar

DIRECTIONS

Cut the guajillo peppers in half lengthwise and remove the seeds. Heat a cast-iron skillet over medium-high heat, about 3 minutes. Add the peppers and toast until starting to brown, about 1 minute per side. Add the water, bring to a boil, and simmer 5 minutes. Put the peppers in a blender or food processor with 1 cup of the water from the pan.

Dry the pan and reheat over medium-high heat, about 3 minutes. Place the coconut oil in the pan and when it's melted, add the onion, carrot, celery, bell pepper, and garlic. Sauté until soft and beginning to turn golden, 5-7 minutes. Add the cumin, salt, and cayenne, stirring until fragrant, about 30 seconds. Turn off heat, add lemon juice and vinegar; stir to combine.

Remove the vegetables from the pan and carefully add them to the blender. Purée until smooth.

Allow the flavors to meld about 10 minutes before using, then eat at room temperature or chilled on EVERYTHING! Store covered in the refrigerator for up to 3 weeks.

TASTY IDEAS

Use as a dipper for raw vegetables and cooked protein – add a kick to grilled chicken! Fire up your morning by spooning onto fried eggs. And you definitely want to drizzle some on Pan-Fried Plantains (p. 184), Plantain Nachos (p. 146), or Tex-Mex Salmon Cakes (p. 138). You can also use it as a simmer sauce for chicken, pork, fish, or shrimp. Simply sauté the protein, then add Lizard Sauce, cover, and simmer until cooked through.

NOTES

ROMESCO SAUCE

GET PIQUANT WITH PIQUILLOS

MAKES 2 cups

PREP	SOAK	COOK
15 MIN.	30 MIN.	20 MIN.

Romesco is a traditional red pepper sauce from Catalonia, Spain. It makes the most of simple Mediterranean ingredients like extra-virgin olive oil, almonds, garlic, and paprika, transforming them into a flavorful, rugged sauce. Served with fish, poultry, pork, and vegetables, it's both rustic and sophisticated. This recipe uses sweetly spicy piquillo peppers – which can be found roasted and jarred in most grocery stores – and results in a texture similar to salsa.

INGREDIENTS

1 dried ancho chile

2-3 cups boiling water

2 tablespoons extra-virgin olive oil

1/3 cup blanched, slivered almonds

4 cloves garlic, peeled and thinly sliced

1/2 teaspoon paprika (smoked is especially nice)

1/4 teaspoon cayenne pepper

1/4 teaspoon salt

1 medium tomato, seeded and chopped (about 2/3 cup)

1 (12 ounce) jar piquillo peppers, drained and chopped

1 tablespoon cider vinegar

DIRECTIONS

Cut the ancho chile in half lengthwise and remove the stem, ribs, and seeds. (It's easiest to do this with kitchen shears, rather than a knife.) Place in a medium-sized bowl, cover with boiling water, and set aside for 30 minutes.

Heat the oil in a large, non-stick skillet over very low heat. Add the almonds and cook, stirring occasionally, until they're golden, about 5-7 minutes. Add the garlic, and stir until lightly brown, about 2 minutes. Add the paprika, cayenne, and salt, stirring until fragrant, about 30 seconds.

Drain the ancho chile and chop it, then add it to the pan. Cook about 2 minutes. Add the tomato; stir, and cook until soft, about 2-3 minutes. Finally, add the piquillo peppers, stirring to combine everyting. Cook an additional 3 minutes or so while you daydream of the craggy shores of the Mediterranean.

Carefully (!) transfer to the bowl of a food processor and run the motor until it's almost smooth – I saw this described in one recipe as "nubbly." Add the vinegar and pulse until combined. Allow to cool to room temperature before eating. Store covered in the refrigerator for up to 10 days.

Piquillo peppers are packed with as much Vitamin C as citrus fruit, so dig into Romesco, and you'll never get scurvy!

TASTY IDEAS

OVEN-FRIED SALMON CAKES, P. 138

PAN-FRIED SARDINES, P. 158

It's excellent on grilled salmon or cooked eggs. Add a dollop to a piece of grilled chicken or steak to turn the meat into a meal. A few spoonfuls mashed into a baked sweet potato elevates it beyond its humble beginnings. Spread it on thick slices of roasted sweet onion for a sublime side dish.

To serve with meat or eggs, warm the sauce gently over low heat. For veg, bring it to room temp for maximum flavor while dipping.

ZINGY GINGER DRESSING

SHOCKINGLY ADDICTIVE

MAKES 1 1/2 *cups*

PREP	COOK
10 MIN.	N/A

Have you ever eaten in one of those Japanese steakhouses where the chef cooks your meal right at the grill table in front of you, and he tries to entertain you by tossing his cleaver and flicking a shrimp tail into someone's pocket and building a miniature, steaming volcano out of onion slices, and all you can think about is how to get the waitress to bring you another salad with that amazingly gingery dressing on iceberg lettuce? THIS is the homemade version of that dressing. It's one of my favorite recipes.

INGREDIENTS

- 1/2 cup light tasting olive oil (not extra virgin!)
- 1/4 cup rice vinegar
- 1 tablespoon coconut aminos
- 2 medium carrots, peeled and cut into chunks
- 1/4 medium yellow onion, peeled and cut into chunks
- 2-inch piece fresh ginger, grated (about 1 tablespoon)
- 1 medium clove garlic, peeled and smashed
- salt and ground black pepper, to taste

NOTES

The Benihana restaurant chain was founded by Hiraoki "Rocky" Aoki on West 56th in New York in 1964. Back in the day, The Beatles and Mohammad Ali ate there.

DIRECTIONS

Combine all ingredients in a food processor and purée until smooth. Add water 1 tablespoon at a time, if necessary, to reach your desired consistency.

Allow the flavors to meld about 10 minutes before eating. Store covered in the refrigerator for up to 2 weeks.

YOU KNOW HOW YOU COULD DO THAT?

You can replace the rice vinegar with cider vineger.

TASTY IDEAS

Dollop it – don't toss – on a salad of iceberg lettuce, cucumbers, and red bell peppers, or use it as a dipper for steamed shrimp and raw veggies. Someone might call you brilliant if you use it as a replacement for the dressing on Spring Chopped Salad (p. 208).

TAHINI DRESSING

IN TRIBUTE TO THE MOST ORNERY, DELIGHTFUL CAT EVER

MAKES 1 *cup*

PREP	COOK
10 MIN.	N/A

This story has nothing to do with a recipe and everything to do with being who you want to be. Once upon a time, we adopted a cat named Sesame. She was a regal calico, and when she was young, we often referred to her as Supermodel. Later, when her true character began to show, we called her Punk Rock Kitty. Social niceties weren't her style, but when she did relent and show some affection, we knew she meant it. She was loud, opinionated, and relentless in her pursuit of what she wanted, including her food, which she ate with gusto for 19 fierce years.

INGREDIENTS

1/2 cup tahini
1/2 cup plus 2 tablespoons water
juice of 1 lemon (about 2 tablespoons)
2 cloves garlic, peeled and smashed
salt and ground black pepper, to taste

NOTES

Grill sliced eggplant and zucchini, then top with tahini dressing and minced fresh parsley.

DIRECTIONS

Place all the ingredients in a blender or food processor and purée until smooth.

Allow the flavors to meld about 10 minutes before eating. Store covered in the refrigerator for up to 2 weeks.

YOU KNOW HOW YOU COULD DO THAT?

SPICE IT UP! *Add 1/2 teaspoon of one or two of the following spices to add a little extra kick:*

- *cayenne pepper*
- *ground cumin*
- *ground coriander*
- *Lebanese Seven-Spice Blend (p. 84)*

TASTY IDEAS

Tahini Dressing is lovely drizzled over grilled protein (especially chicken, lamb, fish, and seafood) and veggies (like Spring Chopped Salad, p. 208 or Herb Salad, p. 196). It's also a good dipping sauce for Stuffed Grape Leaves (p. 148), and it really makes Semi Sabich (p. 136).

MAKE A MEAL! *Cook a pile of veggies; chopped caulifower and spinach are nice. Top the pile with cooked protein: ground beef, grilled chicken, or broiled lamb. Drizzle with Tahini Dressing and sprinkle the top with a minced raw tomato and parlsey.*

DANCE PARTY IN YOUR MOUTH! *Double drizzle with Almost Amba (p. 58) and Tahini Dressing.*

MAGIC DUST

YOU CAN CALL IT "SERÚNDENG KATJANG"

MAKES 1 1/2 *cups*

PREP	SAUTE	BAKE
5 MIN.	15 MIN.	45 MIN.

One of my favorite cookbooks is a tattered, out-of-print copy of Natural Food Feasts, *a super-groovy, '70s cookbook with recipes from Asia and the Middle East. It's handwritten and illustrated with hundreds of sketches that show how to cut vegetables and dismantle hunks of meat. The pages crinkle just right, and it's an encyclopedia of exotic food ideas, with entries like* serundeng katjang. *Which is an Indonesian condiment made from roasted peanuts, shredded coconut, and spices. This version is paleoized and ready to be sprinkled over curries, eggs, and vegetable dishes to add flavor and texture.*

INGREDIENTS

- 1/2 tablespoon coconut oil
- 1/2 medium onion, very finely diced (about 1/4 cup)
- 1 clove garlic, crushed (about 1 teaspoon)
- 1/2 teaspoon powdered ginger
- 1/2 teaspoon ground cumin
- 1/2 teaspoon ground coriander
- 1/2 teaspoon salt
- 1/2 teaspoon ground turmeric
- 1/2 tablespoon lemon juice
- 3/4 cup unsweetened coconut flakes
- 1/2 cup dry-roasted almonds
- 1/3 cup dry-roasted cashews

DIRECTIONS

Preheat oven to 300F and cover a large baking sheet with parchment paper.

Heat coconut oil in a large skillet over medium heat until melted, then add onion and garlic. Cook 2-3 minutes until the onions begin to soften and tickle your nose.

In a small bowl, mix the ginger, cumin, coriander, salt, and turmeric. Add the spices to the onions, stir to combine, and cook an additional 5-7 minutes until the onions are very soft. Add the lemon juice and cook until the mixture forms a paste, about 2 minutes. Add the coconut flakes to the pan and stir until they're coated with the onions and spices.

Transfer to the baking sheet and bake for 30 minutes. Stir with a wooden spoon and add the nuts to the baking sheet. Roast an additional 10-15 minutes until the coconut/onion flakes are very brown, and the nuts are toasted.

Allow to cool completely, then pulse in a food processor until it resembles coarse granola. Store in an airtight container at room temperature and use as a flavoring condiment on cooked foods.

YOU KNOW HOW YOU COULD DO THAT?

Feel free to swap in other nuts or change up the spices. Just replace all the spices with 1 tablespoon of any of the following: Lebanese Seven-Spice (p. 84), Sunrise Spice (p. 78), Jerk Seasoning (p. 82), or Chinese five-spice.

TASTY IDEAS

Magic Dust is enchanting on just about everything! Sprinkle on cooked veggies, mix into meatballs, toss into salads, scatter across the top of soups, stir into Basic Cauliflower Rice (p. 167), or shake onto Zucchini Noodles (p. 168).

TASTY IDEAS

SWEET POTATO SOUP, P. 210
SUNRISE SCRAMBLE, P. 108
PORK RIBS, P. 128
PORK ROAST, P. 132

SUNRISE SPICE

THE TASTE OF SUNSHINE ANY TIME OF DAY

MAKES 1/4 *cup*

PREP	COOK
5 MIN.	N/A

A little bit Russian, a little bit Central European, this spice blend is cozy and spicy-sweet without being hot. Think of it as a jazzed-up version of cinnamon – the Catherine the Great of your spice cabinet, bestowing a touch of the Golden Age on whatever you're cooking. From scrambled eggs to sweet potatoes to beef stew, sprinkle it generously whenever you want to add a regal touch to savory dishes.

INGREDIENTS

- 1 1/2 tablespoons ground cinnamon
- 2 teaspoons ground marjoram
- 1 teaspoon coarse (granulated) garlic powder
- 1 teaspoon salt
- 1/2 teaspoon ground nutmeg
- 1/2 teaspoon paprika
- 1/2 teaspoon ground black pepper
- 1/4 teaspoon ground allspice

DIRECTIONS

Measure all of the spices into a medium bowl and mix with a fork until combined.

Transfer the spice blend to an airtight container and sprinkle into your cooking for a sweet touch of spice to brighten your day.

YOU KNOW HOW YOU COULD DO THAT?

Mix 1 tablespoon per pound into ground beef, pork, lamb, or turkey for instant sausage. Just shape into patties or brown loose in a skillet. Sunrise Spice brightens up baked sweet potatoes, cooked carrots, Pan-Fried Plantains (p. 184), and roasted butternut or acorn squash.

NOTES

Got the original* Well Fed*? This spice blend is an excellent addition to Hot Plates.

MERGUEZ SAUSAGE SEASONING

WEARING A FEZ IS OPTIONAL

MAKES 1/3 *cup*

PREP	COOK
5 MIN.	N/A

Merguez is a spicy lamb sausage popular in North Africa. During their colonial rule of Morocco, the French appropriated the spicy links, and they're now considered part of France's national cuisine. Merguez sausages can be purchased from street vendors and specialty markets from Paris, France to Fes, Morocco. They're fragrant with paprika, cumin, coriander, and fennel. This blend is less fiery than the harissa-spiced original, but it's guaranteed to transport you to the cobbled, winding alleys of an old city. Use it as a rub for meats or sausage-on-demand by mixing into ground meat.

INGREDIENTS

2 tablespoons paprika
1 tablespoon ground fennel seeds
1 tablespoon ground cumin
1 tablespoon salt
1/2 tablespoon ground coriander
1/2 teaspoon ground cinnamon
1/2 teaspoon cayenne pepper
1/2 teaspoon ground black pepper

DIRECTIONS

Measure all of the spices into a medium bowl and mix with a fork until combined.

Transfer the spice blend to an airtight container and bust it out whenever you need to be whisked away to a Moroccan marketplace.

YOU KNOW HOW YOU COULD DO THAT?

Want it fiery like the hot, desert winds known as sirocco? Add an additional 1/4 teaspoon cayenne.

TASTY IDEAS

MERGUEZ BURGERS/BALLS/BANGERS, P. 90
PORK RIBS, P. 128
PORK ROAST, P. 132
DECONSTRUCTED GYRO, P. 126

NOTES ***With a population of one million, Fes is the second largest city in Morocco and is known as the "Athens of Africa."***

JERK

JERK SEASONING

WALK GOOD*

MAKES 1/4 *cup*

PREP	COOK
5 MIN.	N/A

You probably think you know what jerk means – especially if you have a boss, a younger sibling, an annoying roommate, or a lame neighbor. But let me tell you more: Jerk is a Jamaican style of cooking meat and fish that describes both the spice rub and the grilling technique. Street-side jerk stands (insert your own joke here) are found throughout the Caribbean, serving up spicy meat and, presumably, witty banter. This jerk seasoning isn't too hot, and the heat is balanced by the sweet-spiciness of cinnamon, nutmeg, and allspice.

INGREDIENTS

1 tablespoon salt

1 tablespoon allspice

1/2 tablespoon dried thyme leaves

2 teaspoons ground black pepper

1 teaspoon cayenne pepper

1/2 teaspoon ground cinnamon

1/2 teaspoon ground nutmeg

NOTES

****In Jamaica, "walk good" is an intimate way to say "goodbye" or "take care" to friends.***

DIRECTIONS

Measure all of the spices into a medium bowl and mix with a fork until combined.

Transfer the spice blend to an airtight container and sprinkle it on meat and veggies when (1) someone has been a jerk to you and you'd like to put a voodoo curse on them; or (2) you want to add a spicy-sweet-hot kick to whatever's on your plate.

YOU KNOW HOW YOU COULD DO THAT?

If you like fire on your tongue, you can increase the amount of cayenne pepper by 1/4 teaspoon. Go for it!

TASTY IDEAS

OVEN-FRIED SALMON CAKES, P. 138

PINA COLADA CHICKEN, P. 96

SPICY COCONUT MAYO, P. 54

TROPICAL CHOPPED SALAD, P. 140

SHRIMP SCAMPI, P. 114

PAN-FRIED SARDINES, P. 158

PORK ROAST, P. 132

PORK RIBS, P. 128

- *Sprinkle on freshly cooked eggs (or hard-boiled eggs!).*
- *Rub on chicken pieces – along with a little melted ghee or Better Butter (p. 60) – then grill and spritz with lime juice. Serve it up on Citrus Cauliflower Rice (p. 188).*

LEBANESE SEVEN-SPICE BLEND

WHY USE ONE WHEN YOU CAN USE SEVEN?!

MAKES 1/4 *cup*

PREP	COOK
10 MIN.	N/A

A Lebanese Seven-Spice Blend is as common in Lebanese kitchens as salt, and every cook makes her own blend, changing the proportions according to her whims. Recipes are passed down through families and also vary region to region. What's constant is the subtle interplay of flavors and aromatic spices that whisper of Arabian delights.

INGREDIENTS

1 tablespoon ground allspice
1 tablespoon ground black pepper
1 tablespoon ground cinnamon
1 teaspoon ground cloves
1 teaspoon ground coriander
1 teaspoon powdered ginger
1 teaspoon ground nutmeg

NOTES

Use as a rub on steaks, chops, or chicken, or sprinkle onto just-cooked eggs or cooked vegetables with a drizzle of extra-virgin olive oil.

DIRECTIONS

Measure all of the spices into a medium bowl and mix with a fork until combined. Take a sniff!

Transfer the spice blend to an airtight container and sprinkle with abandon on meat and vegetables to add exotic flair.

YOU KNOW HOW YOU COULD DO THAT?

MAKE NINE-SPICE! *Add 1 teaspoon ground cumin and 1 teaspoon ground cardamom.*

TASTY IDEAS

STUFFED GRAPE LEAVES, P. 148
TABBOULEH, P. 172
SCHEHEREZADE OMELET, P. 154
LEBANESE BURGERS/BALLS/BANGERS, P. 90
PORK RIBS, P. 128
CRISPY CHICKEN LIVERS, P. 106
PORK ROAST, P. 132
OVEN-FRIED SALMON CAKES, P. 138
PAN-FRIED SARDINES, P. 158

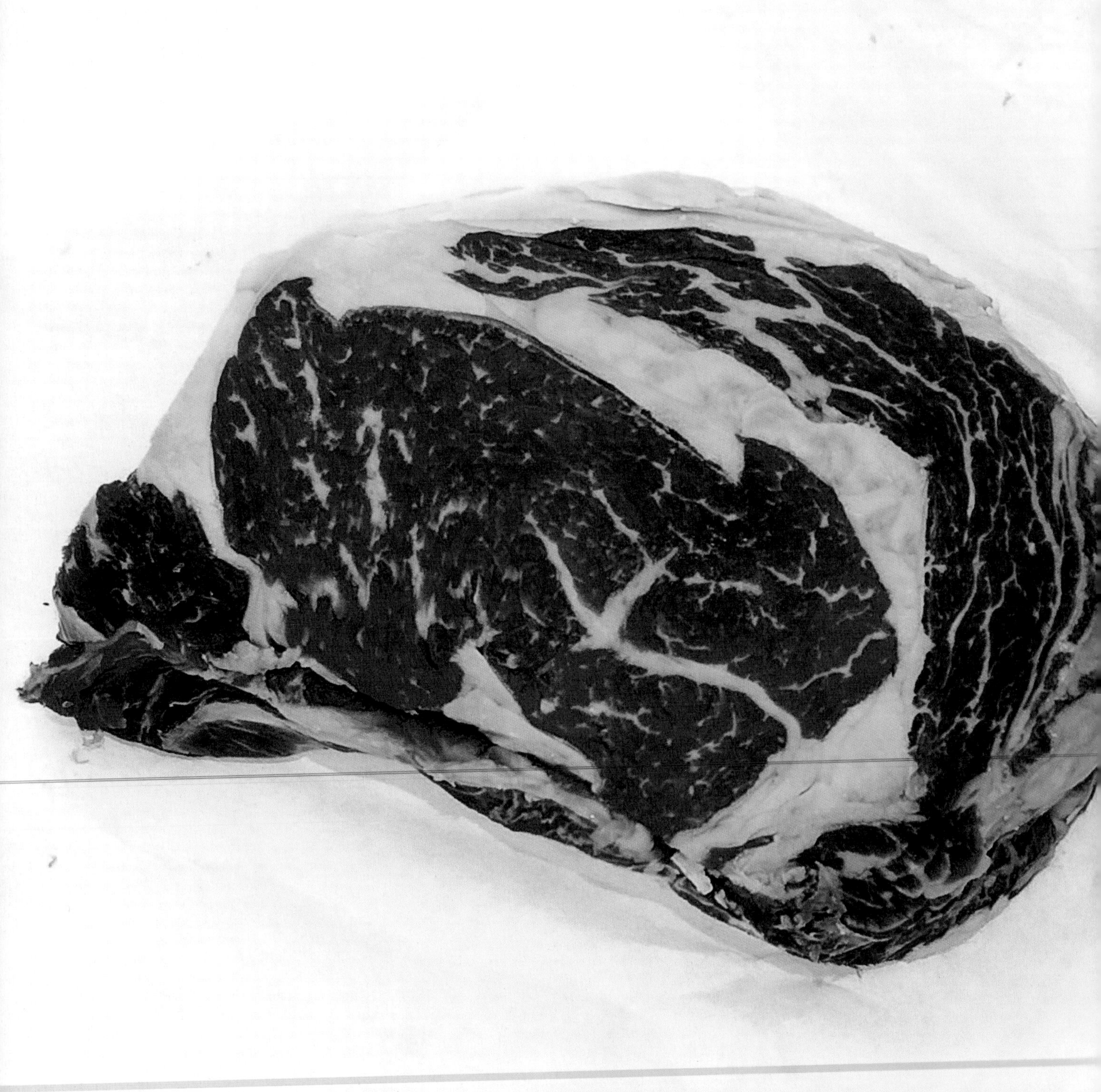

PROTEIN

You know what's delicious? Sausage! You know what's not *delicious? Sausage that's been corrupted with added sugar, unpronounceable ingredients, and preservatives. Sadly, even handmade options from an expert butcher can include sugar.* ***I've got the solution for you!*** *Homemade sausage is as easy as mixing spices and meat in a big ol' bowl.*

These recipes were inspired by traditional sausages and cuisine from around the world – and they can each be made in less than an hour. The result is burger patties, meatballs, and links that are tender in the middle with a satisfying, snappy exterior. These recipes are easy to double and freeze very well, so you can turn your kitchen into a sausage factory. Or something.

HOW IT WORKS

On the next few pages, you'll find assembly instructions and recipes for 15 Burgers, Balls & Bangers. Here are the step-by-step instructions to put it all together.

CHOOSE A RECIPE.

Check out pages 89-92! You'll find the ingredients for 15 varieties of sausages that combine herbs and spices with ground beef, pork, lamb, chicken, and turkey.

SELECT A SHAPE.

Minced meat with spices shows up in a variety of shapes and cooking techniques all over the world. There's no reason you can't feel like a grilled burger today and baked meatballs tomorrow. Page 88 details how to shape the meat and cook it according to your mood.

FOLLOW THE MASTER INSTRUCTIONS.

Glance to your right at the **Master Instructions**. Those are the directions for how to use the ingredients on pages 89-92. The how-to for each variety is the same; just follow those Master Instructions, and you'll be a sausage master.

CHANGE IT UP.

Each of the Burgers, Balls & Bangers recipes includes variations for meat combos and tips on garnishes and go-alongs, so your taste buds will never be bored (and you can happily gobble up the nutritious vegetable odds and ends in the back of your refrigerator).

MASTER INSTRUCTIONS

1. Prep. In a small bowl, mix baking soda and cream of tartar in water. Meanwhile, place meat and all other flavorings in a mixing bowl. Add the baking soda/water to meat.

2. Blend. For a smoother, more tender texture, use a food processor or a standing mixer – fitted with the paddle attachment – to blend the ingredients. For more a traditional texture, mix the meat by hand.

3. Shape & Cook. Form into your desired shape – burgers, balls, or bangers – and chill for 10 minutes in the fridge. Then choose your cooking method – oven baked, gas grilled, or pan fried – and fire it up. (See freeze/reheat details on page 92.)

Helpful Example. To make the Turkish Doner Kebabs on page 89, mix 2 tablespoons water with 1/2 teaspoon cream of tartar and 1/4 teaspoon baking soda; set aside. In a large bowl, mix 1 pound ground lamb with the spices listed, then blend in the baking soda/water. Now you've got "sausage" that can be shaped into burgers, balls, or bangers. Follow cooking instructions on page 88.

WHY CREAM OF TARTAR AND BAKING SODA?

Traditional ground meat recipes are usually tenderized with the addition of breadcrumbs. My recipes use a combination of cream of tartar and baking soda to keep the meat light, delicate, and juicy, but with a nice, crisp exterior, too.

BURGERS!

MAKES
4 burgers per pound

SHAPE
Press into four patties, then gently make an indentation in the center of each until it's about 1/2 inch thick; this keeps them from turning bulbous while cooking. I use a pancake ring to shape the patties. (See p. 25.)

TO BAKE IN THE OVEN...
Cover a rimmed baking sheet with parchment paper. Preheat oven to 400F, then bake patties for 20-25 minutes, until brown and cooked through.

TO BROWN ON THE GRILL...
Preheat a gas grill with all burners on high and lid closed, 15 minutes. Grill patties, uncovered, until they're seared on one side, about 3 minutes. Flip and continue to grill: 3 minutes for rare, 4 minutes for medium, 5 minutes for well-done.

TO COOK ON THE STOVE...
Heat a little fat in a non-stick skillet over medium heat, about 2 minutes. Add patties, indentation side up, and cook until brown, about 5 minutes. Flip the burgers with a spatula and continue to cook: about 3 minutes for rare, 4 minutes for medium, 5 minutes for well-done.

BALLS!

MAKES
20-30 balls per pound

SHAPE
Roll about 1 tablespoon of meat into a 1-inch ball. I like to use a 1-tablespoon scoop to speed up the process. (See p. 25.)

TO BAKE IN THE OVEN...
Cover a rimmed baking sheet with parchment paper. Preheat the oven to 400F and bake meatballs for 20-25 minutes, until browned and sizzling.

TO BROWN ON THE GRILL...
Preheat a gas grill with all burners on high and the lid closed, about 15 minutes. Thread the meatballs onto skewers, leaving a little breathing room between them. Place on the grill grates and cook 4 minutes, then flip the skewers and cook an additional 3-4 minutes, until browned and sizzling.

TO COOK ON THE STOVE...
Heat a little fat in a non-stick skillet over medium heat, about 2 minutes. Add the meatballs in a single layer, leaving wiggle room around them; you might need to do them in batches. Cook 6-8 minutes – turning occasionally for even browning – until caramelized on the outside and cooked through.

BANGERS!

MAKES
5 bangers per pound

SHAPE
Roll about 3 ounces of meat into a sausage shape. You can do it by hand, or use a gadget like the ham dogger. (See p. 25.)

TO BAKE IN THE OVEN...
Cover a rimmed baking sheet with parchment paper. Preheat the oven to 400F, then bake bangers for 20-25 minutes, until browned and cooked through.

TO BROWN ON THE GRILL...
Preheat a gas grill with all burners on high and the lid closed, about 15 minutes. Place the bangers horizontally across the grill grates and cook 4 minutes, then roll and cook an additional 3-4 minutes, until browned and sizzling.

TO COOK ON THE STOVE...
Heat a little fat in a large, non-stick skillet over medium heat, about 2 minutes. Add the bangers to the pan, making sure they don't touch. (I'M NOT TOUCHING YOU!) Cook for 6-8 minutes –turning occasionally for even browning – until pleasingly caramelized.

TURKISH DONER KEBAB

ARABIC STREET FOOD!

2 tablespoons warm water
1/2 teaspoon cream of tartar
1/4 teaspoon baking soda
1 pound ground lamb
2 garlic cloves, minced (about 2 teaspoons)
1 teaspoon dried oregano leaves
1 teaspoon salt
1/2 teaspoon ground black pepper
1/2 teaspoon Italian herb blend
1/2 teaspoon onion powder
1/4 teaspoon cayenne pepper

VARIATIONS:

Beef or a lamb+beef combo.

GO-ALONGS:

Chopped salad of lettuce, red cabbage, onion, cucumber, and tomato dressed with lemon juice and extra-virgin olive oil. Drizzle salad and meat with one or a few sauces: Tahini Dressing (p. 74), Gyro/Kebab Sauce (p. 54), Garlic Mayo (p. 54), hot sauce.

ROMANIAN

YOUR TASTY WEAPON AGAINST VAMPIRES

2 tablespoons warm water
1/2 teaspoon cream of tartar
1/4 teaspoon baking soda
1/2 pound ground lamb
1/4 pound ground beef
1/4 pound ground pork
3 cloves garlic, minced (about 1 tablespoon)
1/2 tablespoon sweet paprika
1 teaspoon salt
1 teaspoon dried oregano leaves
1 teaspoon ground black pepper
1/4 teaspoon ground cloves

VARIATIONS:

Change ratios of meat.

GO-ALONGS:

Mashed Cauliflower (p. 167) or Citrus Cauliflower Rice (p. 188).

TURKEY AND CRANBERRY

COMFORT FOOD GOES PORTABLE

2 tablespoons warm water
1/2 teaspoon cream of tartar
1/4 teaspoon baking soda
1 pound ground turkey
1 tablespoon orange juice
2 cloves garlic, minced (about 2 teaspoons)
1/4 cup dried cranberries, coarsely chopped
1/2 tablespoon rubbed sage
1/2 tablespoon orange zest
1 teaspoon salt
1/4 teaspoon ground black pepper

VARIATIONS:

Sub chicken.

GO-ALONGS:

Mashed sweet potatoes. Make a "Thanksgiving Leftovers Sandwich" by wrapping in a lettuce leaf with Olive Oil Mayo (p. 53).

CLASSIC PORK

PORKY GOODNESS

2 tablespoons warm water
1/2 teaspoon cream of tartar
1/4 teaspoon baking soda
1 pound ground pork
2 tablespoons white wine vinegar
2 cloves garlic, minced (about 2 teaspoons)
1/4 cup fresh parsley leaves, minced (about 1 tablespoon)
1/2 tablespoon dried chives
1 teaspoon salt
1/2 teaspoon ground black pepper
1/2 teaspoon dried tarragon leaves
1/4 teaspoon ground nutmeg
pinch cinnamon
pinch cloves

VARIATIONS:

Sub chicken.

GO-ALONGS:

Mashed Cauliflower (p. 167); mustard mixed with Olive Oil Mayo (p. 53); sauerkraut or fresh cabbage sautéed in ghee.

GREEK

A QUICK TRIP TO THE AEGEAN

2 tablespoons warm water
1/2 teaspoon cream of tartar
1/4 teaspoon baking soda
1/2 pound ground lamb
1/2 pound ground pork
1/2 tablespoon balsamic vinegar
1 clove garlic, minced (about 1 teaspoon)
1 tablespoon lemon juice

1 teaspoon salt
1/4 teaspoon ground fennel seed
1/4 teaspoon ground black pepper
1/4 teaspoon ground marjoram
1/4 teaspoon dried oregano leaves

VARIATIONS:
Sub chicken for pork.

GO-ALONGS:
Citrus Cauliflower Rice (p. 188); Gyro/Kebab Sauce (p. 54); Herb Salad (p. 196); Tabbouleh (p. 172).

CHORIZO

SPICY SAUSAGE FROM IBERIA

2 tablespoons warm water
1/2 teaspoon cream of tartar
1/4 teaspoon baking soda
1 pound ground pork
1 clove garlic, minced (about 1 teaspoon)
2 teaspoons red wine vinegar
1/2 tablespoon dried ancho chili powder
1 teaspoon onion powder
1 teaspoon ground cumin
1 teaspoon paprika
1 teaspoon chipotle chili powder
1 teaspoon salt
1/4 teaspoon dried oregano leaves
1/4 teaspoon dried thyme leaves
1/8 teaspoon ground cinnamon
1/8 teaspoon ground black pepper

VARIATIONS:
Sub beef or a pork+beef combo.

GO-ALONGS:
Eggs scrambled with jalapeños; guacamole; pan-fried or mashed sweet potatoes; Crisp-Sweet Collards (p. 198); Basic Cauliflower Rice (p. 167) sautéed with red and green bell peppers.

LEBANESE

ALMOST LIKE KIBBEH

2 tablespoons warm water
1/2 teaspoon cream of tartar
1/4 teaspoon baking soda
1/2 pound ground lamb
1/2 pound ground beef
1/2 tablespoon white wine vinegar
1 clove garlic, minced (about 1 teaspoon)
1 tablespoon pine nuts, toasted*
1 teaspoon Lebanese Seven-Spice Blend (p. 84)
1 teaspoon salt
1 teaspoon dried mint leaves
1/8 teaspoon ground black pepper

*Toast pine nuts in a non-stick skillet over medium-high heat until golden, 3-5 minutes.

VARIATIONS:
Sub all lamb.

GO-ALONGS:
Tahini Dressing (p. 74) + Almost Amba (p. 58); Gyro/Kebab Sauce (p. 54); Tabbouleh (p. 172); Herb Salad (p. 196); Basic Cauliflower Rice (p. 167); Simple Lemon Spinach (p. 170). Make a wrap with lettuce and a relish of minced onion, cucumber, and tomato dressed with lemon juice and olive oil.

MERGUEZ SAUSAGE

AN AROMATIC TRIP TO A MOROCCAN MARKET

2 tablespoons warm water
1/2 teaspoon cream of tartar
1/4 teaspoon baking soda
1 pound ground lamb
2 cloves garlic, minced (about 2 teaspoons)
2 tablespoons Merguez Sausage Seasoning (p. 80)
1/4 cup fresh parsley or cilantro leaves, minced (about 1 tablespoon)
1/2 tablespoon Aleppo or cayenne pepper

VARIATIONS:
Sub beef or a lamb+beef combo.

GO-ALONGS:
Basic Cauliflower Rice (p. 167); Casablanca Carrots (p. 176); Simple Lemon Spinach (p. 170).

THAI GREEN CURRY

SWEET GREEN CURRY YOU CAN CARRY

2 tablespoons warm water
1/2 teaspoon cream of tartar
1/4 teaspoon baking soda
1 pound ground beef
1/4 cup canned coconut milk
2 teaspoons fish sauce
2 tablespoons green curry paste
2 cloves garlic, minced (about 2 teaspoons)
10-12 basil leaves, minced (about 1/4 cup)
1 teaspoon salt
1/2 teaspoon powdered ginger
1/8 teaspoon ground black pepper

VARIATIONS:
Sub chicken.

GO-ALONGS:
Coconut Cauliflower Rice (p. 202); Thai Pink Grapefruit Salad (p. 212). Use in Faux Pho (p. 130) instead of pork ribs. Make a quick curry sauce: Blend 1 cup coconut milk, 2 tablespoons green curry paste, 1 teaspoon powdered ginger, 1 tablespoon fish sauce, and a handful of basil leaves, then add cooked burgers/balls/bangers, and simmer until hot.

JAPANESE GYOZA

AS CLOSE AS WE CAN GET TO DUMPLINGS

2 tablespoons warm water
1/2 teaspoon cream of tartar
1/4 teaspoon baking soda
1 pound ground pork
1/2 teaspoon sesame oil
3 cloves garlic, minced (about 1 tablespoon)
1 tablespoon coconut aminos*
1/4 pound shitake mushrooms, stemmed and finely chopped*
1/8 head cabbage, very thinly sliced (about 1 cup)*
1/2 cup water chestnuts, minced
2 scallions, very thinly sliced (about 1/4 cup)
1 tablespoon chopped chives (dried or fresh)
1 teaspoon salt
1 teaspoon powdered ginger
1/4 teaspoon crushed red pepper flakes
1/4 teaspoon ground black pepper

*Sauté mushrooms and cabbage in coconut aminos until soft and caramelized. Add to remainder of ingredients.

VARIATIONS:
Sub chicken.

GO-ALONGS:
Basic Cauliflower Rice (p. 167); Wasabi Mayo (p. 54). Make a quick dipping sauce: Blend 1/4 cup rice vinegar, 1/4 cup coconut aminos, 1/2 teaspoon sesame oil, 1/2 clove garlic (minced), 1 scallion (very thinly sliced), 1/2 teaspoon grated fresh ginger root, and 1/4 teaspoon crushed red pepper flakes. Makes about 1/2 cup.

MOROCCAN CHICKEN AND APRICOT

A SWEET AND SAVORY MINI TAGINE

2 tablespoons warm water
1/2 teaspoon cream of tartar
1/4 teaspoon baking soda
1 pound ground chicken
2 cloves garlic, minced (about 2 teaspoons)
4 dried apricots, minced (about 2 tablespoons)
2 tablespoons almonds, chopped
1/4 cup fresh cilantro leaves, minced (about 1 tablespoon)
1/4 cup fresh parsley leaves, minced (about 1 tablespoon)
1 teaspoon salt
1/8 teaspoon ground turmeric
1/8 teaspoon ground cinnamon
1/8 teaspoon powdered ginger
1/8 teaspoon ground black pepper

VARIATIONS:
Sub lamb.

GO-ALONGS:
Eat with extra cilantro leaves; Citrus Cauliflower Rice (p. 188); Casablanca Carrots (p. 176).

BAHN MI

THE BEST PARTS OF THE VIETNAMESE SANDWICH

2 tablespoons warm water
1/2 teaspoon cream of tartar
1/4 teaspoon baking soda
1 pound ground pork
1 tablespoon fish sauce (Red Boat!)
1 tablespoon hot sauce
2 cloves garlic, minced (about 2 teaspoons)
10-12 basil leaves, minced (about 1/4 cup)
4 scallions, thinly sliced (about 1/2 cup)
3/4 teaspoon salt
1 teaspoon ground black pepper

VARIATIONS:
Sub chicken or replace 1/2 pound pork with 1/2 pound minced chicken livers.

GO-ALONGS:
Basic Cauliflower Rice (p. 167); Asian Slaw (p. 178); Spicy Coconut Mayo (p. 54). Make a wrap with lettuce leaves, shredded carrot, minced cilantro, fresh basil leaves, a squeeze of lime juice, and a dollop of Olive Oil Mayo (p. 53).

MOORISH

OLD WORLD TASTE WITH AN AIR OF MYSTERY

2 tablespoons warm water
1/2 teaspoon cream of tartar
1/4 teaspoon baking soda
1 pound ground lamb
1/2 tablespoon hot sauce
2 garlic cloves, minced (about 2 teaspoons)
2 scallions, thinly sliced (about 1/4 cup)
1/4 cup fresh cilantro leaves, minced (about 1 tablespoon)
1/4 cup fresh parsley leaves, minced (about 1 tablespoon)
1/2 tablespoon ground cumin
1/2 tablespoon ground coriander
1/2 tablespoon ground caraway seed
1 teaspoon salt
1 teaspoon chipotle powder
1/2 teaspoon ground fennel seed
1/2 teaspoon cayenne pepper
1/4 teaspoon ground cinnamon

VARIATIONS:

Sub beef or a beef+lamb combo.

GO-ALONGS:

Basic Cauliflower Rice (p. 167); Mashed Cauliflower (p. 167).

ITALIAN

EAT WELL... OR MANGIARE BENE

2 tablespoons warm water
1/2 teaspoon cream of tartar
1/4 teaspoon baking soda
1 pound ground beef
1 clove garlic, minced (about 1 teaspoon)
1 tablespoon tomato paste
1 tablespoon balsamic vinegar
1/2 cup fresh parsley leaves, minced (about 2 tablespoons)
1 teaspoon salt
1/4 teaspoon crushed red pepper flakes
1/2 teaspoon Italian herb blend

VARIATIONS:

Sub a beef+pork combo.

GO-ALONGS:

Zucchini Noodles (p. 168); Crisp-Sweet Collards (p. 198); Pizza Veggies (p. 194). Quick tomato sauce: Gently sauté a few cloves of garlic in olive oil over very low heat. Add 1 can diced tomatoes, salt, and pepper. Bring to boil, then simmer 10 minutes. Adjust salt and pepper, then throw in 8 slivered basil leaves. Mange!

CUBAN

A LITTLE TASTE OF HAVANA

2 tablespoons warm water
1/2 teaspoon cream of tartar
1/4 teaspoon baking soda
1 pound ground beef
1 tablespoon tomato paste
1/2 tablespoon red wine vinegar
2 cloves garlic, minced (about 2 teaspoons)
2 tablespoons blanched almonds, toasted and chopped*
2 tablespoons raisins
2 tablespoons green pimiento-stuffed olives, chopped
1 teaspoon salt
1 teaspoon ground cinnamon
1/2 teaspoon dried oregano leaves
1/4 teaspoon ground black pepper
pinch ground cloves

*Toast almonds in a non-stick skillet over medium-high heat until golden, 3-5 minutes.

VARIATION:

Sub pork or a beef+pork combo.

GO-ALONGS:

Pan-Fried Plantains (p. 184); Lizard Sauce (p. 68).

FREEZE/REHEAT

These recipes can easily be doubled (or tripled!) and frozen for future meals. Just follow these easy instructions for meals-on-demand.

Freeze. Place in a single layer on a baking sheet and freeze until solid, then transfer to a plastic freezer baggie and pop back into the freezer until you're ready to eat.

Defrost. Place the baggie in the refrigerator to defrost overnight.

Oven Reheat. Cover a large, rimmed baking sheet with parchment paper. Preheat the oven to 400F. Place your burgers, balls, or bangers on the baking sheet and cover lightly with foil. Bake 10-15 minutes until heated through.

Stovetop Reheat. Place 1/4 cup water in a large, non-stick skillet. Bring to a boil, then add your burgers, balls, or bangers. Return to a boil, then cover and simmer 10 minutes until water is evaporated and the meat is hot.

TASTES GREAT WITH

ZUCCHINI NOODLES, P. 168

ROASTED SPAGHETTI SQUASH, P. 168

MASHED CAULIFLOWER, P. 167

PIZZA VEGGIES, P. 194

CRISP-SWEET COLLARDS, P. 198

SIMPLE LEMON SPINACH, P. 170

OLD SCHOOL ITALIAN MEAT SAUCE

SUNDAY GRAVY, PALEO STYLE

SERVES 8 *to* 12

PREP	COOK	SIMMER
10 MIN.	40 MIN.	2 1/2 HRS.

In the Italian households I knew growing up, Saturday was sauce and meatball day: You made the sauce in the afternoon so it could simmer all evening. Meanwhile, on Saturday night, you fried up meatballs and put them on the back porch to cool until they were dropped into the sauce on Sunday morning. In addition to quality tomatoes, garlic, and extra-virgin olive oil, a respectable "Sunday Gravy" also included a hefty dose of red wine (both in the sauce and in the cook). But for our good health and happiness, we're replacing pasta with veggie nooodles and wine with balsamic vinegar.

INGREDIENTS

MEAT:

1 teaspoon coconut oil
1 1/2 pounds pork chops (bone in or boneless)
salt and ground black pepper
1 pound Italian sausage (chicken, turkey, or pork)

SAUCE:

2 medium onions, diced (about 2 cups)
1/2 tablespoon dried oregano
3 tablespoons tomato paste
1 tablespoon unsweetened cocoa powder
6 cloves garlic, minced (about 2 tablespoons)
1/4 cup balsamic vinegar
2/3 cup beef broth
2 (28 ounce) cans crushed tomatoes
1/4 cup fresh basil leaves, slivered

MEATBALLS:

2 tablespoons warm water
1/4 teaspoon baking soda
1/2 teaspoon cream of tartar
1/2 pound ground beef
1/2 pound ground pork or turkey
2 cloves garlic, minced (about 2 teaspoons)
1 tablespoon tomato paste
1 tablespoon balsamic vinegar
1/2 cup fresh parsley leaves, minced (about 2 tablespoons)
1 teaspoon salt
1/2 teaspoon Italian herb blend
1/4 teaspoon crushed red pepper flakes

DIRECTIONS

Brown the meats. Heat coconut oil in a large, deep pot. Sprinkle the pork chops with salt and pepper, then brown them on both sides, about 10 minutes. Remove the chops from the pot and place in a bowl to catch the juices. Brown the whole sausage links in the same pot, about 10 minutes, and place in the bowl with the pork chops.

Make the sauce. You're going to make the sauce in the same pot, so add a little coconut oil if there's no fat left in the pan. Cook the onions with the oregano until they're very soft, about 7-10 minutes. Add the tomato paste and cocoa. Sauté until beginning to brown, about 3 minutes. Add the garlic and cook until fragrant, about 30 seconds.

Add the balsamic vinegar and stir, about 1 minute. Add the broth and crushed tomatoes; stir to combine. Nestle the pork chops and sausage into the sauce. Bring to a robust bubble, then cover and simmer, 2 hours. Meanwhile...

Prep the meatballs. Preheat the oven to 400F and cover a large baking sheet with parchment paper or foil. In a small bowl, mix the water, baking soda and cream of tartar with a fork until combined. Crumble the beef and pork into a large bowl, then add the garlic, tomato paste, vinegar, parsley, salt, Italian herb blend, red pepper flakes, and water/baking soda. Mix well with your hands (or if you want it very smooth, with a food processor or mixer) until combined.

Cook the meatballs. Measure 1 tablespoon of the meat and roll into a ball. Line up the meatballs on the baking sheet, then bake 20 minutes, until browned.

The final steps. When the sauce has reached its 2-hour simmer deadline, add the meatballs to the sauce and simmer an additional 15 minutes, uncovered. Remove the sauce from the heat and toss in the fresh basil, then taste and add salt and pepper, if necessary.

If you used bone-in pork chops, the meat could fall right off the bones; you might need to liberate them from the sauce (lest you choke a dining companion). Ladle the sauce over a pile of Zucchini Noodles or Roasted Spaghetti Squash (p. 168) and top with a little of each kind of meat. Mange!

PIÑA COLADA CHICKEN

WHEN IN DOUBT, TRY COCONUT

SERVES 2 *to* 4

PREP	COOK
15 MIN.	35 MIN.

When Dave and I were fairly new to yoga, we went on a week-long yoga retreat in Mexico. Sounds like paradise, right? That's what we thought, but then we became the jerks who complained about their beach paradise. The restaurant served only vegetarian food, the resort had no air conditioning, and at the end of the first night, we were covered in mosquito bites. To turn our vacation around, we watched the sun set each evening with a piña colada and our feet in the sea. I recommend Piña Colada Chicken anytime you need your own escape to a coconut-and-pineapple paradise.

INGREDIENTS

1 pound boneless, skinless chicken breasts or thighs
salt and ground black pepper
1/2 tablespoon plus 1/2 tablespoon coconut oil
1 medium onion, diced (about 1 cup)
1 medium green pepper, diced (about 1 cup)
1 medium red pepper, diced (about 1 cup)
1 teaspoon arrowroot powder
1 cup canned chunk pineapple, packed in its own juice
2 cloves garlic, minced (about 2 teaspoons)
2 teaspoons Jerk Seasoning (p. 82)
juice of 1 lime (about 2 tablespoons)
1/4 teaspoon vanilla extract
1 cup canned coconut milk

DIRECTIONS

Brown the chicken. Cut the chicken into 1-inch cubes. Heat a large, non-stick skillet over medium-high heat, about 3 minutes. Add 1/2 tablespoon coconut oil and allow it to melt. Brown the chicken – cooking in batches, if necessary – until golden all around, about 3-5 minutes per side. Remove the chicken from the pan as it browns and place in a bowl to catch the juices.

Get saucy! To the pan, add 1/2 tablespoon coconut oil. Sauté the onions, peppers, and arrowroot until the vegetables are just-tender, about 5 minutes. Add the pineapple chunks to the pan and stir-fry until they begin to brown, about 3 minutes. Add the garlic and Jerk Seasoning, stirring until fragrant, about 30 seconds. Add the lime juice and stir, scraping up any brown bits stuck to the bottom of the pan. Add the vanilla and coconut milk, stirring to combine. Place the chicken in the sauce and pour in any accumulated juices. Bring to a boil, then simmer, uncovered, until the sauce begins to thicken, about 5 minutes.

NOTES

The pină colada has been the official drink of Puerto Rico since 1978.

YOU KNOW HOW YOU COULD DO THAT?

Substitute boneless pork chops, cut into strips, for the chicken and follow the instructions above. White fish and shrimp are also lovely, just skip the browning step. Make the sauce, then add the seafood to the pan and simmer until cooked through, about 5-7 minutes.

TASTES GREAT WITH

BASIC CAULIFLOWER RICE, P. 167
ZUCCHINI NOODLES, P. 168

When Harry Met Sally... *is my all-time favorite movie. The pickiness of Sally's restaurant orders alone won my heart, but then, there's the deli scene – plus Harry's passion-fueled sprint across Manhattan on New Year's Eve – to really bring it home.*

REUBEN ROLLUPS

I'LL HAVE WHAT SHE'S HAVING...

SERVES 2 *to* 4

PREP 15 MIN. | COOK 30 MIN.

One of my favorite joints for after-hours food in Austin used to be a New York-style deli that served a humongous Reuben, dripping with Russian dressing. Right around the time I stopped eating giant sandwiches at 2:00 a.m., the deli closed. (I can neither verify nor deny those two things are related.) Sauerkraut can help keep your gut in tune and homemade Russian Dressing is a good source of healthy fat, so go ahead and eat this at 2:00 in the afternoon (or maybe even 2:00 a.m.).

Heads up! This recipe requires you to do something in advance; plan prep time accordingly.

INGREDIENTS

1 jar (2 pounds) sauerkraut

1/2 medium onion, diced (about 1/2 cup)

1 teaspoon coconut oil

1 tablespoon caraway seeds

1 pound corned beef, sliced thin

2 teaspoons ghee

GARNISH:

Russian Dressing (p. 54)

kosher pickles, olives

DIRECTIONS

Place the sauerkraut in a sieve and rinse under running water. Allow to drain in the sieve while you dice the onion. Heat a medium saucepan over medium-high, then add the coconut oil. When the oil is melted, add onions and caraway seeds, sauté until the onions are soft and beginning to brown, about 7-10 minutes. Add the sauerkraut, cover, and simmer on low heat, 20-30 minutes.

A few minutes before you're ready to eat, warm a large, non-stick skillet over medium heat and add ghee. When the ghee is melted, add the corned beef and move it around the pan to coat it in melted ghee. Heat through.

Roll slices of warm corned beef around sauerkraut and drizzle with Russian dressing. Dig in immediately!

NOTES

YOU KNOW HOW YOU COULD DO THAT?

Replace the corned beef with smoked or roasted turkey breast.

MAKE IT A RACHEL! *Use pastrami instead of corned beef and replace the sauerkraut with Classic Cole Slaw (p. 178). Keep the Russian Dressing!*

TASTES GREAT WITH

CLASSIC COLE SLAW, P. 178

GREEN BEANS WITH SIZZLED GARLIC, P. 204

CRISP-SWEET COLLARDS, P. 198

SILKY GINGERED ZUCCHINI SOUP, P. 206

GOLDEN CAULIFLOWER SOUP, P. 180

TASTES GREAT WITH
MASHED CAULIFLOWER, P. 167
ZUCCHINI NOODLES, P. 168
BASIC CAULIFLOWER RICE, P. 167
GARLIC-CREAMED SPINACH, P. 214

THYME-BRAISED SHORT RIBS

WHAT'S A FLANKEN?!*

SERVES 4 *to* 6

PREP	COOK
30 MIN.	4 HRS.

Have you ever wondered, Just what is a short rib, anyway? *Does it feel insulted because we keep calling it "short?" Is it a deliberate move to keep us confused that butchers in different regions – like Korea, France, Hawaii, and Eastern Europe – cut their short ribs in different, very specific ways? Did you know that short ribs are known as Jacob's Ladder in the UK? Do the answers to these burning questions really matter much when the end result is succulent shreds of meat so tender they can be eaten with a spoon?*

INGREDIENTS

- 3 to 3 1/2 pounds beef short ribs (about 5-6 ribs)
- salt and ground black pepper
- 1/2 tablespoon coconut oil
- 1/2 medium onion, diced (about 1/2 cup)
- 2 medium carrots, peeled and diced (about 1/2 cup)
- 2 medium ribs celery, diced (about 1/2 cup)
- 5 cloves garlic, peeled and smashed
- 1 tablespoon tomato paste
- 1/2 cup balsamic vinegar
- 1/4 cup water
- 1 tablespoon dried thyme
- 5 cups beef broth
- 4-6 portobello mushroom caps
- 1 tablespoon ghee or coconut oil, melted

GARNISH:
fresh chives, minced

DIRECTIONS

Sprinkle the ribs lavishly with salt and pepper. Heat a large, deep pot over medium-high. Add the coconut oil to the pot, and when it's melted, add the ribs in a single layer and sear on all sides. You want a serious crust, so you'll probably have to work in batches. As the ribs brown, remove them to a bowl to catch their juices.

Add onion, carrots, celery, and garlic to drippings in pan. (Add a little more coconut oil if you need to.) Cook the vegetables until they're soft and beginning to brown, about 7 minutes. Add the tomato paste and fry until brown, about 3 minutes. Add balsamic vinegar, water, and thyme. Bring to a boil and cook until it's syrupy, about 5 minutes.

Return the ribs to the pot and wiggle them into the vegetables. Add the broth and bring to a boil. Reduce heat to simmer and cook, partially covered, 4 hours or until the meat is fall-apart tender. Thirty minutes before the meat is finished...

Preheat oven to 450F. Cover a large baking sheet with parchment paper or aluminum foil. Place the portobello caps on the baking sheet, rib side up. Brush with melted fat and sprinkle gently with salt and pepper. Roast in oven 10-12 minutes, until browned and tender.

When the ribs are done, transfer to a plate, remove bones, and shred with two forks. Strain the cooking liquid through a sieve into another pot to remove the mushy vegetables. Bring the sauce to a boil, then simmer until reduced and thickened. Return the meat to the sauce.Remove mushroom caps from oven. Mound shredded meat on a cap, drizzle with sauce, and sprinkle with minced chives.

YOU KNOW HOW YOU COULD DO THAT?

Replace thyme with dried rosemary.

This shredded meat would also be happy perched atop a Sweet Potato "Waffle" (p. 116).

You can substitute cubed beef stew meat for the short ribs and reduce cooking time to 2 hours for a stew version.

*FLANKEN (FLAHNG-KUHN): *a strip of meat from the front end of the short ribs of beef.*

BUFFALO CHICKEN SALAD

TAKE YOUR TASTEBUDS TO THE END ZONE

PAGE 102

SERVES 2 to 4

PREP	COOK
20 MIN.	35 MIN.

I don't have one favorite team, but I'm a devoted NFL fan and during playoffs, my stat-spouting habit borders very seriously on nerd territory. As you can imagine, the Super Bowl is a Big Deal in my house. But can I honestly call it game day if there are no chicken wings doused in hot sauce? Yes, I can! This recipe recreates the sensation of tender chicken, spicy sauce, and cool go-alongs for a version that still tastes enough like "junk food" to celebrate halftime. Touchdown!

Heads up! This recipe requires you to do something in advance; plan prep time accordingly.

INGREDIENTS

DRESSING:

1/4 cup Garlic Mayonnaise (p. 54)

1/2 tablespoon cider vinegar

1/8 teaspoon paprika

CHICKEN:

1 pound boneless, skinless chicken breasts

2 cups chicken broth or water

3 cloves garlic, peeled and smashed

1 jalapeño, cut into rings

1 bay leaf

1 tablespoon salt

1 teaspoon whole black peppercorns

1/2 teaspoon whole mustard seeds

1 teaspoon dried thyme

2 tablespoons ghee, melted

1/4 cup (or more!) hot sauce (I like Louisiana brand.)

CHOPPED SALAD:

1 head iceberg lettuce, thinly sliced

1 large seedless cucumber, thinly sliced

3 ribs celery, thinly sliced

2 large carrots, peeled and thinly sliced

1/2 medium red onion, thinly sliced

1/2 cup fresh parsley leaves, coarsely chopped

DIRECTIONS

In a small bowl, mix the Garlic Mayo with cider vinegar and paprika. Refrigerate while you make the rest of the salad.

In a large saucepan, place chicken, water, garlic, jalapeño, bay leaf, salt, peppercorns, mustard seeds, and thyme. Bring to a boil, then cover and simmer on low, 15-20 minutes. Turn off the heat and let the chicken relax in its spa, covered, for 20-25 minutes. Remove the chicken from the water and shred with two forks, then toss with melted ghee and hot sauce.

In a large bowl, toss the salad ingredients with the Garlic Mayo using two wooden spoons. Think of it as a mini cardio workout and toss for about two minutes so all the vegetables are coated with dressing. Top with shredded chicken and dig in!

YOU KNOW HOW YOU COULD DO THAT?

Omega-3 shortcut! Replace the poached chicken with canned salmon. Just drain salmon and mix with ghee and hot sauce for Omega-3 power! (Thanks to blog reader Jennifer D. for the suggestion.)

NOTES

When Dave and I visit his family in Cincinnati, we always hit up Skyline Chili for a 3-way. Heh.

CINCINNATI CHILI

WHICH WAY DO YOU GO?

SERVES 6 *to* 8

PREP	COOK
15 MIN.	2 1/2 HRS.

Cincinnati Chili can be endlessly entertaining. First, there's the double-entendre involved in ordering your favorite toppings. Do you want a 2-way (chili+spaghetti) or a 3-way (add onions)? Then there's the legend that it was first served in 1922 at a hot dog stand outside a burlesque theater. This chili is different from its Southwestern cousin because of seasonings like cinnamon, allspice, and cloves – familiar flavors for the immigrant cook from Macedonia who invented it. In this version, you get a paleo 3-way: chili+zucchini noodles+onions.

Heads up! This recipe requires you to do something in advance; plan prep time accordingly.

INGREDIENTS

2 pounds ground beef
4 cups water plus 1/2 cup water
2 medium onions, finely diced (about 2 cups)
4 cloves garlic, minced (about 4 teaspoons)
1/4 cup mild chili powder
1 tablespoon unsweetened cocoa
1/2 tablespoon salt
1 teaspoon cayenne pepper
1 teaspoon ground cinnamon
1 teaspoon ground cumin
1/2 teaspoon ground allspice
1/4 teaspoon ground cloves
1 bay leaf
1 (8 ounce) can tomato sauce
1 (14.5 ounce) can crushed tomatoes
2 tablespoons cider vinegar
1 tablespoon coconut aminos
1 batch Zucchini Noodles (p. 168)

GARNISH:
diced raw onions

DIRECTIONS

Place the ground beef in a large soup pot, cover with 4 cups of cold water, and bring to a boil, stirring and breaking up the beef with a fork to a very fine texture. Slowly simmer until the meat is thoroughly cooked, about 30 minutes.

Stir in the onions, garlic, chili powder, cocoa, salt, cayenne, cinnamon, cumin, allspice, cloves, and bay leaf. Add the tomato sauce, crushed tomatoes, vinegar, coconut aminos, and 1/2 cup water. Stir to combine.

Simmer for 2 hours until slightly thickened. Serve on Zucchini Noodles and top with diced onions.

YOU KNOW HOW YOU COULD DO THAT?

You could replace beef with lamb. It's not authentic, but it is scrumptious. You might also pile your chili on top of Roasted Spaghetti Squash (p. 168).

TASTES GREAT WITH

HERB SALAD, P. 196
SWEET AND SALTY BROCCOLI SALAD, P. 200

TASTES GREAT WITH

CITRUS CAULIFLOWER RICE, P. 188
SPRING CHOPPED SALAD, P. 208
HERB SALAD, P. 196
SWEET POTATO "WAFFLE," P. 116
AWESOME SAUCE, P. 54

Let's be honest: Just about everything tastes great fried. Don't be scared... try 'em!

CRISPY CHICKEN LIVERS

COMFORT FOOD FOR THE SOUL AND BODY

SERVES 2 *to* 4

PREP 10 MIN. | COOK 15 MIN.

I was a strange kid. I preferred reading to playing outside. I roller-skated to the library (in blue-and-yellow sneaker skates). I also voluntarily ate beef liver with onions at my dad's diner and if a restaurant menu offered chicken liver paté, I ordered it. As a surly teenager, I turned up my nose at liver. But now, amidst the barrage of encouragement from the paleo pros to eat more offal, I revisited chicken livers. These are spicy, crispy, and rich, and I encourage you to give them a try. They're offally good. (Yeah, I did that.).

INGREDIENTS

1 pound chicken livers
1/2 cup canned coconut milk
1/3 cup coconut flour
2 tablespoons arrowroot powder
2 teaspoons paprika
2 teaspoons coarse (granulated) garlic powder
1/2 tablespoon ground cumin
2 teaspoons salt
1/2 teaspoon ground black pepper
1/2 teaspoon ground cloves
1/8 teaspoon cayenne pepper
2-4 tablespoons coconut oil

GARNISH:
fresh lemon
chopped fresh herbs (parsley, cilantro, and/or mint)

YOU KNOW HOW YOU COULD DO THAT?

Omit the cumin and cloves, then replace with these seasonings:

BBQISH: *1 teaspoon chili powder; dip in Lizard Sauce (p. 68)*

MIDDLE EASTERN: *1 teaspoon Lebanese Seven-Spice (p. 84); dip in Tahini Dressing (p. 74)*

CHINESE: *1 teaspoon Chinese five-spice powder; dip in Hoisin Sauce (p. 62)*

JAMAICAN: *1 teaspoon Jerk Seasoning (p. 82)*

CLASSIC FRIED CHICKEN: *1 teaspoon rubbed sage leaves*

DIRECTIONS

Cut chicken livers into 2-inch pieces. Place coconut milk in a shallow bowl and add chicken livers; marinate 10 minutes.

In a shallow bowl, mix coconut flour, arrowroot powder, paprika, garlic powder, cumin, salt, pepper, cloves, and cayenne with a fork until blended. Pour the seasoned flour into a large ziplock bag, add the chicken livers, and shake gently until coated evenly.

In a large non-stick skillet, heat 2 tablespoons coconut oil over medium-high until hot, about 3 minutes. Add about half the chicken livers in a single layer – arrange them so they don't touch. Allow the bottom to brown well and form a crisp crust, about 3-5 minutes.

The livers might "pop" while cooking as liquid hits the hot fat, so don't stand with your face over the pan. (No singed eyebrows here!) You might also notice some spots turning bright red and looking something like a horror movie. Avert your eyes and don't worry about it. It's normal and will go away as the livers cook.

Using tongs, flip the livers, and brown the other side. Set aside to drain on paper towels while you cook the second batch. You may need to add more coconut oil to the pan.

Place the livers on a serving plate and garnish with a squeeze of fresh lemon juice and a sprinkle of chopped fresh herbs. These taste their crispy best if you eat them immediately, but I've been known to eat leftovers for breakfast – just re-crisp them in a hot skillet.

SUNRISE SCRAMBLE

LIKE A DANISH, MINUS THE PASTRY

SERVES 2 to 4

PREP 10 MIN.

COOK 10 MIN.

It's kind of stunning to me that there are still places in the world where an apple Danish is considered an ideal breakfast. Don't get me wrong: I agree that apples and cinnamon taste great in the morning (and any time of day, really), but I'm happy to trade the gluten-filled dough for nutrient-dense sweet potatoes and the power of a solid protein infusion. This scramble cooks up quickly, which makes it perfect for busy breakfast time, but the flavors are also savory enough to satisfy after a long, hard day. **Heads up! This recipe requires you to do something in advance; plan prep time accordingly.**

INGREDIENTS

1 tablespoon coconut oil or ghee
8 ounces ground turkey or pork
1 apple, diced (about 1 cup)
2 teaspoons Sunrise Spice (p. 78)
1 cup cooked, diced sweet potato
salt and ground black pepper, to taste
8 large eggs, beaten
6-8 scallions, green tops only, thinly sliced

DIRECTIONS

Heat a large, non-stick skillet over medium-high heat, about 3 minutes. Add coconut oil and allow it to melt. Add the turkey and apple, stirring with a wooden spoon to break up chunks of meat. Cook until no longer pink, about 5-7 minutes. When the meat releases some of its fat, add the Sunrise Spice, sweet potato, salt, and pepper. Stir to mix and cook until sweet potatoes get little brown spots.

Pour the eggs into the pan and stir to combine. Continue to scramble until desired doneness. Top with scallions and eat immediately. Good morning!

NOTES

If this isn't a strong argument in favor of breakfast for dinner, I don't know what is.

YOU KNOW HOW YOU COULD DO THAT?

Make the turkey/apple/sweet potato hash and top with fried or poached eggs, instead of scrambling.

TASTES GREAT WITH

SPRING CHOPPED SALAD, P. 208
ROASTED CABBAGE ROSES, P. 190

Twenty-eight different types of semi-precious and precious gems were used to decorate the Taj Mahal, and its color seems to change, based on the light at different times of day and night.

TAJ MAHAL CHICKEN

IN HOMAGE TO ONE OF THE SEVEN WONDERS OF THE WORLD

SERVES 2 *to* 4

PREP: 15 MIN. | COOK: 1 HR.

Sure, I could have just called this Chicken Curry, but where's the fun in that? This is totally Americanized, combining Indian curry powder, raisins, tomatoes, and chicken into gloppy comfort food. It's warm, soothing, creamy, saucy, and 100 percent inauthentic. It's also ridiculously yummy. It took 20,000 workers 22 years and 1000 elephants (!) to complete the construction of the Taj Mahal, but you only need a little more than an hour to get this meal on the table.

INGREDIENTS

1 pound boneless, skinless chicken thighs
salt and ground black pepper
1/2 tablespoon plus 1/2 tablespoon coconut oil
1 large onion, diced (about 1 cup)
1 large red bell pepper, diced (about 1 cup)
1 large bay leaf
salt and pepper, to taste
4 cloves garlic, minced (about 4 teaspoons)
2-3 tablespoons curry powder
1 teaspoon dried thyme
1 tablespoon tomato paste
1/3 cup raisins
1 (14.5 ounce) can crushed or diced tomatoes
1/2 cup unsweetened apple sauce
1/3 cup water
1/2 cup canned coconut milk

GARNISH:
minced fresh cilantro or parsley leaves

DIRECTIONS

Place the chicken in the freezer for 10 minutes, then cut it crosswise into 1/4-inch strips. Sprinkle the strips with salt and pepper. Heat a large, non-stick skillet over medium-high heat, about 3 minutes. Add 1/2 tablespoon coconut oil and allow it to melt. Add the chicken in a single layer and brown well on both sides, about 10 minutes. Cook in batches if you need to and remove the chicken to a bowl to catch the juices.

In the same pan, add the onions, bell pepper, and bay leaf. Sauté until the veggies are tender and beginning to brown, about 5-7 minutes. Season with salt and pepper, then add the garlic and stir until fragrant, about 30 seconds.

If the pan is looking dry, add 1/2 tablespoon coconut oil. Add the curry powder, thyme, and tomato paste. Stir to blend and fry about 1 minute, then add the raisins, tomatoes, apple sauce, and water. Stir to combine and bring to a boil. Return the chicken to the pan with any accumulated juices. Reduce the heat to simmer and cook, covered, 20-30 minutes until sauce thickens.

Add the coconut milk and stir to combine. Heat through, about 5 minutes, then sprinkle with chopped herbs.

TASTES GREAT WITH

ROASTED SPAGHETTI SQUASH, P. 168
BASIC CAULIFLOWER RICE, P. 167
CRISP-SWEET COLLARD GREENS, P. 198
SIMPLE LEMON SPINACH, P. 170

YOU KNOW HOW YOU COULD DO THAT?

You can use chicken breast or turkey in place of chicken thighs. This is a spicy way to turn leftover Thanksgiving turkey into a welcome rerun, just skip the browning step, and add cubed or shredded poultry to the sauce along with the raisins.

If you have a sensitive tongue, replace the serrano with a milder jalapeño – or even half a jalapeño. If your grocery or farmer's market has Thai chiles (a.k.a., Bird's Eye Chiles), go for it. Carefully.

THAI BASIL BEEF

A SLIGHTLY MORE ELEGANT STIR-FRY

SERVES 2 *to* 4

PREP	MARINATE	COOK
10 MIN.	10 MIN.	20 MIN.

If you're anything like me, a stir-fry loaded with veggies was one of the first "international" recipes you learned to cook. A stir-fry is easy, fast, nutritious, and a great way to use up odds and ends of veggies you find in the back of the fridge. This stir-fry is different. Maybe a little more special. But just as easy to pull together on a weeknight. Thanks to its Thai origins, Thai Basil Beef balances sour, sweet, salty, and bitter tastes. Think of it as grown-up stir-fry that pleases eaters of all ages.

INGREDIENTS

MEAT & MARINADE:

1 pound flank steak

2 teaspoons coconut aminos

2 teaspoons rice vinegar

2 cloves garlic, minced (about 2 teaspoons)

STIR-FRY:

1 1/2 tablespoon fish sauce (I like Red Boat!)

1 tablespoon coconut aminos

1 tablespoon lime juice

1/2 cup water

1/2 pound green beans, cut into 1-inch pieces

1/2 tablespoon coconut oil

1 large red bell pepper, thinly sliced

4 scallions, cut into 1-inch pieces

1 small serrano chile, stems and seeds removed, thinly sliced

2 cloves garlic, minced (about 2 teaspoons)

1 cup fresh basil leaves

DIRECTIONS

Place flank steak in the freezer for 10-15 minutes. Slice very thinly, across the grain to make 1/4-inch strips. Place the steak in a medium mixing bowl and add the coconut aminos, rice vinegar, and garlic. Toss with two wooden spoons to combine, then cover and refrigerate 10 minutes or up to 1 hour.

In a small bowl, mix the fish sauce, coconut aminos, and lime juice. Set aside.

Place water in a large, non-stick skillet, and bring to a boil. Add the green beans and steam until just tender, about 4-5 minutes. Drain the beans, discarding any remaining water, and rinse under cold water to stop cooking. Set aside.

Reheat the pan over medium-high heat and add coconut oil. Allow it to melt, about 2 minutes. Brown the meat without crowding the pan; work in batches, if necessary. As the meat cooks, remove it to a bowl to catch its juices.

In the same pan, stir-fry the bell pepper, scallions, serrano, and garlic until the peppers are just tender, about 2 minutes. Add the reserved beef, green beans, and sauce, tossing with two wooden spoons until heated through. Remove from heat, add basil leaves, and toss until the leaves are wilted. Serve immediately.

TASTES GREAT WITH

COCONUT CAULIFLOWER RICE, P. 202

THAI PINK GRAPEFRUIT SALAD, P. 212

ASIAN SLAW, P. 178

YOU KNOW HOW YOU COULD DO THAT?

Replace the steak with ground beef, sliced lamb, or chicken breast.

MAKE IT A CURRY! *After stir-frying, add 1 cup coconut milk, 2 tablespoons Thai green curry paste, 1 teaspoon powdered ginger, and a splash of fish sauce. Bring to a quick boil, then simmer until slightly thickened. Stir in basil leaves and attack!*

SHRIMP SCAMPI

SIMPLICITY AS ITS FINEST

SERVES 2 to 4

PREP: 10 MIN.

COOK: 20 MIN.

I think it's pretty obvious from my recipes that (1) I'm not intimidated by long lists of ingredients; and (2) I enjoy the alchemy of playing with plenty of spices. But sometimes, when the right flavors come together in just the right proportions, simplicity wins the day. Because of the super low heat in this recipe, the shrimp are plump and firm, but still tender, and the garlic is sweet and rich. By dividing the cooking fat between extra-virgin olive oil and ghee, you get a double-dose of lusciousness brightened by a kiss of lemon.

INGREDIENTS

- 1 pound large shrimp
- 4 teaspoons extra-virgin olive oil
- 6 cloves garlic, thinly sliced lengthwise
- 1/2 teaspoon Aleppo pepper (or crushed red pepper flakes)
- 1/2 teaspoon ghee
- 1/2 fresh lemon
- salt, to taste
- 1/2 cup fresh parsley leaves, minced (about 2 tablespoons)

DIRECTIONS

With a small, sharp knife, pierce the shrimp at the head end and carefully cut along the back toward the tail, removing the dark vein. Rinse in running water and pat dry.

In a large, non-stick skillet, heat the olive oil on low heat – VERY low heat – just enough heat to warm the oil. Add the garlic and Aleppo pepper, and cook until the garlic is golden and very soft, about 7-10 minutes.

Add the shrimp and cook until opaque and beginning to curl, about 6-8 minutes. Drop the ghee into the pan and toss gently to coat the shrimp. Spritz with a squeeze of lemon juice, then add a few shakes of salt, and sprinkle with parsley. Devour immediately.

YOU KNOW HOW YOU COULD DO THAT?

Shrimp are welcoming to many international flavors. Replace the Aleppo pepper, lemon juice, and parsley with the following:

TEX-MEX: *1/2 teaspoon chili powder; lime juice; cilantro*

SUNNY: *orange juice; chives*

ASIAN: *1/2 teaspoon crushed red pepper flakes; coconut aminos; scallions*

AFRICAN: *replace olive oil with Better Butter (p. 60); cilantro*

TROPICAL: *1/2 teaspoon Jerk Seasoning (p. 82); lime juice; cilantro*

TASTES GREAT WITH

CITRUS CAULIFLOWER RICE, P. 188
HERB SALAD, P. 196
SPRING CHOPPED SALAD, P. 208
ROASTED SPAGHETTI SQUASH, P. 168

NOTES

Mmmmm... extra-virgin olive oil** and **ghee is so indulgent.

The beef can be replaced with pork shoulder.

TASTES GREAT WITH

CRISP-SWEET COLLARDS, P. 198
MUSTARD-GARLIC BRUSSELS SPROUTS, P. 182
GREEN BEANS WITH SIZZLED GARLIC, P. 204

BBQ BEEF "WAFFLE" SANDWICH

YOU'RE GONNA NEED A LOT OF NAPKINS

SERVES 6 *to* 8

PREP	COOK
10 MIN.	4-7 HRS. IN SLOW COOKER

There's an old joke: I'm not from Texas but I got here as fast as I could. If I'd known how good the BBQ could be, I probably would have gotten here even sooner. I tip my hat to the BBQ experts in Texas, and I respectfully assert that while the recipe below is not authentic, it's pretty good for a Yankee. Plus, it doesn't take 18+ hours of smoking to get it on the table. Plate-licking good and messy!

Heads up! This recipe requires you to do something in advance; plan prep time accordingly.

INGREDIENTS

BBQ BEEF:

1 tablespoon paprika
1/2 tablespoon coarse (granulated) garlic powder
1/2 tablespoon salt
1 teaspoon chili powder
1/4 teaspoon dry mustard powder
2 pounds beef stew meat (chuck or round)
3 tablespoons cider vinegar
1 tablespoon coconut aminos

SWEET POTATO "WAFFLE:"

2 large sweet potatoes, grated (about 6 cups)
1 large egg, beaten
1 teaspoon salt
1/4 teaspoon baking soda
1/2 teaspoon cream of tartar
a little melted fat (coconut oil or ghee)

NOTE: THE "WAFFLE" IS NOT WHOLE30 APPROVED.

GARNISH:

1 batch Classic Cole Slaw (p. 178)
1 batch BBQ Sauce (p. 56)
dill pickles, fresh jalapeño

DIRECTIONS

Make the BBQ beef. In a small bowl, mix the paprika, garlic powder, salt, chili powder, and dry mustard. Place the beef in the slow cooker and sprinkle with the spices, tossing to coat. Pour the vinegar and coconut aminos into the bottom of the slow cooker. Cover and cook 4 hours on high or 7 hours on low.

Make the "waffles." About 20-30 minutes before you want to eat, preheat the oven to 200F. Place the shredded sweet potatoes in a clean dish towel and wring out the excess moisture. Squeeze with purpose and commitment; you want the sweet potatoes as dry as possible. Place them in a large bowl, then add the egg, salt, baking soda, and cream of tartar. Stir to combine.

Preheat a waffle iron to medium-high heat and brush the grates with melted fat. Place 1 cup of sweet potatoes in the waffle iron, close the lid, and cook for 10-15 minutes, until browned and cooked through. Place the waffle directly on the oven rack to keep warm and to make crisp. Repeat to make 2-3 waffles. Meanwhile...

Finish the BBQ beef. When the meat is finished braising, transfer it from the slow cooker to a bowl and shred with two forks. Place the shredded meat in a large saucepan and add the juice from the slow cooker; stir to combine. Bring to a simmer, then add 3/4 to 1 cup BBQ sauce; stir and simmer, covered, until the waffles are done.

Make your sandwiches! Pile BBQ Beef on a waffle, top with cole slaw and garnishes, then drizzle with a little extra BBQ sauce.

YOU KNOW HOW YOU COULD DO THAT?

Doing a Whole30? Too impatient to make the waffles? Pile the BBQ Beef on half a baked sweet potato instead. Or eat it Texas style: On a piece of butcher paper, with your hands.

I find it nearly impossible to resist celebrity magazines, especially if they feature "Stars Without Their Makeup." But I don't buy them anymore. I just flip through them as fast as I can at the grocery store checkout.

DELI TUNA SALAD

TO-GO TUNA WITH HOMEMADE TASTE

SERVES 2

PREP	COOK
20 MIN.	N/A

Good ol' tuna. Salmon gets all the attention like the popular girl in high school, but tuna is the reliable friend you call on when you need a sympathetic ear or, more accurately, when it's time to eat and you want something nutritious and easy. This recipe is a riff on classic takeout tuna from a deli. It uses traditional mix-ins – onion, celery, pickles, and mayo – and pumps up the flavor by adding a short, simple marinade step.

Heads up! This recipe requires you to do something in advance; plan prep time accordingly.

INGREDIENTS

- 2 (5 ounce) cans oil-packed tuna
- 1/4 medium onion, minced (about 1/4 cup)
- 1/4 cup fresh parsley leaves, minced (about 1 tablespoon)
- 1/2 tablespoon lemon juice
- 1/4 teaspoon ground black pepper
- 1/8 teaspoon salt
- dash cayenne pepper
- 1 rib celery, finely diced
- 2 tablespoons dried chives
- 1/4 cup minced dill pickle
- 2-3 tablespoons Olive Oil Mayo (p. 54)

NOTES

DIRECTIONS

Drain the tuna and keep 1 tablespoon oil from the can. In a large bowl, flake the tuna with a fork and add the reserved oil. Add the onion, parsley, lemon juice, black pepper, salt, and cayenne. Mix and allow to marinate 10-15 minutes.

To the tuna, add the celery, chives, and pickle. Mix with a rubber scraper. Add the mayo and gently fold until all the ingredients are combined. Eat immediately or store in the fridge for 2-3 days.

YOU KNOW HOW YOU COULD DO THAT?

Replace the tuna with wild-caught, canned salmon.

Add minced jalapeños – fresh or pickled – to up the ante.

TASTY IDEAS

WRAP IT UP! *Wrap the tuna salad in lettuce leaves or sheets of toasted nori, or spoon it into bell pepper halves or cucumber boats.*

Replace the Olive Oil Mayo with Garlic Mayo or with Green Goddess Dressing (p. 54).

FIESTA PORK CHOPS

MAKE YOU SAY OLÉ!

SERVES 2 to 4

PREP 10 MIN.

COOK 30 MIN.

With its festive flavors, this could quickly become a weeknight favorite at your house, transforming even a mundane Monday or a tiresome Tuesday into a fiesta that feels like Friday. Quick-browned pork chops are simmered in a sauce bursting with south of the border flavors: chiles, lime juice, cilantro, and the tasty trinity of chili powder, cumin, and oregano. This party in your mouth is piquant enough to please adults and mild enough for little amigos.

INGREDIENTS

4 large pork chops, bone in or boneless
salt and ground black pepper
1/2 tablespoon ghee plus 1/2 tablespoon ghee
1/2 medium onion, diced (about 1/2 cup)
1/2 teaspoon arrowroot powder
2 cloves garlic, minced (about 2 teaspoons)
1 teaspoon chili powder
1/2 teaspoon ground cumin
1/4 teaspoon dried oregano leaves
2/3 cup chicken broth
1 tablespoon lime juice
1 (4 ounce) can diced mild green chiles
1/4 cup fresh cilantro leaves, minced (optional)

GARNISH:

diced avocado
chopped scallions

DIRECTIONS

Sprinkle the pork chops exuberantly with salt and pepper. Heat 1/2 tablespoon ghee in a large, non-stick skillet over medium-high heat, about 3 minutes. Add the pork chops to the pan with a little wiggle room around them (work in batches if you need to) and cook on one side, undisturbed, for 4-5 minutes. With tongs, flip the pork over and brown the other side, 4-5 minutes.

Remove the pork from the pan, reduce the heat to medium, and add the onion and arrowroot to the pan. Sauté until soft and golden, about 5-7 minutes. Add the garlic, chili powder, cumin, and oregano. Cook until fragrant, about 30 seconds. Add the chicken broth, lime juice, and diced green chiles, then use a wooden spoon to scrape up any brown bits from the bottom of the pan.

Bring to a boil, then simmer and allow to thicken a bit, about 3 minutes. Add 1/2 tablespoon ghee to the pan, stir to combine, then place the pork chops back into the pan to reheat and coat them in sauce. Remove from the heat, sprinkle with cilantro. *Olé!*

YOU KNOW HOW YOU COULD DO THAT?

Replace pork chops with chicken breast, shrimp, or flank steak.

AVOCADO SIDE SALAD: *Fill an avocado half with diced onion and tomato tossed with minced cilantro and a spritz of lime juice.*

TASTES GREAT WITH

BASIC CAULIFLOWER RICE, P. 167
GREEN BEANS WITH SIZZLED GARLIC, P. 204
ROASTED CABBAGE ROSES, P. 190
SIMPLE LEMON SPINACH, P. 170

If you're an olive person, replace the canned black olives with the more traditional, stronger-flavored Niçoise olives. (Be sure to remove the pits!)

BEEF STEW PROVENÇAL

SAVOR THE SUN-RIPENED FLAVORS OF THE MEDITERRANEAN

SERVES 4 *to* 6

PREP	MARINATE	COOK
15 MIN.	2-3 HRS.	2 HRS.

Forget everything you think you know about beef stew. Bid adieu to waterlogged carrots and white potatoes, mushy gray-green peas, and bland, brown gravy. Instead, imagine thyme-scented beef, just-tender zucchini, bright orange carrots, and briny black olives in a flavor-infused broth. It's both comforting on a chilly evening and special enough to serve to company.

INGREDIENTS

3/4 cup balsamic vinegar
1/2 tablespoon salt
3/4 teaspoon ground black pepper
1 tablespoon dried thyme leaves
2 medium oranges
2 pounds boneless beef chuck
2 teaspoons ghee
1 medium onion, diced (about 1 cup)
2 cloves garlic, minced (about 2 teaspoons)
2 bay leaves
1 (14.5 ounce) can fire-roasted, diced tomatoes
1 cup beef broth
2 pounds zucchini, cut into 1-inch thick rounds
1 pound carrots, peeled, cut into 1/2-inch thick rounds
1 (6 ounce) can large black pitted olives

GARNISH:
minced fresh parsley leaves, extra-virgin olive oil

TASTES GREAT WITH

BASIC CAULIFLOWER RICE, P. 167
MASHED CAULIFLOWER, P. 167
SPRING CHOPPED SALAD, P. 208

DIRECTIONS

In a medium bowl, mix the vinegar, salt, and black pepper. Use your fingers to crush the dried thyme into the bowl. With a peeler or sharp knife, carefully cut the peel from an orange to make two strips that are 1 inch wide by 3 inches long. Add the peel to the bowl, then squeeze the juice from the oranges to make about 1/3 cup; add to the bowl. Stir with a fork to combine.

Cut the beef into 1-inch cubes. Add the beef to the marinade and mix well to coat. Cover and refrigerate for 2 to 3 hours or up to overnight. Remove the meat from the marinade and keep the marinade; you'll add it to the stew later. Pat the meat dry with paper towels, then sprinkle with plenty of salt and ground black pepper.

Heat a large, deep pot over medium-high heat, then add the ghee. When the ghee is melted, add the beef cubes to the pan in a single layer, being careful not to crowd the pan. (Everyone appreciates a little wiggle room when the heat is on.) Brown the beef on all sides in batches; remove the beef to a bowl as it browns.

When the meat is browned, add the onions and garlic to the drippings (add a little more ghee, if necessary) and cook until soft and golden, about 7 to 10 minutes. Return the beef to the pot and add the bay leaves, tomatoes, broth, and reserved marinade. Stir to combine. Bring to a boil, then reduce heat and simmer, covered, for 90 minutes.

Place the zucchini, carrots, and olives on top of the meat in the pot, then cook an additional 20 minutes, covered, until the beef and vegetables are tender. Serve topped with minced parsley and a gentle drizzle of extra-virgin olive oil.

TASTES GREAT WITH

BASIC CAULIFLOWER RICE, P. 167
ZUCCHINI NOODLES, P. 168

CHICKEN NANKING

PERFECT FOR A FIRST DATE OR ANNIVERSARY DINNER

SERVES 2 to 4

PREP 20 MIN. | MARINATE 30 MIN. | COOK 30 MIN.

My first official date with my husband Dave was at the House of Nanking in San Francisco's Chinatown, in 1992. It's a hole-in-the-wall restaurant, the windows smeared with steam and decades of grease. When the door opens, aromas drift out to tease hungry crowds waiting to get inside to sample the namesake dish. Dave told me it was a litmus test: If I liked the chicken, there'd be a second date. We've been eating together ever since.

Heads up! This recipe requires you to do something in advance; plan prep time accordingly.

INGREDIENTS

CHICKEN:

1 pound boneless, skinless chicken thighs
1/4 cup coconut aminos
1 tablespoon sesame oil
1 teaspoon arrowroot
1-inch piece fresh ginger, grated (about 1 tablespoon)
2 cloves garlic, minced (about 2 teaspoons)
1 teaspoon coconut oil

VEGETABLES:

1 pound green beans
1 large sweet potato (about 10-12 ounces)

SAUCE (OPTIONAL):

1/2 cup chicken broth
1/3 cup unsweetened apple sauce
1/4 cup coconut aminos
1 tablespoon Kickass Ketchup (p. 64)
4 cloves garlic, peeled and smashed
1 dried date (or dried fig), pit removed
1 teaspoon arrowroot powder
1/8 teaspoon ground black pepper
1/8 teaspoon ground cinnamon
dash cayenne pepper

GARNISH:

toasted sesame seeds
sliced scallions

DIRECTIONS

This is two dishes in one. With the sauce, it's tangy, sweet, and well... saucy. Without, it's flavorful and clean. Either way, prep all the components in advance, then fry it up just before eating.

Prep the chicken. In a medium bowl, mix the coconut aminos, sesame oil, arrowroot, ginger, and garlic. Cut the chicken into 1-inch pieces and add to the bowl. Mix well, then cover and refrigerate at least 2 hours or up to overnight.

Prep the veggies. Peel the sweet potato and cut in half lengthwise, then cut into 1/4-inch slices. Set aside. Wash and trim the green beans, then cut in half cross-wise. Set aside.

Prep the sauce. Place all the sauce ingredients in a blender or food processor and purée until smooth. When you're ready to start stir-frying the chicken and veggies, pour the sauce into a small saucepan, bring to a boil, then reduce heat to a gentle simmer so the sauce thickens.

Cook the veg. In a large, non-stick skillet or wok, bring 1/2 cup water to a boil, then add the sweet potatoes. Cover and steam until tender, 4-5 minutes. Remove the sweet potatoes to a large bowl. Add another 1/2 cup water to the pan, bring to a boil, then add the green beans. Cover and steam until tender, 4-5 minutes. Remove the beans from the pan and add to the bowl with the sweet potatoes.

Cook the chicken. In the same skillet, dry out any remaining water and heat 1 teaspoon coconut oil over medium-high heat. Remove the chicken from the marinade (and discard remaining marinade). Working in batches, if necessary, add the chicken in a single layer and cook until well browned, about 4-5 minutes per side. Try not to crowd the pan or the chicken won't attain the crispy, brown exterior that makes this dish feel decadent. As the chicken browns, add it to the bowl with the vegetables.

If using the sauce: Return the chicken and veggies to the sauté pan, add the sauce, and stir-fry until coated with sauce and heated through. Garnish with toasted sesame seeds and scallions.

If not using the sauce: Return the chicken and veggies to the sauté pan and season with a few dashes of coconut aminos. Garnish with toasted sesame seeds and scallions.

DECONSTRUCTED GYRO

OPA! OPA! OPA!

SERVES 6 *to* 8

PREP	COOK	ALERT
5 MIN.	2 HRS.	15 MIN.

This recipe requires very little effort but the cooking technique creates lovely caramelized bits, and caramelized bits are one of the best things on the planet. Plus it uses cumin. What else could you possibly need? How about mint to add the right bite and lemon juice to slyly tenderize the meat while you go about your business? This deconstructed salad delivers all the flavor of a gyro by keeping just the good stuff: fresh veggies, succulent lamb, creamy dressing, while dumping the dairy and gluten. **Heads up! This recipe requires you to do something in advance; plan prep time accordingly.**

INGREDIENTS

LAMB:

1 tablespoon dried mint leaves
1/2 tablespoon dried oregano leaves
1 tablespoon ground cumin
1 teaspoon Aleppo pepper or crushed red pepper flakes
1/2 tablespoon coarse (granulated) garlic powder
1 teaspoon salt
1 teaspoon ground black pepper
2 pounds lamb stew meat (Shoulder is nice!)
1/3 cup lemon juice
water

SALAD:

shredded lettuce: romaine, leaf, and iceberg are all good!
diced tomatoes, red onion, and cucumber
fresh parsley or mint (or both!), coarsely chopped
black olives

DRESSING:

Gyro/Kebab Sauce (p. 54)

DIRECTIONS

In a small bowl, rub the mint and oregano leaves between your palms to crush them. Add the cumin, Aleppo pepper, garlic powder, salt, and black pepper; mix with a fork until blended. Add the spice blend to a large plastic storage bag, add the lamb cubes, zip it closed, and shake with conviction until all the lamb pieces are coated with the spices. Place the lamb in a large, deep pot. Pour the lemon juice into the bottom of the pot, then add water to just cover the meat.

Place the pot on high heat and bring the water to a rip-roaring boil. When it's rolling, reduce the heat to keep a steady, strong simmer with the pan uncovered. The liquid should bubble a fair amount, but should not be a vigorous boil. While it's cooking, it will probably look like gray soup straight out of Dickens. Keep heart! As the water evaporates, the acid in the lemon juice tenderizes and flavors the meat.

At about the 2-hour mark, check the pot. The water should be much lower and maybe even almost gone. Allow all the water to cook out of the pot and watch as the meat fries and caramelizes in the fat and fruit juice.

Carefully turn the hunks of meat to brown all sides, then remove the hunks to a plate and let them rest for 5 minutes before eating. Arrange the salad on the plate, add the lamb, drizzle with the Gyro/Kebab Sauce, and sprinkle with minced, fresh herbs.

TASTES GREAT WITH

CITRUS CAULIFLOWER RICE, P. 188
STUFFED GRAPE LEAVES, P. 148
TABBOULEH, P. 172

YOU KNOW HOW YOU COULD DO THAT?

Serve the lamb with Herb Salad (p. 196); try Tahini Dressing (p. 74) or Almost Amba (p. 58) instead of Gyro/Kebab Sauce.

HEAD TO MOROCCO! *Replace mint, oregano, and cumin with 1 tablespoon Merguez Sausage Seasoning (p. 80).*

Chow down on the ribs with raw jalapeños, thin slices of sweet onion, and fresh cilantro leaves.
This is also a knockout with beef ribs instead of pork.

CHINESE FIVE-SPICE PORK RIBS

SLOW COOKED, SUPER TENDER

SERVES 3 *to* 4

PREP	COOK
5 MIN.	6-12 HRS. IN SLOW COOKER

Want to be a kitchen wizard (while doing minimal work)? Of course you do! Thanks to succulent pork, good spices, and a slow cooker, this recipe results in fall-off-the-bone-if-you-look-at-them-askance ribs that are infused with the complex and comforting flavors of Chinese five-spice powder. The kicker? Your time investment is about five minutes. Now ***that*** *is magic.*

INGREDIENTS

3-4 pounds baby back or St. Louis pork ribs

salt and ground black pepper

2 teaspoons Chinese five-spice powder

3/4 teaspoon coarse (granulated) garlic powder

1 fresh jalapeño, cut into rings

2 tablespoons rice vinegar

2 tablespoons coconut aminos

1 tablespoon tomato paste

DIRECTIONS

Cut the ribs into pieces that will fit standing up in the slow cooker. Lay the ribs on a cutting board and sprinkle generously with salt and pepper. In a small bowl, mix the Chinese five-spice and garlic powder together, then massage onto the meat to coat the ribs.

Toss the jalapeño rings into the bottom of the slow cooker, and add the rice vinegar, coconut aminos, and tomato paste. Stir until the tomato paste is combined with the other liquids. Add the ribs, standing up so they're not lying in the liquid – or use a roasting rack inside the cooker so the ribs are not lying on the bottom – cover, and cook 6 hours on high or 8-10 hours on low.

When the ribs are fall-apart tender, remove them from the cooker. Pour the liquid into a heat-proof container and refrigerate until the fat separates from the juices. Remove the fat and bring the remaining liquid to a boil, then simmer for a few minutes. Use as a dipping/drizzle sauce for the meat.

Want 'em crispy? Throw the ribs in a 400F oven for 10 minutes while you boil the sauce.

YOU KNOW HOW YOU COULD DO THAT?

NO SLOW COOKER? *Place the ribs in a baking dish with the sauce ingredients and bake, covered, at 275F for 4 hours. Place the ribs on a baking sheet, brush with the sauce from the baking dish, and broil for 5 minutes.*

Replace Chinese five-spice and coconut aminos with these:

BBQ: *1/2 teaspoon each chili powder, cumin, paprika; cider vinegar*

MIDDLE EASTERN: *2 teaspoons Lebanese Seven-Spice (p. 84); lemon juice*

JAMAICAN: *2 teaspoons Jerk Seasoning (p. 82); lime juice*

SPICY-SWEET: *2 teaspoons Sunrise Spice (p. 78); orange juice*

MOROCCAN: *2 teaspoons Merguez Sausage Seasoning (p. 80); orange juice*

TASTES GREAT WITH

FAUX PHO, P. 130

BASIC CAULIFLOWER RICE, P. 167

ASIAN SLAW, P. 178

SESAME CUCUMBER NOODLES, P. 192

FAUX PHO

SLURP!

SERVES 2 *to* 4

PREP: 10 MIN.

COOK: 15 MIN.

This recipe begins with the simplicity of Chinese Five-Spice Pork Ribs and is transformed into a nourishing bowl of broth spiked with plenty of ginger, oh-so-green bok choy, and morsels of spiced-just-right pork. And thanks to Zucchini Noodles, you can twirl, splash, and slurp to your heart's content.

Heads up! This recipe requires you to do something in advance; plan prep time accordingly.

INGREDIENTS

1 tablespoon coconut oil

2-inch piece fresh ginger, grated (about 2 tablespoons)

3 cloves garlic, minced (about 1 tablespoon)

4-6 cups beef broth

4-6 cups chicken broth

1 pound Chinese Five-Spice Pork Ribs, off the bone (p. 128)

1 head fresh bok choy, coarsely chopped

1 batch Zucchini Noodles, sweated, not cooked (p. 168)

4 teaspoons ghee

4 hard-boiled eggs, cut in half lengthwise

8 scallions, thinly sliced

GARNISH:

chopped fresh cilantro, fresh jalapeños, fresh lime juice

DIRECTIONS

Heat a saucepan over medium-high heat and add coconut oil. When it's melted, add the ginger and garlic, stirring frequently, until fragrant, about 30 seconds. Add the beef and chicken broth. Bring to a boil, then simmer, covered, about 10 minutes.

To the pot, add the pork and bok choy. Stir and simmer until the bok choy is tender and the meat is hot, about 5 minutes.

To serve, place some raw zucchini noodles in the bottom of a deep bowl. Add pork, greens, and broth. Drop 1 teaspoon of ghee into the bowl, place 2 hard-boiled egg halves into the broth, and sprinkle with the scallions. Garnish with cilantro, jalapeños, and lime juice, if that's how you slurp.

YOU KNOW HOW YOU COULD DO THAT?

Replace zucchini noodles with Basic Cauliflower Rice (p. 167).

Replace the bok choy with kale, collards, chard, or spinach.

MAKE IT THAI(ISH): *To the broth, add 1 cup coconut milk and 2 tablespoons red or green curry paste.*

NOTES

You could eat this with a spoon, but where's the fun in that? Grab your chopsticks!

TASTES GREAT WITH

ASIAN SLAW, P. 178

ITALIAN PORK ROAST

A NO-WORK RECIPE THAT MAKES YOU LOOK LIKE A GENIUS

SERVES *a lot!*

PREP	COOK
10 MIN.	16 HRS. IN SLOW COOKER

I have a passionate dislike for stews and soups made in the slow cooker. The ingredients don't caramelize enough for my taste and what comes out of the cooker is always too watery. But I recently fell in love with my slow cooker as a countertop oven. This roasting recipe requires just a few minutes of hands-on work, and the result is succulent: tender meat that lasts for multiple meals and flavorful juice that can be quickly simmered into a sauce. I suppose you could say the slow cooker is the genius, but don't you think we cooks are pretty smart to use it?

INGREDIENTS

- 5-7 pound pork roast, boneless or bone in
- 4 cloves garlic, cut into slivers
- 1 tablespoon salt
- 1 tablespoon Italian herb blend
- 2 teaspoons ground black pepper
- 1 teaspoon ground fennel seeds (optional)
- 1 teaspoon crushed red pepper flakes (optional)

YOU KNOW HOW YOU COULD DO THAT?

Replace the Italian herb blend & fennel with these seasonings instead:

BBQ: *1 teaspoon each chili powder, cumin, and paprika*

MIDDLE EASTERN: *1 tablespoon Lebanese Seven-Spice Blend (p. 84)*

JAMAICAN: *1 tablespoon Jerk Seasoning (p. 82)*

SPICY-SWEET: *1 tablespoon Sunrise Spice (p. 78)*

MOROCCAN: *1 tablespoon Merguez Sausage Seasoning (p. 80)*

TASTES GREAT WITH

ZUCCHINI NOODLES, P. 168
MASHED CAULIFLOWER, P. 167
CRISP-SWEET COLLARDS, P. 198
ROASTED CABBAGE ROSES, P. 190
GREEN BEANS WITH SIZZLED GARLIC, P. 204

DIRECTIONS

Pat the pork roast dry with paper towels. Use a small, sharp knife to make slits all over the pork, then insert the garlic slivers into the slits.

In a small bowl, mix the salt, Italian herb blend, black pepper, fennel, and red pepper flakes, using your fingers to crush the leaves and mix them with the spices. Rub the mixture all over the pork roast, working into the nooks and crannies.

Place the pork roast in the slow cooker and cook on low for 14 to 16 hours. As the pork roasts, the pan of the slow cooker will fill with liquid. You have two choices: (1) let it go and pour off the liquid when the meat is finished cooking; or (2) halfway through cooking, remove the lid and carefully pour off the liquid. Put the lid back on the pork and let it continue roasting. Refrigerate the liquid in a glass bowl, jar, or BPA-free container so the grease can separate from the flavorful juice. I like to pour off the liquid so the outside of the roast gets crispier.

When the meat is finished roasting, it's fall-apart tender. You can either shred it with forks, mixing the crusty bits with the interior, tender bits, or break it into serving-size hunks. It's crazy-good either way.

Remember the juice you put in the fridge? Now you can easily skim off the excess fat, reheat the juice in a pan on the stove, and use it as a sauce for the cooked meat.

NO SLOW COOKER? *Roast in a 425F oven for 20 minutes, then reduce heat to 325F and cook 1 hour per pound of meat until internal temp reaches 185-190F.*

PERFECT STEAK

JUST THE WAY YOU LIKE IT, EVERY TIME

SERVES *varies*

PREP	CHILL	COOK
5 MIN.	1 HR	30-60MIN

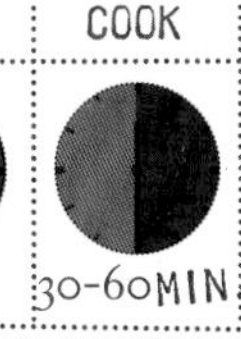

I'm just going to come right out and say it: Most of the time, grass-fed steak doesn't taste as good to me as a slab of beef from a big, corn-fed, Midwestern steer. But that's not the fault of the grass! It's the cooking. Grass-fed beef needs gentle, loving care to retain its sweet, meaty flavor and tender texture. That means a blast of high heat to crisp it, followed by slow, low heat to cook through. I cobbled together the following technique from a handful of kitchen scientists. It's persnickety, but neither time consuming nor difficult, and the results are 100 percent reliable.

INGREDIENTS

Your favorite cut of steak, 3/4- to 1-inch thick

PER STEAK:

1/4 teaspoon salt

1/2 teaspoon arrowroot powder

1 teaspoon ghee

YOU KNOW HOW YOU COULD DO THAT?

MAKE IT FANCY! *Melt 2 tablespoons ghee in a saucepan. Add 1 tablespoon finely chopped pistachios, 1 clove crushed garlic, 1 tablespoon chopped chives (fresh or dried), and 2 minced, dried figs. Warm on the stove until the steaks are done, then drizzle on the hedonism.*

TASTES GREAT WITH

GARLIC-CREAMED SPINACH, P. 214
BALSAMIC-GRILLED BUTTERNUT, P. 174
GREEN BEANS WITH SIZZLED GARLIC, P. 204
MASHED CAULIFLOWER, P. 167
SPAGHETTI SQUASH FRITTERS, P. 216

DIRECTIONS

Pat steak dry with paper towels. In a small bowl, mix the salt and arrowroot powder, then rub both sides of the steak with the salt.

Place the steak on a roasting rack on a baking sheet in the freezer. Or you could also just place the steak directly on the shelf in the freezer. Chill for 1 hour.

Preheat oven to 200F and cover a large baking sheet with parchment paper. Heat a cast-iron skillet on the stovetop until it's very, *very*, ***VERY*** hot – like, "make you kinda scared of it" hot – about 10 minutes. Carefully add the ghee and when it's melted, place the steak in the pan. Sear it on each side, pressing down with another pan, if necessary, to get an even crust, about 3-5 minutes per side.

Remove steak to the baking sheet and roast in the oven to desired temperature: about 30 minutes for rare (125F), about 45 minutes for medium (145F), and about 1 hour for well-done (165F). Remove the pan from the oven and lightly cover with a piece of foil. Let the steak rest 10 minutes before cutting.

NOTES ***You'll never overcook your steak again. Rejoice!***

Sabich was brought to Israel by Jews from Iraq in the 1940s and '50s. Cooking isn't allowed on the Sabbath, so sabich ingredients were cooked in advance for assembly on the Sabbath.

SEMI SABICH

IRAQI JEWISH FOOD FROM ISRAEL... OY VEY

SERVES 2 *to* 4

PREP	SWEAT	COOK
15 MIN.	30 MIN.	20 MIN.

I've never eaten an authentic Sabich (sounds like suh-beach*) from a street vendor in Israel. But I like to travel with my taste buds, so I dug into research to learn more about this popular sandwich. I read many magazine articles and recipes, and all of them gushed about this irresistible combination of eggplant, hard-boiled eggs, amba sauce, and tahini. Like most traditional foods, each cook customizes their recipe, so my version includes spiced lamb with raisins. All of the components can be made in advance then assembled when it's time to eat.* **Heads up! This recipe requires you to do something in advance; plan prep time accordingly.**

INGREDIENTS

EGGPLANT:
1 large eggplant
salt
2 tablespoons coconut oil, melted
za'atar, to taste

RELISH:
2 teaspoons extra-virgin olive oil
2 teaspoons lemon juice
1 large seedless cucumber, diced
1 medium tomato, diced
1/2 cup fresh parsley leaves, minced (about 2 tablespoons)
1/4 medium red onion, minced (about 2 tablespoons)
salt and ground black pepper, to taste

LAMB:
1 pound ground lamb
1/2 medium onion, diced (about 1/2 cup)
1 clove garlic, minced (about 1 teaspoon)
2 tablespoons raisins
1/2 teaspoon ground cumin
1/2 teaspoon dried oregano
1/2 teaspoon dried mint
1/4 teaspoon Aleppo pepper or crushed red pepper flakes
1/2 teaspoon salt
1/4 teaspoon ground black pepper

GARNISH:
Almost Amba (p. 58)
Tahini Dressing (p. 74)
sliced hard-boiled eggs
fresh mint leaves
hot pepper rings
toasted sesame seeds
pickles or cornishons

DIRECTIONS

Sweat the eggplant. Cut eggplant into 1/4-inch thick slices. Sprinkle the slices aggressively with salt on both sides and place in a colander or sieve to sweat for 30 minutes.

Prep the relish. In a medium bowl, mix olive oil and lemon juice with a fork. Add cucumber, tomato, parsley, and red onion. Toss to combine, then season with salt and pepper. Set aside.

Roast the eggplant. Preheat oven to 450F and cover a large baking sheet with parchment paper. Rinse the eggplant slices and pat dry with paper towels or a clean dish towel, then brush with coconut oil and sprinkle with za'atar. Bake for 20 minutes, until browned and beginning to crisp. Meanwhile...

Brown the lamb. Heat a large, non-stick skillet over medium-high heat, about 3 minutes. Add the lamb and cook until browned, breaking up big chunks with a wooden spoon. Add the onion, garlic, and raisins. Cook until the onions are soft, 5-7 minutes. Toss in the cumin, oregano, mint, Aleppo pepper, salt, and pepper. Stir to combine and cook until fragrant.

Assemble! To serve, place eggplant slices on a plate and top with lamb, relish, and other optional garnishes. Drizzle with sauces.

YOU KNOW HOW YOU COULD DO THAT?

Replace lamb with beef.

TASTES GREAT WITH

CASABLANCA CARROTS, P. 176
HERB SALAD, P. 196
BASIC CAULIFLOWER RICE, P. 167

OVEN-FRIED SALMON CAKES

PROTEIN & CARBS IN A CAKE

SERVES 2 *to* 4

PREP 25 MIN.

COOK 30 MIN.

I predict that this is going to become one of your go-to recipes. It's fast – less than an hour from pantry to plate. It uses ingredients you probably have in your kitchen right now. It's great for breakfast, lunch, or dinner. And like a favorite little black dress that makes you feel good and goes with everything, it's easy to adapt to your mood. Plus, it has cake in the name. How could it not be a favorite?

INGREDIENTS

1 (14.75 ounce) can wild-caught pink or red salmon
1 cup cooked (or canned) sweet potato, mashed
2 large eggs, beaten
1/2 cup almond flour
1/2 cup fresh parsley leaves, minced (about 2 tablespoons)
2 scallions, white and green, very thinly sliced
1 tablespoon Old Bay Seasoning
1 teaspoon salt
1 teaspoon hot sauce
1/2 teaspoon paprika
1/4 teaspoon ground black pepper
zest from 1 lemon
2 tablespoons ghee, melted

GARNISH:
Tartar Sauce (p. 54)
Remoulade (p. 54)
Awesome Sauce (p. 54)
minced fresh parsley

DIRECTIONS

Preheat the oven to 425F and cover a large baking sheet with parchment paper.

Drain the liquid from the salmon and using your fingers, crumble the fish into a large mixing bowl, removing the bones and flaking the fish. Add the sweet potato, eggs, almond flour, parsley, scallions, Old Bay Seasoning, salt, hot pepper sauce, paprika, black pepper, and lemon zest. Mix well and refrigerate for 10 minutes.

Brush the parchment paper with some of the melted ghee, then use a 1/3 measuring cup to scoop the cakes and drop them onto the parchment. The patties should be about 2 1/2 inches wide and about 1 inch thick. Brush the tops of the cakes with ghee, then bake for 20 minutes. Carefully flip each patty with a spatula and return to the oven. (Brush with more ghee if that tickles your fancy.) Bake an additional 10 minutes until golden brown and crisp. Serve with a squeeze of lemon juice and your sauce of choice.

YOU KNOW HOW YOU COULD DO THAT?

Replace Old Bay Seasoning with these spices and top with sauces listed.

INDIAN: *2 teaspoons curry powder (I like Penzeys Maharajah.)*
MIDDLE EASTERN: *2 teaspoons Lebanese Seven-Spice Blend (p. 84) + Almost Amba (p. 58) + Tahini Dressing (p. 74)*
MEDITERRANEAN: *2 teaspoons dried rosemary leaves + Romesco Sauce (p. 70)*
TROPICAL: *1/2 teaspoon powdered ginger, 1 clove crushed garlic + Spicy Coconut Mayo (p. 54)*
SPICY-SWEET: *2 teaspoons Sunrise Spice (p. 78)*
ASIAN: *2 teaspoons Chinese five-spice powder*
TEX-MEX: *2 teaspoons chili powder, 1 teaspoon ground cumin, lime zest + Lizard Sauce (p. 68)*
JERKY: *2 teaspoons Jerk Seasoning (p. 82)*

NOTES ***Use Better Butter (p. 60) for another taste explosion! Serve these on top of Simple Lemon Spinach (p. 170).***

TROPICAL CHOPPED SALAD

TINY PAPER UMBRELLA OPTIONAL

SERVES 2 to 4

PREP	COOK
20 MIN.	N/A

There are many azure-blue-and-white-sand beaches that top lists of "The Ten Best Tropical Islands." Their exotic names – Fiji, Bora Bora, Tahiti – evoke images of dramatic sunsets, the warm kiss of the sun, and flavors like sweet mango and citrus. This salad is perfect for a lazy day when your biggest ambition is to flip over from sunning your front to sunning your back. If you find yourself in a snowsquall, wishing for an island breeze, you can use defrosted, frozen mango in this recipe to import sunshine into your day.

Heads up! This recipe requires you to do something in advance; plan prep time accordingly.

INGREDIENTS

- 1 pound shrimp (any size will do)
- 1 tablespoon lime juice
- 1 tablespoon lemon juice
- 1 tablespoon extra-virgin olive oil
- 1/2 medium red onion, finely minced (about 1/4 cup)
- 1/2 teaspoon Jerk Seasoning (p. 82)
- 1/4 cup fresh cilantro leaves, minced (about 1 tablespoon)
- 1 ripe mango
- 1 medium ripe avocado
- 2 medium red bell peppers
- salt and ground black pepper, to taste

DIRECTIONS

With a small, sharp knife, pierce the shrimp at the head end and carefully cut along the back toward the tail, removing the dark vein. Rinse in running water. Bring a saucepan of water to boil and add the shrimp. Set a timer for 4 minutes and let the shrimp enjoy the hot tub; no need to bring it to a boil again. When time is up, drain the shrimp and let them cool just until you can handle them without burning your fingertips. Cut them into 1/2-inch pieces.

In a medium bowl, mix the warm shrimp with the lime juice, lemon juice, olive oil, onion, Jerk Seasoning, and cilantro. Let the shrimp marinate while you prep the other ingredients.

While the shrimp is in the flavor spa, dice the mango, avocado, and red pepper into equal-sized dice. I like 1/2-inch cubes. Toss everything together and eat languidly.

NOTES

Bula! Bula! ***In Fiji, the islanders use "bula" as a greeting and all-purpose interjection. It embodies life and love, a wish for others' health and happiness.***

YOU KNOW HOW YOU COULD DO THAT?

MAKE IT SALSA! *Omit the protein in the salad and spoon it over a lovely piece of grilled chicken, pork, or fish instead.*

Replace the shrimp with lump crabmeat, lobster (!), or poached chicken breast. Try pineapple in lieu of mango, or fire it up with a fresh jalapeño.

TASTES GREAT WITH

COCONUT CAULIFLOWER RICE, P. 202

TASTES GREAT WITH

BASIC CAULIFLOWER RICE, P. 167
SPRING CHOPPED SALAD, P. 208
HERB SALAD, P. 196
CASABLANCA CARROTS, P. 176
IMPLE LEMON SPINACH, P. 170

LEMON LAMB TAGINE

SLOW-BRAISED BERBER STEW

SERVES 2 *to* 4

PREP	COOK	SIMMER
15 MIN.	35 MIN.	1 1/2 HRS

"Tagine" is both the name of the dish and the special earthenware pot in which it's slow cooked. Found primarily in Morocco, a tagine is a savory combination of meat, vegetables, aromatic spices, and, sometimes, dried fruit. Unlike curries and gravy-ish stews, a tagine produces just enough broth to braise the ingredients and flavor the bed of (cauliflower) rice on which it's served. This recipe is adapted to work on the stovetop in a standard soup pot, but if you're fortunate enough to own a cone-shaped cooking tagine, these instructions will work for that, too.

INGREDIENTS

1 medium lemon
1/2 teaspoon extra-virgin olive oil
1 clove plus 2 cloves garlic, minced (about 3 teaspoons)
3/4 teaspoon paprika
1/4 teaspoon ground cumin
1/8 teaspoon Aleppo pepper (or cayenne pepper)
1/8 teaspoon powdered ginger
1/8 teaspoon ground cinnamon
1 pound lamb stew meat
salt and ground black pepper
1/2 tablespoon coconut oil or ghee
1/2 large onion, cut into 1/2-inch thick half-moons
1/2 pound carrots, peeled and cut into 1/2-inch thick rounds
1 cup chicken broth
3/4 pound zucchini, cut into 1/2-inch thick half-moons
1/4 large head cabbage, cut into 2-inch pieces
1/4 cup green olives
1/4 cup fresh cilantro leaves, minced (about 1 tablespoon)

YOU KNOW HOW YOU COULD DO THAT?

Replace lamb with chicken thighs (bone in or out).

DIRECTIONS

Remove all the peel from the lemon with a vegetable peeler and cut it into 2-inch long strips. Mince one strip and place in a small bowl, along with the olive oil and 1 clove minced garlic. Cover with plastic wrap and set aside. Squeeze the juice from the lemon into another small bowl and set aside. Save the remaining strips of peel for later.

In another small bowl (last one!), use a fork to mix 2 cloves of the minced garlic with the paprika, cumin, Aleppo pepper, ginger, and cinnamon. Save for later.

Pat the lamb dry with paper towels and sprinkle heartily with salt and pepper. In a large pot or Dutch oven, heat the coconut oil over medium-high, then add the meat in batches and sear on all sides. With tongs, remove the browned pieces to a bowl to catch their juice. Repeat with the remaining cubes.

Add the onion and reserved lemon peel to the pot, cook over medium heat, stirring occasionally, until crisp-tender, about 3 minutes. Add the garlic-spice blend and cook until fragrant, about 30 seconds. Stir in the carrots and broth, scraping up any brown bits in the bottom of the pot. Return the lamb and accumulated juices to the pot and tuck the meat into the broth. Bring to a boil, then reduce heat to simmer and cook, covered, 25 minutes.

Add the zucchini and cabbage to the pot, piling it on top of the meat. Cover and cook an additional 45 minutes, until meat and vegetables are tender. Add the olives to the pot and stir to combine all the ingredients. Increase the heat to medium-high and cook, uncovered, until the sauce is slightly thickened, about 5-10 minutes. Stir in the reserved lemon juice, garlic-infused olive oil, and cilantro. Taste and add salt and pepper, if necessary.

If you can't find fresh shitake and wood ear mushrooms, you can used jarred mushrooms from the Asian section of your grocery store.

TASTES GREAT WITH

BASIC CAULIFLOWER RICE, P. 167

HU PORK

AMERICAN-CHINESE FOOD FROM THE SWINGIN' SIXTIES

S 2 *to* 4

ARINATE	COOK
2 HRS.	15 MIN.

What I love best about Moo Shu Pork is that it requires me to play with my food. This version substitutes butter lettuce for traditional pancakes, but the drizzle of hoisin sauce and sticky-fingered rolling process remain blessedly similar. A few (appetizing) words of warning: This makes a mountain of vegetables, so you'll need a Very Big Bowl. You can swap simple white mushrooms for the shitakes, but there is no substitute for the chewy, dark flavor of the wood ear mushrooms.

Heads up! This recipe requires you to do something in advance; plan prep time accordingly.

REDIENTS

& MARINADE:

und pork loin (or boneless chops)
cup coconut aminos
ablespoon toasted sesame oil
teaspoon arrowroot powder
-inch piece fresh ginger, grated (about 1 tablespoon)
2 cloves garlic, minced (about 2 teaspoons)

STIR-FRY:

1 ounce wood ear mushrooms
4 ounces shitake mushrooms
1 (8 ounce) can bamboo shoots, drained and julienned
1 (14.4 ounce) can bean sprouts, drained (optional)
4 scallions, very thinly sliced (about 1/4 cup)
4 cups very thinly sliced green cabbage
coconut oil, for stir-frying
2 large eggs, beaten
3 cloves garlic, minced (about 1 tablespoon)

TO SERVE:

1 batch Hoisin Sauce (p. 62)
1 head butter or Boston lettuce

DIRECTIONS

Marinate the pork. Place pork in the freezer for 10 minutes to chill, then slice into very thin ribbons (about 1/4 inch wide). In a medium bowl, mix the coconut aminos, sesame oil, arrowroot, ginger, and garlic. Add the pork and toss to coat. Cover and refrigerate 2 hours or up to overnight.

Prep the mushrooms and gather vegetables. Place the wood ear mushrooms in a small bowl and cover with boiling water. Soak for 30 minutes while you prep the rest of the veggies. Remove the stems from the shitakes and slice very thin. The stir-fry process goes pretty quickly, so make sure all veggies are ready to go. Ready? GO!

Cook the eggs. Heat a large, non-stick skillet over medium-high, about 3 minutes. Add 2 teaspoons coconut oil. When it's melted, pour in the eggs and let them spread like a pancake. Reduce the heat to medium and cover, letting the eggs cook until set and beginning to brown, about 3-4 minutes. Flip and brown the other side. Remove from the pan and cut into strips. Place in a Very Big Bowl. Very Big.

Stir-fry! In the same pan, add 1/2 teaspoon coconut oil, and when it's melted, cook the pork with the garlic, 3-5 minutes. Add to the Very Big Bowl. Add all the mushrooms to the pan and cook until heated through, about 1 minute. Add to the Very Big Bowl. Throw the bean sprouts and bamboo shoots into the pan and heat, then add them to the Very Big Bowl.

In the same pan, add 1 teaspoon oil, then stir-fry the cabbage and scallions until wilted, about 1 minute. Add to the Very Big Bowl. Using two wooden spoons, toss all the ingredients in the Very Big Bowl until combined.

Eat! Serve family style with a platter of butter lettuce leaves, the Very Big Bowl of Moo Shu, and Hoisin Sauce for drizzling. The messier the better!

YOU KNOW HOW YOU COULD DO THAT?

- *Replace the pork with chicken breast, flank steak, or shrimp.*
- *Use hearts of romaine lettuce instead of butter lettuce.*

TASTES GREAT WITH

SIMPLE LEMON SPINACH, P. 170
BASIC CAULIFLOWER RICE, P. 167

PLANTAIN NACHOS

CRISPY, SALTY, SPICY, SLOPPY

SERVES 2 *to* 4

PREP 20 MIN. COOK 30 MIN.

Tacos versus nachos. It's a timeless rivalry with no clear winner. I think we can all agree that a basket of crispy things, ready to be smothered in tender, spicy meat and fresh toppings can perk up the most mundane Monday or woeful Wednesday. So why choose? This recipe combines the best of tacos and nachos, while ditching the soy, sugar, and grains hidden in most commercial taco seasonings. It's impossible to argue and stuff chips into your mouth at the same time, so let's just declare a peace treaty between tacos and nachos. Buen apetito!

INGREDIENTS

PLANTAINS:

2 green plantains

1 tablespoon coconut oil, melted

TACO MEAT:

2 teaspoons coconut oil

1/2 medium onion, minced (about 1/2 cup)

3 cloves garlic, minced (about 1 tablespoon)

2 tablespoons chili powder

1 teaspoon ground cumin

1 teaspoon ground coriander

1/2 teaspoon dried oregano leaves

1/4 teaspoon cayenne pepper

3/4 teaspoon salt

1 pound ground beef

2 tablespoons tomato paste

1/2 cup chicken broth

2 teaspoons cider vinegar

GARNISH:

minced scallions

jalapeño slices

diced avocado

shredded lettuce

chopped tomato

fresh lime juice

YOU KNOW HOW YOU COULD DO THAT?

Did your plantains get too ripe to make these crispy "chips?" Make Pan-Fried Plantains (p. 184) instead.

DIRECTIONS

Preheat oven to 350F. Cover two large baking sheets with parchment paper and set aside.

Prep the plantains. Cut off both ends of the plantain, then with the tip of a sharp knife, make shallow slits lengthwise along the skin. Use your fingers to pry off the strips. With a mandoline slicer on its thinnest setting, slice the plantains into coins. Use two wooden spoons to toss the slices in a large bowl with the melted coconut oil.

Bake the plantains. Use four coins to make each "tortilla:" Lay them flat on the baking sheet with edges slightly overlapping and sprinkle with salt. While they bake, the natural starches make them stick together. Bake for about 30 minutes until very crisp and beginning to brown. Remove from the oven and sprinkle with additional salt, if you're feeling it. Meanwhile...

Make the taco meat. Heat the coconut oil in a large, non-stick skillet over medium heat, about 2 minutes. Add onion and cook until softened, about 7-10 minutes. In a small bowl, mix the garlic, chili powder, cumin, coriander, oregano, cayenne, and salt. Add to the onions and stir until fragrant, about 30 seconds.

Crumble the ground beef into the pan and cook, breaking up the meat with a wooden spoon, until no longer pink, about 5 minutes. Push the meat to the side of the pan and drop in the tomato paste, frying until it darkens a bit, about 3 minutes. Add the chicken broth and vinegar; stir to combine. Bring to a boil, then reduce to simmer and cook, uncovered, 10 minutes, until the liquid has reduced and thickened. Add salt and pepper, to taste.

Dig in! Pile the meat on top of the plantain chips and top with your favorite garnishes.

TASTES GREAT WITH

TABBOULEH, P. 172
HERB SALAD, P. 196
BELLY DANCE BEET SALAD, P. 186
CASABLANCA CARROTS, P. 176

STUFFED GRAPE LEAVES

YOU CAN CALL 'EM DOLMAS, IF YOU WANT

SERVES 2 *to* 4

PREP	COOK
35 MIN.	30 MIN.

I've probably eaten thousands of stuffed grape leaves in my life, and about 99 percent of them were made by my dad. We always called them "stuffed grape leaves," never dolmas, and we'd soak the leaves in the sink, never in a bowl. Then my dad and I would divvy up the responsibilities: one to scoop filling, the other to roll and place in the pot. This recipe comes together quicker than you might think, but it can also inspire lingering with friends and family. It's amazing how quickly the pot fills with rows of rolls when the stories and laughter are flowing.

Heads up! This recipe requires you to do something in advance; plan prep time accordingly.

INGREDIENTS

- 1 8-ounce jar grape leaves (I like Mezzeta.)
- 1/2 head raw cauliflower (about 1 pound)
- 3 tablespoons pine nuts (optional)
- 3 tablespoons raisins or currants (optional)
- 1 pound ground lamb
- 1/2 medium raw onion
- 1 tablespoon dried mint
- 2 teaspoons Lebanese Seven-Spice Blend (p. 84)
- 1/2 cup fresh parsley leaves
- 2 garlic cloves, peeled and smashed
- 1/2 tablespoon salt
- 1 teaspoon ground black pepper
- 2-3 cups water, boiling hot
- 2 fresh lemons
- 2 large egg yolks (optional)

Jarred grape leaves can be found in most grocery stores in the international section.

DIRECTIONS

Remove the grape leaves from the jar and place in a large mixing bowl. Cover with hot water and soak 15 minutes. Meanwhile, break the cauliflower into florets, removing the stems. Place the florets in a food processor and pulse until the cauliflower looks like rice. This takes about 10 to 15 one-second pulses. Place rice in a large mixing bowl and return the food processor bowl to its base; no need to clean it.

Heat a dry skillet over medium high heat, then add the pine nuts and raisins, stirring often and cooking until the pine nuts are lightly toasted, about 3-5 minutes. Set aside to cool, then coarsely chop. Add the nuts and raisins to the rice in the bowl.

Place the lamb, onion, mint, Lebanese Seven-Spice, parsley, garlic, salt, and pepper in the bowl of the food processor and purée until the ingredients form a paste. Add the lamb paté to the rice and mix well. The easiest way to do this is with your hands: run them under a little cold water and dig in.

In a 3-quart saucepan, place a few reject leaves to cover the bottom of the pan. Drain the water from the rest of the leaves and get ready to start rolling…

Place a leaf on a flat surface with the shiny side facing down, snip off the stem, and place 1 tablespoon of lamb/rice filling on the end of the leaf closest to you. Roll from the bottom, fold in the sides, and keep rolling until you have a cigar shape. Roll them tightly so they don't come apart during cooking. Place the rolls in the pan and cuddle them up against each other.

Cut one of the lemons into thin slices and arrange on top of the dolmas in the pan. Place a plate or saucer on top of the dolmas and press down, then pour boiling water into the pan to cover the plate (about 2 cups). Put the lid on the pot and simmer. (Keep an eye on it; you want a few bubbles but not a rolling boil.) Cook 25-30 minutes, until the leaves are tender but still snappy.

Carefully remove the plate and drain the water from the pan. Cover with the lid so they stay hot. In a small bowl, whisk the juice from the remaining lemon with the egg yolks until frothy. Pour over the dolmas, then put the lid back on the pot. The hot dolmas gently cook the egg/lemon sauce to create a tangy coating.

Remove the dolmas from the pan, place covered in the fridge, and wait until they're chilled. They taste great cold, room temp, or hot – but are best if reheated, rather than eaten immediately when they come out of the pan. I like to eat them cold with a sprinkle of coarse salt, za'atar, and a tiny drizzle of extra-virgin olive oil.

VIDEO! *Check out my Dolmas Rolling Demo Video at www.theclothesmakethegirl.com/wellfed2*

To toast almonds, brown them in a dry skillet over medium-high heat for 3-5 minutes, until lightly golden.

MULLIGATAWNY STEW

"PEPPER WATER" FROM INDIA

SERVES 6 to 8

PREP	COOK	SIMMER
15 MIN.	25 MIN.	55 MIN.

This aromatic stew with a light touch of creaminess originated in India and became popular in Britain during the UK occupation. I learned about mulligatawny in college when I subscribed to the monthly installments of McCall's Cooking School. *I was smitten with the photo of a brass tureen shaped like a crown and filled to the brim with golden soup flecked with coconut. The taste lives up to the visual: it's silky, rich without cloying, and balances the warmth of curry with the sweetness of apples.*

Heads up! This recipe requires you to do something in advance; plan prep time accordingly.

INGREDIENTS

2 pounds boneless, skinless chicken thighs
salt and ground black pepper
1/2 tablespoon plus 1/2 tablespoon coconut oil
2 medium onions, diced (about 2 cups)
3/4 pound carrots, peeled and cut into 1/2-inch coins
2 medium stalks celery, diced (about 1/2 cup)
2 medium apples, peeled and diced (about 2 cups)
3/4 cup unsweetened coconut flakes
3 cloves garlic, minced (about 1 tablespoon)
1 tablespoon arrowroot powder
1 1/2 tablespoons curry powder
1 tablespoon salt
1/2 teaspoon chili powder
1/4 teaspoon ground allspice
pinch cayenne
1 bay leaf
4 cups chicken broth
2 cups water
1 cup canned coconut milk
1 batch Basic Cauliflower Rice (p. 167)

GARNISH:
minced fresh parsley leaves
sliced almonds, toasted

DIRECTIONS

Sprinkle the chicken assertively with salt and pepper. Heat a large, deep pot over medium-high heat, then add 1/2 tablespoon coconut oil. When the oil is melted, add the chicken in a single layer with some elbow room around each piece. Brown in batches so a golden crust forms, about 5 minutes per side. Remove cooked chicken to a bowl to catch the juice.

Add 1/2 tablespoon coconut oil to the pot. Add onions, carrots, celery, apples, coconut flakes, and garlic. Sauté 7-10 minutes, scrape up any brown bits stuck to the bottom of the pan. In a small bowl, mix the arrowroot, curry powder, salt, chili powder, allspice, cayenne, and bay leaf. Stir-fry until the spices are fragrant, about 30 seconds.

Add the broth and water to the pot and stir to combine. Nuzzle the chicken into the liquid and bring to boil. Reduce heat to simmer and cook, covered, 45 minutes. Stir the coconut milk into the pot and simmer uncovered, 10 more minutes.

Serve on top of Basic Cauliflower Rice and sprinkle cheerfully with parsley and almonds.

TASTES GREAT WITH

Roasted Cabbage Roses (p. 190), or if you're feeling a little lazy, simply sauté shredded greens – cabbage, kale, spinach, and collards are all good choices – in a little ghee and use as a bed for the stew. You could also try it on a bed of Mashed Cauliflower (p. 167) instead of rice.

YOU KNOW HOW YOU COULD DO THAT?

Use chicken breast or a combo of breasts and thighs, or replace the chicken with lamb stew meat.

This was inspired by a burger at the charming 26 Beach restaurant in Venice, California.

SB&J BURGER

LIKE A PALEO PB&J

SERVES 2 *to* 4

PREP: 10 MIN.

COOK: 10 MIN.

At first glance, you're probably going to think this recipe looks kooky. And you're right: It's pretty kooky. It's also totally scrumptious and satisfying. The creamy texture of the sunflower seed butter is a slinky contrast to the grilled meat, and the strawberries on top are a tangy treat without the cloying sweetness of traditional jelly. Together, these seemingly contradictory ingredients combine for a mouth explosion of the very best kind.

INGREDIENTS

- 2 cups strawberries, hulled and sliced
- 1 teaspoon lemon juice
- 1/2 teaspoon powdered ginger
- 1 pound ground beef
- 3/4 teaspoon salt
- 1/4 teaspoon ground black pepper
- 1/4 cup sunflower seed or almond butter (no sugar added)
- 4-6 scallions, green tops only, thinly sliced

YOU KNOW HOW YOU COULD DO THAT?

CHANGE THE MEAT! *Use turkey, pork, or a meat combo.*
CHANGE THE JELLY! *Use other berries or stone fruits, like peaches or apricots.*
MAKE AN ELVIS! *Replace strawberry jelly with sautéed bananas and add crumbled bacon.*

NO GRILL? *Heat a little fat in a large, non-stick skillet over medium heat, about 2 minutes. Add patties, indentation side up, and cook until browned, about 5 minutes. Using a spatula, flip the burgers and continue cooking, about 4 minutes for medium-well or 5 minutes for well-done.*

DIRECTIONS

In a small bowl, mix the strawberries, lemon juice, and ginger. Set aside. Preheat a gas grill with all burners on high, lid closed, 10-15 minutes.

Mix the ground beef with salt and pepper and shape into four patties. Gently press down the center of each patty until it's about 1/2-inch thick to make a slight depression; this will prevent them from turning bulbous when you cook them. Grill patties, uncovered and without pressing down on them, until they're seared on one side, about 3 minutes. Flip the burgers and continue grilling to desired temperature: 3 minutes for rare, 4 minutes for medium, and 5 minutes for well-done.

While the burgers are cooking, heat a small saucepan over medium-high. Pour the strawberries and their juice into the pan and sauté the berries until they're very soft and syrupy. They should be reduced to about 1/2 cup. Allow to cool a bit.

Place the sunflower butter in a microwave-safe dish (or saucepan) and heat until thinned, about 40 seconds in the microwave.

When the burgers are good to go, top each with 1 tablespoon of melted sunflower butter and a few tablespoons of the strawberry "jelly," then sprinkle with scallions.

TASTES GREAT WITH

COCONUT CAULIFLOWER RICE, P. 202
ASIAN SLAW, P. 178
PAN-FRIED PLANTAINS, P. 184
SPRING CHOPPED SALAD, P. 208

SCHEHERAZADE OMELET

NEVER UNDERESTIMATE THE POWER OF A GOOD STORY

SERVES 4 to 6

PREP	COOK
15 MIN.	1 HR.

Scheherazade was a legendary Persian queen who used her studies of philosophy, art, and science to evade being murdered by the King. For 1001 nights, she charmed him with stories of romance and magic, leaving him with a cliffhanger just as dawn approached. This ensured his curiosity and her continued existence. When she'd completed telling her tales, he was smitten and became a wiser, kinder man. Likewise, this frittata-like dish – rich with lamb, walnuts, herbs, and spices – will transform all those who take a bite, any time of day or night. **Heads up! This recipe requires you to do something in advance; plan prep time accordingly.**

INGREDIENTS

- 1 tablespoon coconut oil or ghee
- 1 medium onion, finely diced (about 1 cup)
- 1 pound ground lamb
- 1 tablespoon arrowroot powder
- 1 tablespoon Lebanese Seven-Spice Blend (p. 84)
- 1/2 teaspoon plus 1/2 teaspoon salt
- 1/2 teaspoon plus 1/2 teaspoon ground black pepper
- 1/2 teaspoon ground turmeric
- 2 cloves garlic, minced (about 2 teaspoons)
- 6 large eggs
- 1/4 teaspoon baking soda
- 1/2 teaspoon cream of tartar
- 1 cup finely chopped romaine lettuce
- 4 scallions, minced (about 1/2 cup)
- 1 cup fresh parsley leaves, minced (about 1/3 cup)
- 1 cup fresh cilantro leaves, minced (about 1/3 cup)
- 1/2 cup chopped walnuts

DIRECTIONS

Preheat oven to 400F.

Heat the coconut oil in a cast iron skillet (or other oven-safe pan), about 2 minutes. Add the onions and cook until crisp-tender and translucent, about 5 minutes. Add the lamb, arrowroot, Lebanese Seven-Spice Blend, 1/2 teaspoon salt, 1/2 teaspoon pepper, turmeric, and garlic. Cook the meat, breaking up chunks with a wooden spoon, until it's browned, then set aside until it's cool to the touch.

Crack eggs into large mixing bowl and whisk in the baking soda, cream of tartar, 1/2 teaspoon salt, and 1/2 teaspoon pepper. Using a rubber scraper, gently fold in lettuce, scallions, parsley, cilantro, walnuts, and the cooled meat. Be careful not to overmix; just introduce the ingredients to each other and let them get to know each other on their own.

Return the cast iron skillet to the stove and heat over medium-high heat. Add 1/2 tablespoon coconut oil and when it's hot, about 2 minutes, pour the egg mixture into the skillet. Use a wooden spoon to stir, gently scraping the bottom of the skillet to make large curds, about 2 minutes. Shake the pan to evenly distribute the ingredients then allow it to cook undisturbed so the bottom sets, about 30 seconds. Place the pan in the oven and bake until the top is puffed and getting brown, about 20 minutes. Remove the skillet from the oven, allow the omelet to set for 5 minutes, then cut into wedges to serve.

YOU KNOW HOW YOU COULD DO THAT?

Replace lamb, Lebanese Seven-Spice, and turmeric with:

ITALIAN: *beef; 1 tablespoon Italian herb blend; omit cilantro*

TEX-MEX: *beef; 1/2 tablespoon chili powder, 1 teaspoon cumin; omit parsley, double cilantro*

CHINESE: *pork; 1 tablespoon Chinese five-spice powder; omit parsley, double cilantro*

ALL-AMERICAN JOE: *beef; 1 teaspoon paprika; omit cilantro; use 2 cups spinach instead of lettuce*

THAI: *pork; omit parsley, double cilantro; add 1 tablespoon fish sauce and 1/2 tablespoon lime juice*

TASTES GREAT WITH

SPRING CHOPPED SALAD, P. 208

HERB SALAD, P. 196

BASIC CAULIFLOWER RICE, P. 167

TOD MUN CHICKEN CAKES WITH CUCUMBER RELISH

THAI STREET FOOD

SERVES 4 *to* 6

MAKES	PREP	COOK
about 14 cakes	15 MIN.	25 MIN.

Our favorite local Thai joint makes a version of these crispy, spicy cakes served with a refreshing cucumber relish. Sadly, the cakes are deep-fried, and the cucumber salad is dressed with both sugar and peanuts. My home version swaps pan-frying in coconut oil for the swim in peanut oil, and the cucumber relish is tangy, tart, and dressed up with cashews. The fish sauce in both recreates that distinctive Thai flavor, but if you don't have any on hand, you can substitute 1 anchovy (or 1 teaspoon anchovy paste) mixed with 1 tablespoon coconut aminos.

INGREDIENTS

CHICKEN CAKES:

2 pounds boneless, skinless chicken breasts and thighs
6 scallions, trimmed and cut in thirds
1 bunch chives, trimmed and cut in thirds
1 cup fresh cilantro leaves
1 jalapeño, seeds removed, minced (about 2 tablespoons)
1 tablespoon lime juice
3 tablespoons red curry paste
2 large eggs
2 tablespoons fish sauce (I like Red Boat.)
1/4 teaspoon baking soda
1/2 teaspoon cream of tartar
coconut oil for cooking

CUCUMBER RELISH:

1 large seedless cucumber, very thinly sliced
salt
1/4 medium red onion, very thinly sliced (about 1/4 cup)
1/2 cup fresh cilantro leaves, chopped (about 2 tablespoons)
1 tablespoon lime juice
3 tablespoons orange juice
a few healthy splashes of fish sauce or coconut aminos
2 tablespoons cashews, finely chopped

DIRECTIONS

Toss the cucumber slices with a generous amount of salt and let them sit for 20-30 minutes in a colander to remove excess moisture. Rinse with running water, drain, and pat dry. Place in a large mixing bowl, along with the onion, cilantro, lime juice, orange juice, and fish sauce. Toss with two wooden spoons until the vegetables are coated with dressing. Allow flavors to meld and add chopped cashews just before serving.

Cut the chicken into 3-inch chunks and place them in the bowl of a food processor. Process on high until the chicken is chopped and beginning to form a paste. Remove from the food processor and place in a large mixing bowl.

To the food processor, add the scallions, chives, cilantro, jalapeño, lime juice, curry paste, eggs, fish sauce, baking soda, and cream of tartar. Process on high until it's puréed, then pour into the bowl with the chicken. Mix the chicken and herb purée until combined, then cover with plastic wrap and refrigerate for 30 minutes.

Place 1/2 tablespoon coconut oil in a large, non-stick skillet and heat on medium-high, about 3 minutes. Measure 1/3 cup of the chicken and drop into the hot pan, flattening a bit to make a patty; repeat. You should be able to get 3 to 4 in the pan. Don't pack them in there like they're riding a Bangkok subway – give 'em breathing room so they can get crisp. Brown on one side, about 5 minutes, then flip and brown the other side, about 5 minutes. Keep patting and flipping until they're done, then serve with cucumber relish.

YOU KNOW HOW YOU COULD DO THAT?

Replace chicken with white fish, shrimp, or a combo.

Serve with Sunshine Sauce from the original Well Fed.

TASTES GREAT WITH

ASIAN SLAW, P. 178
COCONUT CAULIFLOWER RICE, P. 202

Get serious about dinner and serve these on a bed of Simple Lemon Spinach (p. 170).

PAN-FRIED SARDINES

IT'S DINNER FOR ONE – EAT WHAT YOU WANT

SERVES 1

PREP	MARINATE	COOK
5 MIN.	30-60 MIN.	2 MIN.

When I was growing up, my family ate dinner together at 5:00 p.m. most nights. Now, I cook for my husband Dave and I nearly every evening. When I cook for myself and eat alone – in my pajamas, maybe watching TV with my plate in my lap, and my cat Smudge next to me – I indulge in weird stuff that no one else would want to eat. Sometimes I shock myself and land on something so worth eating, it becomes a real recipe. That's how these fried, canned sardines came to be. I know this recipe seems strange and maybe it is. You know what else it is? Salty, crispy, nourishing, and ridiculously savory.

INGREDIENTS

1 (3.75 ounce) can sardines, packed in olive oil
1 tablespoon lemon juice
1 clove garlic, minced (about 1 teaspoon)
1/4 cup fresh parsley leaves, minced (about 1 tablespoon)
1 tablespoon arrowroot powder
1/4 teaspoon ground cumin
pinch Aleppo pepper (or cayenne pepper)
pinch paprika
a few shakes of salt and ground black pepper
2 teaspoons coconut oil
a few handfuls of shredded lettuce

DIRECTIONS

Dump the sardines and about half their oil into a small bowl. Add the lemon juice, garlic, and parsley, then cover and refrigerate 30-60 minutes.

In a medium bowl, mix the arrowroot powder with the cumin, Aleppo pepper, and paprika. Add a few shakes of salt and pepper and mix with a fork. Remove the sardines from the marinade (keep the marinade) and add the fish to the bowl with the spices. Gently roll the sardines in the spices until they're coated. In a separate bowl, toss the shredded lettuce with the reserved marinade and place on a serving plate.

Heat a non-stick skillet over medium-high heat, about 3 minutes. Add coconut oil and allow it to melt. Fry the sardines about 2 minutes per side, until they're crisp and heated through. Pile on top of the shredded lettuce and eat like an animal. If you want to make it fancy, you can sprinkle with fresh lemon juice and minced parsley, but I never make it that far.

YOU KNOW HOW YOU COULD DO THAT?

SPANISH: *omit cumin and Aleppo pepper, increase paprika to 1/4 teaspoon, then top with Romesco Sauce (p. 70)*

MIDDLE EASTERN: *add 1/4 teaspoon Lebanese Seven-Spice Blend (p. 84)*

JAMAICAN: *omit cumin, add 1/4 teaspoon Jerk Seasoning, then top with Lizard Sauce (p. 68)*

CLASSIC SEAFOOD: *omit cumin, add 1/4 teaspoon Old Bay Seasoning, then top with Remoulade (p. 54)*

BETTER! *Use Better Butter (p. 60) in place of coconut oil*

TASTES GREAT WITH

TAHINI DRESSING, P. 74
CASABLANCA CARROTS, P. 176
BELLY DANCE BEET SALAD, P. 186

This recipe makes one serving, but if you're willing to crack open more cans, you can easily feed a crew.

Your food is supposed to be your medicine and your medicine is supposed to be your food. – African Proverb

WEST AFRICAN CHICKEN STEW

ABE BAAKON NA SÉI ENSA. (ONE BAD NUT SPOILS ALL.)

SERVES 2 *to* 4

PREP: 15 MIN.

COOK: 70 MIN.

I have a thing for peanut butter, where "thing" is that I love it to distraction. I especially adore peanut butter in unexpected places, like soups and savory dishes. It was a heart-breaking day when I learned that peanuts are a legume and, therefore, do not love me back. But sunflower seed butter is an excellent rebound partner, and this stew will win you over with its savory combination of creamy sunflower seed butter, just the right bite of heat (from the ginger and cayenne), and the underlying sweetness of vanilla and coriander.

INGREDIENTS

- 1/2 tablespoon coconut oil
- 1 pound boneless, skinless chicken thighs
- salt and ground black pepper
- 1/2 medium onion, diced (about 1/2 cup)
- 1-inch piece fresh ginger, grated (about 1 tablespoon)
- 3 cloves garlic, minced (about 1 tablespoon)
- 1/2 tablespoon ground coriander
- 1/2 teaspoon cayenne pepper
- 1 bay leaf
- 1 cup canned crushed tomatoes
- 1/4 cup water
- 1/4 cup sunflower seed butter (no sugar added)
- 1/4 teaspoon vanilla extract

GARNISH:
minced fresh parsley leaves, sunflower seeds

DIRECTIONS

Sprinkle the chicken enthusiastically with salt and pepper. Heat a large soup pot over medium-high heat, about 3 minutes. Add coconut oil and allow it to melt. Add the chicken in a single layer and brown well on both sides, about 10 minutes. (Don't crowd the pan; cook in batches if you need to.) Remove the chicken to a bowl to catch the juices.

In the same pot, cook the onions and ginger until soft, about 5-7 minutes. Add the garlic, coriander, cayenne, and bay leaf, and cook until fragrant, about 30 seconds. Add the tomatoes and water, stirring to combine. Nestle the chicken into the sauce, along with any juices it released. Increase the heat to bring the pot to a boil, then reduce to a simmer and cook, covered, for 25 minutes.

Remove the chicken from the pot; it will be very tender. Break the chicken into large pieces with the side of a wooden spoon. Add the sunflower seed butter and vanilla to the pot and mix to combine. Return the chicken to the pot and cover. Heat through, about 5 minutes, then serve, sprinkled with parsley and sunflower seeds.

TASTES GREAT WITH

SPRINKLE WITH MAGIC DUST! P. 76
COCONUT CAULIFLOWER RICE, P. 202
CRISP-SWEET COLLARDS, P. 198
SIMPLE LEMON SPINACH, P. 170
ROASTED CABBAGE ROSES, P. 190

YOU KNOW HOW YOU COULD DO THAT?

REPLACE THE CHICKEN WITH WHITE FISH:
Skip the browning step and jump right to making the tomato sauce. Poach fish (cod, haddock, sea bass) in the sauce for 6 minutes. Remove the fish, add sunflower seed butter and vanilla to pan and heat through. To serve, spoon the sauce over the fish.

I wanted to call these Vietnamese Tostadas, but I thought that would be too incongruous. Sadly, "Jicamadas" didn't make the cut, either.

TASTES GREAT WITH

COCONUT CAULIFLOWER RICE, P. 202

VIETNAMESE CHICKEN SALAD

LIKE A BAHN MI SANDWICH SANS BREAD

SERVES 2 *to* 4

PREP	COOK
20 MIN.	45 MIN.

Let's get something straight: This is not authentic Vietnamese food. But it is inspired by a bahn mi sandwich I ate during a legendary vacation to New York City. The jicama is a sweet, crunchy foil for the peppery bite of the relish, and the smear of creamy mayo pulls it all together. Cool, crisp, flavorful, and light, these are easy to make and fun to eat. Some of the toppings might fall off on their way to your mouth, but that means after you've devoured your last bit of jicama, you can scoop up the remnants from the plate for one last, perfect bite.
Heads up! This recipe requires you to do something in advance; plan prep time accordingly.

INGREDIENTS

VEGETABLES:
1 large jicama
2 medium carrots, peeled and minced (about 1/2 cup)
1 red bell pepper, minced (about 1 cup)
4 scallions, thinly sliced (about 1/2 cup)
1 jalapeño, seeds removed, minced (about 2 tablespoons)
2 cloves garlic, minced (about 2 teaspoons)
3 tablespoons dry roasted cashews, chopped
6-8 large basil leaves, finely chopped (about 2 tablespoons)
10 fresh mint leaves, finely chopped (about 1 1/2 tablespoons)

CHICKEN:
1 pound boneless, skinless chicken breasts
2 cups water
1 tablespoon salt
1 teaspoon whole peppercorns
3 cloves garlic, peeled and smashed
1 tablespoon coconut aminos
1 tablespoon lime juice
a few fresh basil leaves

DRESSING:
1 tablespoon lime juice
1 tablespoon rice vinegar
1/2 tablespoon olive oil
1 tablespoon fish sauce (I like Red Boat!)
salt and ground black pepper, to taste
Olive Oil Mayo (p. 53)

DIRECTIONS

Prep the jicama. Wash and peel the jicama, cut it in half, then slice into 1/4-inch thick ovals. Place in a covered container in the fridge to chill while you prep the rest of the ingredients.

Poach the chicken. In a large saucepan, place chicken, water, salt, peppercorns, garlic, coconut aminos, lime juice, and basil. Bring to a boil, then cover and simmer on low, 15-20 minutes. Turn off the heat and let the chicken chillax in the bath for 20-25 minutes. Remove the chicken from the water and shred with two forks. Set aside. While the chicken is cooking…

Prep the salad: In a large bowl, mix the carrots, red pepper, scallions, jalapeño, garlic, cashews, basil, and mint.

Dress the salad. In a small bowl, whisk the lime juice, rice vinegar, oil, and fish sauce. Pour over the vegetables and toss with two wooden spoons until the veggies are coated. Add salt and pepper to taste, then add the chicken and let the salad sit at room temperature so the flavors can meld, about 10 minutes. Adjust the seasonings. You may need to add salt after mixing in the chicken.

Assemble! Spread a slice of jicama with a bit of mayo, then sprinkle lightly with salt and black pepper. Pile chicken salad on the jicama, top with additional minced herbs, then eat with your hands, licking your fingers often.

YOU KNOW HOW YOU COULD DO THAT?

- *Replace chicken with pork, fish, shrimp, crab, or a combo.*
- *Replace the jicama slices with butter lettuce cups.*

VEGGIES

& SALADS

Go ahead and say it! It's OK to complain a little among friends. At first, saying "no" pasta, rice, and potatoes – to replace them with vegetables! – is no fun. I understand. We all go through it. But here's the thing: We have choices. Tasty choices. There's no reason to give up the fun of twirling long, strands of yumminess on a fork, or to abandon the idea of a bed of "rice" under a spicy curry. With a little patience, some ingenuity, and the loving support of vegetables, you can have all the joy of noodles, rice, and mashed comfort without the troublesome anti-nutrients of grains and white potatoes.

Remember: It's nearly impossible to eat too many vegetables. They're so good for you! I eat about six or seven cups of veggies every day, which is so much chopping and cooking! That's why once a week, I turn into a Veg-O-Matic and make it my mission to prepare at least four different vegetables so they're ready to be transformed into meals when I need them.

In the next few pages, I'll show you how to make steam-sautéed veggies, so you always have plenty of nutritious vegetation ready to throw into a skillet – and you'll learn how zucchini, spaghetti squash, and cauliflower can replace starchy pantry staples.

STEAM-SAUTÉED VEGGIES

SERVES *a lot* | PREP + COOK 15 *min.*

INGREDIENTS

water + your favorite vegetables, like:

bell pepper, sliced
carrots, sliced
leafy greens, chopped
green beans, whole
Brussels sprouts, cut in half
eggplant, chopped
broccoli florets
cabbage, chopped
cauliflower florets
zucchini, sliced

DIRECTIONS

Wash your veggies under running water, then using a sharp knife, cut or slice into the desired size, depending on your mood and tastes. It's best if you keep the pieces roughly the same size, so they'll cook evenly.

Heat a large skillet over medium-high heat. Toss the still-wet-from-washing vegetable into the pan, cover with a lid, and allow the residual water to soften the veggies a bit. Remove the lid, and stir vigorously with a wooden spoon until the vegetable is softened, but not completely cooked. If the veggies stick to the pan or begin to brown, add a tablespoon of water to continue the steaming process.

Place each vegetable in its own container and store in the fridge. Be sure to pop the containers into the refrigerator while warm. Cooling at room temperature allows bacteria to grow. I usually reserve the bottom shelf of my fridge for hot veggies.

When it's time to eat, heat about 1-2 teaspoons of coconut oil or ghee in a non-stick skillet, then toss in the partially cooked veggies and seasonings.

BASIC CAULIFLOWER RICE

SERVES 2 *to* 4 | PREP + COOK 20 *min*

INGREDIENTS

1 large head fresh cauliflower
1 tablespoon plus 1 tablespoon coconut oil or ghee
1/2 medium onion, diced (about 1/2 cup)
1 clove garlic, minced (about 1 teaspoon)
salt and ground black pepper, to taste

DIRECTIONS

Break the cauliflower into florets, removing the stems. Place the florets in the food processor bowl and pulse until the cauliflower looks like rice. This takes about 10 to 15 one-second pulses. You may need to do this in two batches to avoid overcrowding (which leads to mush).

Heat a large skillet over medium-high heat, about 3 minutes. Add the cooking fat and allow it to melt. Toss the onion and garlic into the pan, stir with a wooden spoon to coat with fat, then cook until the onions are translucent, about 5 minutes.

Push the onions to the side of the pan and add the remaining 1 tablespoon of coconut oil. Add the riced cauliflower to the pan and sauté until the cauliflower is tender, about 7-10 minutes. Try a bite, then season with plenty of salt and a hint of pepper.

PRO TIP! *You can store raw, riced cauliflower, covered, in the fridge until you're ready to cook it. Be sure to avert your nose when you open the container.*

MASHED CAULIFLOWER

SERVES 2 *to* 4 | PREP + COOK 15 *min*

INGREDIENTS

1 (16 ounce) bag frozen cauliflower florets
1 garlic clove, crushed (about 1 teaspoon)
1 1/2 tablespoons coconut oil
1/2 cup canned coconut milk
salt and ground black pepper, to taste
1 tablespoon plus 2 teaspoons dried chives

DIRECTIONS

Cook the cauliflower according to the package directions until it's very soft, but not waterlogged.

In a microwave-safe bowl or small saucepan, heat the garlic, coconut oil, coconut milk, salt, pepper, and 1 tablespoon chives, about 1 minute. Add the cauliflower, stir to combine, and heat through, about 5 minutes.

Pour the cauliflower and liquids into the bowl of a food processor and purée, scraping down the sides, as necessary. Taste and adjust seasonings, then sprinkle with remaining chives before serving. Eat right away or store in the refrigerator for 4-5 days.

ROASTED SPAGHETTI SQUASH

SERVES 4 *to* 6 | PREP + COOK 50 *min*

INGREDIENTS

1 large spaghetti squash

3 tablespoons water

DIRECTIONS

Preheat the oven to 375 F. Cover a large baking sheet with parchment paper.

Cut the squash in half lengthwise. The easiest way to do this is, surprisingly, with a small knife. Use a sharp paring knife to carefully create a shallow slit along the top of the squash, lengthwise. Now, using a LARGE knife, place the blade in the slit and bang the squash carefully with some force on the cutting board. It should crack along the fault line created by the small knife. Scoop out the seeds and pulp with a large spoon.

Place squash, cut side down, on the baking sheet. Sprinkle the water onto the paper around the squash. Roast until the squash is tender, but not mushy, 30-40 minutes. Place the baking sheet on a cooling rack, and, using a hot pad, turn the squash cut side up to cool.

When it's cool enough to handle, scrape the inside with a fork to shred the squash into gorgeous spaghetti strands. Eat right away or store in the refrigerator for 4-5 days.

For tips on how to remain injury free while cutting spaghetti squash, visit www.theclothesmakethegirl.com/wellfed2

ZUCCHINI NOODLES

SERVES 2 *to* 4 | PREP + COOK 40 *min*

INGREDIENTS

4 zucchini, julienned with a julienne peeler (about 4 cups)

1 tablespoon extra-virgin olive oil

salt and ground black pepper, to taste

DIRECTIONS

Place the julienned zucchini in a colander or wire strainer and toss generously with salt until the strands are lightly coated. Allow the zucchini to sit for 20-30 minutes to remove excess water. Rinse with running water, drain well, and pat dry with paper towels. You can proceed to the next step right away or – for absolutely *al dente* noodles that do not get mushy – return the noodles to the colander and place in the fridge, uncovered, for 1-2 hours. This allows the strands to dehydrate even further.

Heat a large non-stick skillet over medium-high heat and add the prepared zucchini noodles. Sauté them in the dry pan until just tender, about 1-2 minutes. Reduce the heat to low and drizzle the olive oil over the noodles, stirring gently to coat the strands. Taste and season with salt and pepper.

PRO TIP! *You can julienne and sweat the zucchini in advance, then store raw noodles in a covered container in the fridge for 4-5 days. Quick pasta whenever you need it!*

To toast pine nuts, heat a small sauté pan over medium heat and toss the nuts until light brown, about 2-3 minutes.

SIMPLE LEMON SPINACH

POPEYE WAS ONTO SOMETHING

SERVES 2

PREP	COOK
5 MIN.	25 MIN.

I have a confession to make: I'm not spinach's number one fan. In fact, on my list of favorite greens – doesn't everyone keep timely documentation of favorite greens? – spinach is my number two. But thanks to this recipe, inspired by my dad, it's become a solid competitor for the top spot. Simple Lemon Spinach is a change of pace for a few reasons: It relies on onions instead of garlic. There's no cumin, a.k.a., my favorite spice. It requires minimal ingredients, but delivers an abundance of flavor. Simple is beautiful.

INGREDIENTS

1 pound fresh spinach (or 16-ounce package frozen)

1 tablespoon extra-virgin olive oil

1/2 medium onion, diced (about 1/2 cup)

1 tablespoon pine nuts, toasted (optional)

salt and ground black pepper

juice of 1 lemon (about 2-3 tablespoons)

YOU KNOW HOW YOU COULD DO THAT?

MAKE IT A MEAL! *Top with browned ground lamb, beef, or chicken, then drizzle with Tahini Dressing (p. 74). A fried egg on top (and/or a diced, juicy tomato) would also be a tasty touch.*

TASTES GREAT WITH

PERFECT STEAK, P. 134
SHRIMP SCAMPI, P. 114
WEST AFRICAN CHICKEN STEW, P. 160
SCHEHERAZADE OMELET, P. 154
PLANTAIN NACHOS, P. 146
LEMON LAMB TAGINE, P. 142
PAN-FRIED SARDINES, P. 158
OVEN-FRIED SALMON CAKES, P. 138

DIRECTIONS

If using fresh spinach, rinse well (very well! no grit here!) and dry the leaves. If the leaves are large, you should probably coarsely chop them. If using frozen spinach, defrost the package, then squeeze out all excess water; fluff the leaves before cooking.

In a large, non-stick skillet, heat the olive oil on low heat. VERY low heat, just enough heat to warm it up. Add the onion and pine nuts and cook, stirring only occasionally, until the onions are translucent, soft, and beginning to get brown bits. This can take 10-12 minutes at low heat. (This is a nice time to meditate: For three minutes, breathe in through your nose for 4 beats, then out through your nose for 4 beats. Stir the onions, then repeat for another three minutes. Stir the onions, repeat. Done!)

Add the spinach to the pan, stirring gently to allow the leaves to wilt. When they're beginning to get soft, add the lemon juice and stir with a little more fervor. Sprinkle with salt and pepper, then eat immediately.

MY FAVORITE GREENS

1. Collards
2. Spinach
3. Kale
4. Bok Choy
5. Turnip Tops
6. Beet Tops
7. Chard
And around 1,000,000 or so... Mustard Greens

This is great on day one, tastes even better on day two, is still very much worth eating on day three, and starts to look a little sad after that. If you can't eat a full batch in 2-3 days, cut the recipe in half.

TABBOULEH

IT'S GRASSY GOOD

SERVES 6 to 8

PREP	COOK	CHILL
20 MIN.	25 MIN.	1 HR.

For what appears to be a simple salad, tabbouleh presents a few challenges. There's the ratio of lemon juice to olive oil to consider, radishes or no, curly vs. flat-leaf parsley, and to spice or not to spice. These are the questions! I opted for a slightly tart dressing with a lovely olive oil slinkiness. No radishes (too muddy). Curly parsley because that's what we always used in our kitchen when I was a kid. And yes, yes, yes! *to spices. I always say* yes *to spices.*

Heads up! This recipe requires you to do something in advance; plan prep time accordingly.

INGREDIENTS

SALAD:

1 head raw cauliflower (about 3 pounds)
1/2 tablespoon ghee, melted
2 seedless cucumbers, diced
4 medium tomatoes, diced
salt
4 cups curly parsley leaves (about 2 bunches), minced
1 cup fresh mint leaves, minced
6 scallions, very thinly sliced

DRESSING:

1/3 cup lemon juice (about 3 lemons)
3/4 teaspoon salt
1/2 teaspoon ground black pepper
zest of 1 lemon
1/2 teaspoon Lebanese Seven-Spice Blend (p. 84)
1/2 cup extra-virgin olive oil

TASTES GREAT WITH

STUFFED GRAPE LEAVES, P. 148
SCHEHERAZADE OMELET, P. 154
SEMI SABICH, P. 136
DECONSTRUCTED GYRO, P. 126
DELI TUNA SALAD, P. 118

DIRECTIONS

Preheat the oven to 400F. Cover two large baking sheets with parchment paper.

Use a food processor to "rice" the cauliflower: Break the cauliflower into florets, removing the stems. Place the florets in the food processor bowl and pulse until the cauliflower looks like rice. This takes about 10 to 15 one-second pulses. You may need to do this in two batches to avoid overcrowding.

In a large bowl, toss the cauliflower rice with the melted ghee, then divide the cauliflower between the baking sheets. Spread it in a single layer so it can toast in the oven. Bake for 20 minutes or so, checking at the 15-minute mark to make sure it's golden but not burning. (I like mine pretty dark so it retains a nice bite, even after being tossed with the dressing.)

Place the cucumber and tomato in a colander, sprinkle generously with salt, and let the vegetables "sweat" out their excess moisture while the cauliflower is in the oven, about 15-20 minutes.

When the cauliflower is toasted, remove from the oven and allow to cool. While it's cooling, drain the cucumbers and tomatoes of the released liquid, then place the vegetables in a large mixing bowl, and add the parsley, mint, and scallions. Toss with a rubber scraper to combine.

In a small bowl, use a fork to mix the lemon juice, salt, pepper, lemon zest, and Lebanese Seven-Spice Blend. Slowly drizzle in the olive oil while you continue to mix with the fork. Pour the dressing over the vegetables and toss gently, but with purpose, until all the ingredients are coated. Cover and refrigerate for at least an hour before eating so the flavors can meld.

BALSAMIC-GRILLED BUTTERNUT

WHO KNEW A HUMBLE PUMPKIN COULD BE SO ALLURING?!

SERVES 2 to 4

PREP	MARINATE	COOK
10 MIN.	1 HR.	25 MIN.

For the longest time, butternut squash made me go "Meh [shrug]" until my pal Stacey told me she likes to cook hers on the grill. Hmmm… sweet butternut squash + intense heat = caramelization… and caramelization is just about the best thing that can happen to food. Marinating the butternut starts the tenderizing process and the focused heat of the grill finishes it, sealing in the citrusy, garlic flavors. This tastes great straight off the grill and leftovers can be reheated in a skillet alone, or chopped and mixed into other can't-wait-to-eat-it things.

INGREDIENTS

- 1 butternut squash (about 3 pounds)
- 1 tablespoon coconut oil, melted
- 2 tablespoons balsamic vinegar
- 1 teaspoon dried thyme
- 3 cloves garlic, minced (about 1 tablespoon)
- zest from 1/2 orange (about 2 teaspoons)
- salt and ground black pepper, to taste

DIRECTIONS

Cut squash in half crosswise, then in half lengthwise. Cut into slices, about 1/4 inch thick. Mix with melted coconut oil, vinegar, thyme, garlic, and zest. Marinate 1 hour at room temperature.

Remove squash from marinade and save marinade. Preheat grill on high until hot, about 10 minutes. Place squash on the grill, close lid, and grill 5 minutes per side to brown. Reduce heat to medium high and continue to grill until tender, about 5-10 minutes. (You'll need to check it periodically to see when it's reached your desired level of bite.) Toss the cooked squash in the reserved marinade and season with salt and pepper. Let it rest 10 minutes then dig in.

NOTES

Butternut squash is a solid source of manganese, magnesium, and potassium, as well as vitamins C, A, and E. Style and substance!

YOU KNOW HOW YOU COULD DO THAT?

- *Replace thyme with rosemary*
- *Replace orange zest with lemon zest*

TASTES GREAT WITH

PERFECT STEAK, P. 134
ITALIAN PORK ROAST, P. 132
OVEN-FRIED SALMON CAKES, P. 138

CASABLANCA CARROTS

HERE'S LOOKING AT YOU, CARROT

SERVES 4

PREP	COOK	CHILL
5 MIN.	10 MIN.	20 MIN.

Who is responsible for the unwritten rule that salads must be made from raw vegetables? And can we force that person to spend eternity paring vegetables with a dull peeler? In Morocco, many of the ambrosial (yeah, I said ambrosial*) salads begin with lightly steamed vegetables. When hot veggies meet spices and oils, wonderful things happen. Forget about dressing on your vegetables, this dressing is* in *the vegetables – and that somehow makes the dressing both more impactful and less overwhelming. It's a culinary conundrum.*

INGREDIENTS

- 1 pound carrots
- 1 clove garlic, minced (about 1 teaspoon)
- 1/2 teaspoon paprika
- 1/2 teaspoon ground cumin
- 1/8 teaspoon ground cinnamon
- dash cayenne pepper
- juice of 1 lemon (about 2-3 tablespoons)
- salt and ground black pepper, to taste
- 1 tablespoon extra-virgin olive oil
- 1/2 cup fresh parsley leaves, minced (about 2 tablespoons)

NOTES

DIRECTIONS

Wash and peel the carrots; cut on the diagonal into 1/2-inch pieces. Steam for 10-15 minutes until tender and drain.

In a large bowl, mix the *warm* carrots with garlic, paprika, cumin, cinnamon, cayenne, lemon juice, salt, and pepper. Place in the refrigerator until the carrots are chilled.

Remove from refrigerator, drizzle with olive oil and toss to coat. Add the parsley, toss for 2 minutes, then taste and adjust seasonings. Serve cool or at room temperature.

TASTES GREAT WITH

MERGUEZ BURGER/BALLS/BANGERS, P. 90
MOROCCAN CHICKEN BURGER/BALLS/BANGERS, P. 91
SB&J BURGER, P. 152
DECONSTRUCTED GYRO, P. 126
SEMI SABICH, P. 136
STUFFED GRAPE LEAVES, P. 148
PAN-FRIED SARDINES, P. 158

WHO DOESN'T LOVE THE MOVIE CASABLANCA? ENJOY THIS SNIPPET OF HARD-BOILED DIALOGUE.

CAPTAIN LOUIS RENAULT: *What in heaven's name brought you to Casablanca?*

RICK BLAINE: *My health. I came to Casablanca for the waters.*

RENAULT: *The waters? What waters? We're in the desert!*

BLAINE: *I was misinformed.*

Make it a little sweeter by adding 1 cup crushed canned pineapple (unsweetened, packed in its own juice), 1 cup diced mango, or 1/3 cup raisins.

CLASSIC COLESLAW

KEEPIN' IT CRISP AND COOL

SERVES 4

PREP	COOK
10 MIN.	N/A

It's so easy for coleslaw to go so wrong. Limp vegetables. Too-sweet, watery dressing. A disproportionate ratio of mayo to salad. The trick is to keep it simple. The best coleslaw allows the conflicting flavors and textures to find their way to a peaceful détente negotiated by just-right dressing. The tang of vinegar balances the creamy mayo. Crisp-sweet carrots and cabbage relax the hot-sweet bite of red onion, and the fresh parsley brightens the whole affair.

Heads up! This recipe requires you to do something in advance; plan prep time accordingly.

INGREDIENTS

2/3 cup Olive Oil Mayo (p. 53)
1/2 small red onion, grated (about 2 tablespoons)
1 tablespoon lemon juice
1 tablespoon white wine vinegar
1/2 teaspoon salt
1/4 teaspoon ground black pepper
1/2 head green cabbage, very thinly sliced (about 5-6 cups)
1/2 head red cabbage, very thinly sliced (about 4 cups)
3 large carrots, peeled and shredded (about 1 1/2 cups)
1/2 cup loosely packed parsley leaves, roughly chopped

DIRECTIONS

In a small bowl, make the dressing by whisking together the mayonnaise, red onion, lemon juice, vinegar, salt, and pepper. Set aside.

In a large bowl, toss the cabbage, carrots, and parsley with two wooden spoons. Add the dressing and toss vigorously for 2 minutes to ensure the vegetables are evenly coated. Cover and refrigerate for at least 1 hour before serving. This colelsaw tastes great on the first day and even better the second day, so make it in advance for maximum impact.

TASTES GREAT WITH

BBQ BEEF "WAFFLE" SANDWICH, P. 116
REUBEN ROLLUPS, P. 98
OVEN-FRIED SALMON CAKES, P. 138

YOU KNOW HOW YOU COULD DO THAT?

SAME DIRECTIONS, DIFFERENT INGREDIENTS.

ASIAN SLAW

2/3 cup Olive Oil Mayo (p. 53)
1/2 small red onion, grated (about 2 tablespoons)
1 tablespoon lime juice
1 tablespoon rice vinegar
1 tablespoon fish sauce (Red Boat!)
1/2 teaspoon salt
1/4 teaspoon ground black pepper
1/2 head green cabbage, very thinly sliced (about 5-6 cups)
1/2 head red cabbage, very thinly sliced (about 4 cups)
3 large carrots, peeled and shredded (about 1 1/2 cups)
1 large red bell pepper, julienned
1/2 cup fresh cilantro leaves, roughly chopped
1/2 cup fresh basil leaves, slivered

NOTES

"Coleslaw" is an anglicized take on "koolsla," the short version of the Dutch word "koolsalade," which means "cabbage salad."

This is an easy way to get extra vegetables! Just eat a cup while you're making dinner – or go formal and begin dinner with a soup course. Feel free to slurp at the table!

GOLDEN CAULIFLOWER SOUP

SOMETIMES IT SEEMS LIKE CAULIFLOWER IS JUST SHOWING OFF

SERVES 6 to 8

PREP	COOK
10 MIN.	1 HR.

It's rarely soup weather here in Austin, Texas, but that doesn't mean that I can't eat soup. In fact, I enjoy my soup so defiantly, I often eat it for breakfast. Soup in the morning is an easy, cheater way to get extra vegetables into my belly, and it's a good stand-in for coffee or tea. It's comforting, warm, cozy, and bonus! it gets eaten instead of drunk. 'Cause being drunk that early in the morning would be a bad way to start the day.

INGREDIENTS

1 large head cauliflower (about 3 pounds)
1 tablespoon coconut oil
1 medium onion, diced (about 1 cup)
2 large carrots, peeled and diced (about 1 cup)
2 cloves garlic, peeled and smashed
2 cups beef broth
1 cup water
1 teaspoon salt
1/2 teaspoon ground black pepper
1/2 cup canned coconut milk

GARNISH:
extra-virgin olive oil, ground nutmeg

YOU KNOW HOW YOU COULD DO THAT?

Replace the beef broth with chicken broth. The chicken version tastes more like gravy and could easily masquerade as such on a classic roast chicken.

TASTY IDEAS

TOP YOUR SOUP WITH SOMETHING SPECIAL:
CHOPPED PARSLEY + CHOPPED WALNUTS
TOASTED, SLIVERED ALMONDS + GHEE
MINCED DRIED DATES + CHOPPED PECANS

DIRECTIONS

Wash and core the cauliflower, then coarsely chop. Set aside.

Heat a large, deep pot over medium-high heat and add the coconut oil. When the oil is melted, add onions, carrots, and garlic. Stir with a wooden spoon and cook until they're soft and golden, about 5 minutes. Add the chopped cauliflower and cook until beginning to brown, about 5 minutes.

Add the broth and water, then bring to a boil. Reduce heat to simmer and cook, covered, until the vegetables are very tender, about 45 minutes.

Purée the vegetables and broth in a blender or food processor. Be careful! Do this in batches and fill the canister only halfway, holding a towel over the lid while you purée. Hot soup expands in the canister and can spurt out if you're not vigilant.

Pour the purée back into the soup pot, then add the salt, pepper, and coconut milk. Stir to combine and cook over medium until heated through. Serve immediately with garnishes, or store covered in the refrigerator. To reheat, warm the soup gently over medium-low heat until bubbly.

NOTES

MUSTARD-GARLIC BRUSSELS SPROUTS

TINY IS MIGHTY

SERVES 4

PREP 15 MIN.

COOK 40 MIN.

A few facts: Tiny things are cute. People love cute things. Brussels sprouts are really just stupid-cute, tiny cabbages. So if Brussels sprouts are loveable, then Brussels sprouts caramelized with tangy mustard and pungent garlic must be adored. And if you prepare food that's adored, you will be revered and lauded. Absolutely lauded. (I'm fairly certain that these exact arguments are used to teach logic at universities around the globe.)

INGREDIENTS

1 pound fresh Brussels sprouts

1 head garlic, peeled and separated into cloves

1 tablespoon ghee, melted

3 cloves garlic, minced (about 1 tablespoon)

1 tablespoon coconut aminos

1/2 tablespoon Dijon mustard

ground black pepper

NOTES

DIRECTIONS

Preheat the oven to 400F. Cover a large baking sheet with parchment paper.

Cut the Brussels sprouts in half lengthwise, keeping the leaves that fall off. (They'll turn into crispy chips in the oven!)

In a large bowl, mix the Brussels sprouts and the whole garlic cloves with the ghee, minced garlic, coconut aminos, mustard, and a robust sprinkle of black pepper.

Spread the sprouts in a single layer on the baking sheet. Roast 35-40 minutes. Take a bite, then add more pepper (and a pinch of salt), if necessary.

YOU KNOW HOW YOU COULD DO THAT?

FEELING BOHEMIAN? *Toss in 1 tablespoon of caraway seeds and a healthy pinch of smoked salt before roasting.*

TASTES GREAT WITH

PERFECT STEAK, P. 134

OVEN-FRIED SALMON CAKES, P. 138

BBQ BEEF "WAFFLE" SANDWICH, P. 116

PAN-FRIED PLANTAINS

THE SALTY-SWEET TASTE OF THE TROPICS

SERVES 4

PREP 5 MIN.

COOK 10 MIN.

How cool is it that bananas come in two version: sweet and savory? Sure, sweet bananas are like acceptable candy, but let's talk about plantains. I'm gonna stick my neck out with a bold statement: I like them even more than potatoes. There, I said it! And – bonus! – they're a "safe starch," which means you get a nutritional kick along with your high-quality carbs. You could eat these as a post-workout recovery food – or you can enjoy them for, say, Tuesday dinner or Sunday brunch, too. For this recipe, look for plantains that are dark yellow and have a few brown spots.

INGREDIENTS

- 2 ripe (yellow and brown) plantains
- 1 tablespoon coconut oil or ghee
- plenty of salt
- dash ground cumin
- juice of 1 lime

DIRECTIONS

Peel the plantains. The easiest way is to cut off both ends, then make shallow slits along the ridges in the skin that run the length of the plantain. Use your fingers to pry off the strips of skin. Slice the plantains into 1/4-inch thick coins.

Heat a large, non-stick skillet over medium-high heat, about 3 minutes. Add coconut oil and allow it to melt. Add the plantain slices in a single layer and allow to brown on the bottom, 2-3 minutes. Flip and brown the other side. Keep a close eye on them; the sugars in the plantains can turn from brown to black in a blink.

When you're happy with the color, sprinkle generously with salt and a bit of cumin. Remove to a serving plate and squeeze fresh lime juice over the top. Eat immediately. Fork optional.

YOU KNOW HOW YOU COULD DO THAT?

Plantains don't discriminate: They greet many spice blends as friends. Try these! Jerk Seasoning (p. 82), Sunrise Spice (p. 78), Lebanese Seven-Spice Blend (p. 84), or keep it simple with cinnamon.

BETTER! *For another taste sensation, replace the coconut oil with Better Butter (p. 60).*

CRUNCH! *Are your plantains too green to pan fry? Make Plantain Nachos (p. 146) instead.*

NOTES

These are really good alongside eggs at breakfast (or breakfast for dinner).

TASTES GREAT WITH

LIZARD SAUCE, P. 68
MAGIC DUST, P. 76
CUBAN BURGERS/BALLS/BANGERS, P. 92
CINCINATTI CHILI, P. 104
SB&J BURGER, P. 152
PINA COLADA CHICKEN, P. 96

BELLY DANCE BEET SALAD

MAKES YOU WIGGLY, IN A GOOD WAY

SERVES 4

PREP: 15 MIN.

COOK: 1 HR.

The Western form of belly dancing – with gauzy costumes and jangling jewelry – is based on the Ghawazi dancers of Egypt. The Arabic word "ghawazi" means "conqueror," a reference to the way the dancer conquered the heart of her audience. It makes me wonder: If the way to a man's heart is through the stomach, doesn't Belly Dance Beet Salad double our heart-winning powers? This salad is exotic, but not fussy or too challenging. The flavors make sense but are also magically unexpected. I like to eat it at room temperature, but you can dance with it the way you like.

INGREDIENTS

- 2 bunches beets (about 2 pounds)
- 1 tablespoon coconut oil, melted
- 1/3 cup shelled pistachios
- juice of 1/2 large orange (about 2 tablespoons)
- 1 tablespoon red wine vinegar
- 1/8 teaspoon ground cumin
- 1/8 teaspoon ground coriander
- 1/8 teaspoon ground cinnamon
- 1 clove garlic, minced (about 1 teaspoon)
- 1/8 teaspoon salt
- a few shakes of ground black pepper
- 1 tablespoon extra-virgin olive oil
- 3 scallions, white and green, thinly sliced (about 1/2 cup)

YOU KNOW HOW YOU COULD DO THAT?

SHORTCUT! *Use 2 (14.5 oz.) cans of beets of instead of fresh and toast the pistachios in a skillet over medium-high heat for 2-3 minutes.*

TASTES GREAT WITH

STUFFED GRAPE LEAVES, P. 148
SEMI SABICH, P. 136
PAN-FRIED SARDINES, P. 158
SCHEHERAZADE OMELET, P. 154
CASABLANCA CARROTS, P. 176

DIRECTIONS

Preheat the oven to 375F. Cover two large baking sheets with parchment paper.

Wash the beets, and cut off the stem and root ends – no need to peel them! Cut the beets in half and toss with melted coconut oil. Roast for about 45-60 minutes, until tender.

To toast the pistachios, spread them in a single layer on the other baking sheet and add to the oven during the last 7-10 minutes of roasting the beets. Allow them to cool, then coarsely chop them.

While the beets and pistachios are roasting, whisk the orange juice, vinegar, cumin, coriander, cinnamon, garlic, salt, and pepper in a small bowl. Whisking continuously, drizzle in the olive oil and set the dressing aside.

When the beets are done, allow them to cool enough to handle and cut into 1/2-inch cubes. (**PRO TIP:** Use the parchment paper from the baking sheet on top of your cutting board for easier cleanup.)

Place the beets in a large bowl and toss with the dressing. Add the scallions and pistachios and toss well with two wooden spoons. Allow to cool to room temperature before eating. Taste and add more salt and pepper, if necessary.

EAT YOUR BEET GREENS! *Wash thoroughly to remove grit, then chop and throw in a pan with a little water and steam 'til tender. Toss with Better Butter (p. 60), salt, pepper, and a clove of crushed garlic. Eat under the room temp beet salad!*

CITRUS CAULIFLOWER RICE

BUTTERY SUNSHINE IN A BOWL

SERVES 4

PREP	COOK
15 MIN.	10 MIN.

Before I made the switch to paleo, a bowl of seasoned rice was my go-to comfort food. Something about white food that can be eaten with a spoon makes it practically irresistible. White rice is so humble and unassuming, eating it was like finally exhaling after a tough day... aaaaaah. But no more! Because now I know that rice isn't really my friend. Happily, cauliflower is steadfast and true. Sautéed with herbs and finished with ghee, this pilaf is just the thing for the days that make you crave a soft landing.

INGREDIENTS

1 large head fresh cauliflower (about 2-3 pounds)
1/2 tablespoon coconut oil
1/2 medium onion, diced (about 1/2 cup)
1 clove garlic, minced (about 1 teaspoon)
1/2 teaspoon Aleppo pepper (or crushed red pepper flakes)
1 tablespoon ghee
zest from 1 lemon (about 1 tablespoon)
2 teaspoons lemon juice
1/2 cup fresh parsley leaves, minced (about 2 tablespoons)
salt and ground black pepper, to taste

DIRECTIONS

Break the cauliflower into florets, removing the stems. Place the florets in the food processor bowl and pulse until the cauliflower looks like rice. This takes about 10 to 15 one-second pulses. You may need to do this in two batches to avoid overcrowding (which leads to mush).

Heat a large, non-stick skillet over medium-high heat, about 3 minutes. Add coconut oil and allow it to melt. Add the onion and cook until the onions are translucent, about 5 minutes. Add the garlic and Aleppo pepper and stir-fry until fragrant, about 30 seconds.

Add the ghee to the pan, along with the cauliflower, lemon zest, and lemon juice. Stir everything together and sauté until the cauliflower is tender, about 5-7 minutes. Stir in the parsley, try a bite, then season with plenty of salt and a little pepper.

NOTES

Top a pile of Citrus Cauliflower Rice with grilled chicken, then drizzle with Tahini Dressing (p. 74).

YOU KNOW HOW YOU COULD DO THAT?

- *Replace the lemon zest and parsley with orange or lime zest and cilantro*
- *Replace fresh parsley with fresh or dried rosemary*
- *Replace ghee with Better Butter (p. 60)*

TASTES GREAT WITH

CRISPY CHICKEN LIVERS, P. 106
SHRIMP SCAMPI, P. 114
OVEN-FRIED SALMON CAKES, P. 138
DECONSTRUCTED GYRO, P. 126

This totally looks
like a rose, right?

ROASTED CABBAGE ROSES

THE SIDE DISH THAT'S SHABBY CHIC

SERVES 4

PREP	COOK
10 MIN.	35 MIN.

I know it's an odd choice, but cabbage is my favorite vegetable. I understand why you might turn up your nose at this cruciferous veggie, especially if you've been victim of overcooked cabbage or its lingering aroma. But let's talk about what makes cabbage so much fun! It's a solid source of beta-carotene and vitamin C; it comes in stylish green and purple hues; and back in the day, it was widely used as a cure for hangovers. Plus, you can impress your friends by dropping old-timey slang into conversation. Who wouldn't think it's cool to refer to money as "cabbage" or describe yourself as "cabbaged" after a tough workout?

INGREDIENTS

1 head green cabbage

2 tablespoons ghee, melted

1/2 teaspoon paprika

1/2 teaspoon coarse (granulated) garlic powder

1/2 teaspoon dried thyme

salt and ground black pepper, to taste

NOTES

DIRECTIONS

Preheat the oven to 400F. Cover two large baking sheets with parchment paper.

Remove the tough outer leaves from the cabbage and trim the stem. Cut the head into 3/4-inch thick vertical slices, keeping the core intact. Arrange the slices on the baking sheets in a single layer and brush with melted ghee.

In a small bowl, mix the paprika, garlic powder, and thyme together with a fork. Sprinkle over the cabbage, then vigorously sprinkle the slices with salt and black pepper. Roast 30-40 minutes until golden, crispy on the edges, and tender in the middle. Taste and sprinkle with additional salt and pepper, if necessary.

YOU KNOW HOW YOU COULD DO THAT?

Use Better Butter! (p. 60)

TASTES GREAT WITH

WEST AFRICAN CHICKEN STEW, P. 160
SUNRISE SCRAMBLE, P. 108
OVEN-FRIED SALMON CAKES, P. 138
MULLIGATAWNY STEW, P. 150
ITALIAN PORK ROAST, P. 132
FIESTA PORK CHOPS, P. 120

According to Sam Sifton of The New York Times: *"Shorty Tang... cooked the best cold sesame noodles Manhattan ever tasted." There are so many things to love about that sentence.*

SESAME CUCUMBER NOODLES

A CELEBRATION OF THE JULIENNE PEELER... AND SEED BUTTER

SERVES 2

PREP	SWEAT	COOK
25 MIN.	30 MIN.	N/A

Sometimes, especially when I'm stressed, my desire for the good ol' days of takeout is almost unbearable. In my romanticized memories, Chinese takeout was a carefree experience: pick up the phone, order a pile of food, and 45 minutes later, inhale a bowl of cool, creamy, nutty sesame noodles in all their MSG-starchy-sugary glory. In reality, I did mental gymnastics to make it OK with myself to overeat foods I knew weren't doing me any favors. When the gluttony was done, I made promises to myself about how I'd "start over tomorrow." This recipe requires no recriminations or rueful promises.

INGREDIENTS

- 2 large cucumbers (or 1 large English cucumber)
- salt
- 1 teaspoon sesame seeds
- 4 teaspoons tahini
- 2 teaspoons sunflower seed butter (no sugar added)
- 1 teaspoon toasted sesame oil
- 1 tablespoon coconut aminos
- 1/2 tablespoon rice vinegar
- 1 tablespoon water
- 1/4 teaspoon crushed red pepper flakes
- 2 cloves garlic, minced (about 2 teaspoons)
- 1/4 teaspoon powdered ginger
- 1 scallion, green only, thinly sliced

DIRECTIONS

With a julienne peeler, turn the cucumber into noodles. Place the julienned cucumber in a colander or wire sieve and toss generously with salt until the strands are lightly coated. Allow the noodles to sweat for 20-30 minutes to remove excess water. Rinse with running water, drain well, and pat dry with paper towels. (You may be tempted to skip this step. I strongly advise against it. This step prevents watery noodles.)

While the cucumber is sweating in the colander, heat a small sauté pan over medium, and toast the sesame seeds until light brown, about 2-3 minutes. Set aside to cool.

In a small bowl or food processor, mix the tahini, sunflower seed butter, sesame oil, coconut aminos, rice vinegar, water, red pepper flakes, garlic, and ginger until smooth.

Place the cucumber noodles in a large mixing bowl, add the dressing, and toss gently with two wooden spoons until evenly coated. Mound on a plate and sprinkle with the sliced scallions and toasted sesame seeds. Enjoy the first creamy, nutty bite, then ask yourself, "Who needs takeout?"

YOU KNOW HOW YOU COULD DO THAT?

MAKE IT A MEAL! *Add sliced, cooked chicken, pork, beef, or seafood.*

Replace the sunflower butter with almond butter or cashew butter (or a combo!).

TASTES GREAT WITH

CHICKEN NANKING, P. 123

TOD MUN CAKES, P. 156

NOTES

Got the original Well Fed? *Replace the herbs with 1/2 tablespoon Pizza Seasoning (p. 49).*
Applegate Farms makes paleo-friendly pepperoni, and their prosciutto would also be a good addition to this recipe.

PIZZA VEGGIES

A SNEAKY WAY TO EAT PEPPERONI

SERVES 4

PREP 10 MIN.

COOK 40 MIN.

Apparently, the per-capita consumption of pizza is 23 pounds per year; that means in the United States, people are chowing down on 350 slices of pizza per second. Someone is eating my share! It should surprise exactly no one that pepperoni is the most popular topping, but here's a shocker: Americans eat about 251,770,000 pounds of pepperoni annually. Thanks to this recipe, we can all do our part to contribute to that number.

INGREDIENTS

- 1/2 head cauliflower (about 1 pound)
- 1 pound broccoli
- 2 1/2 ounces uncured pepperoni, julienned
- 1/4 cup black olives, pitted and quartered
- 1 tablespoon ghee
- 2 cloves garlic, minced (about 2 teaspoons)
- 2 tablespoons tomato paste
- 1 tablespoon balsamic vinegar
- 1/2 teaspoon dried oregano leaves
- 1/2 teaspoon dried basil leaves
- 1/2 teaspoon dried parsley leaves
- 1/4 teaspoon crushed red pepper flakes
- salt and ground black pepper, to taste
- 1/2 tablespoon extra-virgin olive oil

DIRECTIONS

Preheat the oven to 400F. Cover a large baking sheet with parchment paper.

Break the cauliflower and broccoli into small florets and place in a large mixing bowl. Add the pepperoni and olives.

In a small saucepan, melt the ghee, then add the garlic, tomato paste, balsamic vinegar, oregano, basil, parsley, and red pepper flakes. Mix to combine. Pour the flavored ghee over the vegetables and toss with two wooden spoons to coat evenly.

Spread the vegetables in a single layer on the baking sheet and roast 25-30 minutes, until the florets are tender and the pepperoni is crisp. Taste and add salt and pepper, then drizzle with olive oil and serve.

TASTES GREAT WITH

OLD SCHOOL ITALIAN MEAT SAUCE, P. 94
ITALIAN PORK ROAST, P. 132
ITALIAN BURGERS/BALLS/BANGERS, P. 92

YOU KNOW HOW YOU COULD DO THAT?

PIZZA FOR BREAKFAST! *Top a pile of Pizza Veggies with fried eggs and a sprinkle of minced parsley.*

HEAD FOR THE BORDER! *Omit pepperoni. Replace basil and parsley with 1/2 teaspoon each chili powder and paprika. Bonus points if you add in a little homemade chorizo (p. 90).*

MAKE IT A MEAL! *Add slices of cooked Italian sausage during the last 5 minutes of roasting.*

HERB SALAD

THE VERY BEST RABBIT FOOD

SERVES 2

PREP	COOK
15 MIN.	N/A

My friend Sara used to joke that salad is "foods' food" as she tucked into a steak after a grueling workout. Between us friends, I have to admit, this salad is particularly grassy. In place of the typical cucumber+pepper+lettuce combo, this sunny, sharp mix of greens is all about the leaves. The flavors are unexpected – bold mint, garlicky chives, almost-sweet toasted walnuts – but drizzled with peppery extra-virgin olive oil and bright lemon juice, it tastes just right.

INGREDIENTS

2 tablespoons chopped walnuts

1/2 cup (tightly packed) parsley leaves, coarsely chopped

1/2 bunch fresh chives, cut in 1-inch pieces (about 1/3 cup)

16 fresh mint leaves, coarsely chopped (about 2 tablespoons)

2 medium scallions, very thinly sliced (about 1/4 cup)

1 head butter lettuce, julienned (about 4 cups)

1 tablespoon lemon juice

1 tablespoon extra-virgin olive oil

salt and ground black pepper, to taste

NOTES

DIRECTIONS

Heat a small skillet over medium heat. Add the walnuts and toast until golden, 3-5 minutes. Set aside.

In a large bowl, mix the parsley, chives, mint, scallions, and lettuce. Drizzle with lemon juice and olive oil, then sprinkle with walnuts and toss with two wooden spoons until the salad is evenly dressed, at least two minutes. Taste and season with salt and pepper. Enjoy immediately.

YOU KNOW HOW YOU COULD DO THAT?

- *Replace butter lettuce with romaine hearts, or try pecans instead of walnuts.*
- *Sub cilantro for the parsley and dress with lime juice instead of lemon.*

MAKE IT A MEAL! *Top with steamed shrimp or flaked salmon.*

TASTES GREAT WITH

STUFFED GRAPE LEAVES, P. 138

SHRIMP SCAMPI, P. 114

SCHEHERAZADE OMELET, P. 154

LEMON LAMB TAGINE, P. 142

CRISPY CHICKEN LIVERS, P. 106

THYME-BRAISED SHORT RIBS, P. 100

This also works remarkably well with frozen, chopped collards. Just defrost, pat dry, and start with the last step of the directions.

CRISP-SWEET COLLARDS

BERRIES AND NUTS ARE THE REWARD FOR EATING YOUR GREENS

SERVES 2

PREP 20 MIN. COOK 15 MIN.

The traditional way to cook collard greens is to fry up some bacon as a base, then stew the bejesus out of them. This makes them soft, for sure, but also gray-green and bland, despite the heroic effort on the part of the bacon. I like my collards to talk back with some attitude still left in the leaves and some crispy brown bits on the edges. And between you and me, I think tart cranberries and crunchy pecans trump the bacon.

INGREDIENTS

- 1 bunch collard greens (about 1 pound)
- 1/2 cup water
- 1/2 tablespoon coconut oil or ghee
- 2 cloves garlic, minced (about 2 teaspoons)
- 1 tablespoon chopped pecans
- 1 tablespoon dried cranberries (sugar free!)
- salt and ground black pepper, to taste

DIRECTIONS

Wash the greens. Remove the tough ribs, then stack the leaves and cut into 1/2-inch strips.

Heat a large, non-stick skillet over medium-high heat. Toss the still-wet-from-the-washing greens into the pan, add 1/2 cup water, cover with a lid, and steam 5 minutes or so, until almost all the water is evaporated.

Remove the lid, toss the greens with two wooden spoons until they are very dark green. The leaves and the pan should be dry. This takes about 2-3 minutes.

Push the greens to the side. Add coconut oil or ghee and when it's melted, drop the minced garlic, pecans, and cranberries into the fat. Cook until fragrant, about 30 seconds. Toss everything together and allow the greens to cook another 5 minutes. Add salt and pepper to taste, then eat your vegetables!

YOU KNOW HOW YOU COULD DO THAT?

Replace the collard greens with kale, Swiss chard, spinach, or turnip greens – or swap pine nuts and raisins for the pecans and cranberries. (You might also try chopped dates with walnuts. Just sayin'...) You could also nod to tradition by adding a slice or two of crumbled, sugar-free bacon.

TASTES GREAT WITH

PERFECT STEAK, P. 134
OLD SCHOOL ITALIAN MEAT SAUCE, P. 94
THYME-BRAISED SHORT RIBS, P. 100
ITALIAN PORK ROAST, P. 132
BBQ BEEF "WAFFLE" SANDWICH, P. 116
WEST AFRICAN CHICKEN STEW, P. 160
TAJ MAHAL CHICKEN, P. 110

NOTES

salad!
pecans + raisins

bacon ♡

mayo

onion

broccoli

SWEET AND SALTY BROCCOLI SALAD

BACON AND RAISINS? OK!

SERVES 4

PREP	COOK
15 MIN.	N/A

My mom's version of this salad was a summer-time staple at picnics and potlucks. Unfortunately, it included shredded cheese and store-bought mayo along with the bacon, raisins, and pecans. We get to keep the bacon, which completely drowns out any disappointment about the cheese, right? Right!

Heads up! This recipe requires you to do something in advance; plan prep time accordingly.

INGREDIENTS

4 slices sugar-free, nitrate-free bacon
1 tablespoon white wine vinegar
1/3 cup Olive Oil Mayo (p. 53)
1 pound fresh broccoli, broken into small florets
1/4 medium red onion, finely diced (about 1/4 cup)
2 tablespoons raisins
2 tablespoons pecans, chopped
salt and ground black pepper, to taste

DIRECTIONS

Cut the bacon crosswise into 1/4-inch wide pieces. Place the chopped bacon in a large, cold skillet, turn the heat to medium-high, and fry the bacon until it's crisp, about 3-4 minutes. Remove from the pan and drain on a paper towel.

In a large bowl, whisk the vinegar and mayo until smooth. Add the broccoli, onion, raisins, and pecans. Toss with two wooden spoons to coat. Add the bacon and toss again. Taste, then add salt and pepper as needed.

NOTES

Find Whole30-friendly bacon at US Wellness Meats.

YOU KNOW HOW YOU COULD DO THAT?

Have trouble digesting raw broccoli? Blanch broccoli in boiling, salted water for about 3 minutes, then drain and rinse under cold water until cool. Bingo! Friendlier broccoli.

Swap dried cranberries for the raisins (and maybe even walnuts for the pecans).

TASTES GREAT WITH

TURKEY & CRANBERRY BURGERS/BALLS/BANGERS, P. 89
REUBEN ROLLUPS, P. 98
BBQ BEEF "WAFFLE" SANDWICH, P. 116

COCONUT CAULIFLOWER RICE

SERVES 4

PREP 15 MIN.

COOK 10 MIN.

Coconut and cauliflower are the shape-shifting superheroes of paleo. Coconut gives us milk, butter, flakes, and oil, while cauliflower can be mashed, roasted, and riced. Together, they're like the Wonder Twins: Shape of a waterfall of coconut milk! Form of... OK. That doesn't really work because there's no animal related to cauliflower. But you feel me, right? This recipe infuses cauliflower rice with the rich, creaminess of coconut milk to make a dish that's kind of like Thai sticky rice and is the perfect bed for all kinds of curries and stews. Or just a bowl and a spoon.

INGREDIENTS

- 1 medium head cauliflower (about 2 pounds)
- 1 shallot, minced (about 3 tablespoons)
- 1/2 tablespoon coconut oil
- 1/4 teaspoon ground cardamom
- 3/4 cup canned coconut milk
- salt and ground black pepper, to taste

DIRECTIONS

Break the cauliflower into florets, removing the stems. Place the florets in the food processor bowl and pulse until the cauliflower looks like rice. This takes about 10 to 15 one-second pulses. You may need to do this in two batches to avoid overcrowding (which leads to mush).

Heat a large, non-stick skillet over medium-high, about 3 minutes. Add the coconut oil and allow it to melt. Add the shallot and sauté until tender, about 5 minutes. Add the cardamom and stir with a wooden spoon until fragrant, about 30 seconds.

Add the cauliflower and coconut milk, stirring to combine. Simmer/sauté the cauliflower for about 10-12 minutes until the coconut milk is absorbed. **Warning:** This will look like wet, mushy oatmeal for a while, and you will be convinced it's ruined. Be strong of heart! Eventually, the coconut milk is absorbed, the cauliflower dries out a bit, and flavorful brown bits begin to appear. Taste and season with plenty of salt and a little black pepper.

YOU KNOW HOW YOU COULD DO THAT?

MAKE IT A ONE-POT MEAL! *Add diced cooked protein and steamed veggies to the cooked "rice." Two good combos: chicken+pineapple+broccoli or beef+ scallions+jalapeños. You could also multiply the coconut quotient by mixing 1/3 cup toasted coconut into the cooked rice (then top with minced cilantro and a squeeze of lime juice).*

TASTES GREAT WITH

TOD MUN CHICKEN CAKES, P. 156
THAI PINK GRAPEFRUIT SALAD, P. 212
THAI BASIL BEEF, P. 112
THAI GREEN CURRY BURGERS/BALLS/BANGERS, P. 90
WEST AFRICAN CHICKEN STEW, P. 160
TROPICAL CHOPPED SALAD, P. 140

NOTES

GREEN BEANS WITH SIZZLED GARLIC

YOU'LL BE TEMPTED TO EAT THE GARLIC ON ITS OWN

SERVES 4

PREP 15 MIN. | COOK 10 MIN.

Green beans can be tricky devils. Undercooked, they remain unyielding and wooden, but caught in the maelstrom of boiling water, they can quickly turn drab and waterlogged. The way to make them behave is a two-step process: a fairly quick steam bath blanches them bright green and begins the tenderizing process, followed by a gentle rest in garlic-infused olive oil to wear down their resistance. The low heat in this recipe crisps the garlic, while coaxing out its sweeter side, and the cumin seeds add their own, earthy crunch.

INGREDIENTS

1/2 tablespoon whole cumin seeds
1 pound green beans, trimmed
1/2 cup water
4 teaspoons extra-virgin olive oil
5 cloves garlic, thinly sliced lengthwise
salt and ground black pepper, to taste
juice of half lemon

NOTES

Sizzled garlic is friendly. Feel free to introduce it to other veggies.

DIRECTIONS

Heat a large, non-stick skillet over medium-high. When the pan is hot, toss in the cumin seeds and stir constantly until they're light brown and fragrant, about 90 seconds. Set aside.

In the same pan, place the green beans and water. Cover and bring to a boil, steaming for 3-4 minutes until tender. Drain the green beans, set aside, and dry out the pan.

Return the pan to the stove and turn the heat to low. VERY low heat; just enough heat to make it warm. Add the olive oil and garlic slivers; cook until golden and tender, about 7 minutes. Add the cumin seeds and green beans; toss with two wooden spoons to coat the beans with the oil and allow to heat through, 3-4 minutes. Season with salt and pepper, then spritz with lemon juice – use a light hand! Eat immediately.

YOU KNOW HOW YOU COULD DO THAT?

Replace the cumin seeds with caraway seeds (and skip the lemon juice) for a completely different taste.

TASTES GREAT WITH

PERFECT STEAK, P. 134
REUBEN ROLLUPS, P. 98
FIESTA PORK CHOPS, P. 120

SILKY GINGERED ZUCCHINI SOUP

A HEALTHY HUG IN A BOWL

SERVES 4 to 6

PREP	COOK
10 MIN.	1 HR.

The ginger and garlic in this recipe give it a little bit of zing, and you'll be shocked – shocked! – at how creamy this soup is, without the benefit of dairy or coconut milk. I'm halfway obsessed with eating soup for breakfast, and this is one of my favorites. It's an easy way to make sure I get a dose of veggies in the morning, and because a bowl of this soup is warm and cozy, it fills in for tea or coffee but ***I can eat it.*** *Bonus!*

INGREDIENTS

1 tablespoon coconut oil
1/2 medium onion, coarsely chopped
4 large cloves garlic, peeled and smashed
1 teaspoon powdered ginger
1 teaspoon ground coriander
1 teaspoon salt
1/2 teaspoon ground black pepper
4 zucchini, chopped (about 2 pounds)
2 cups chicken broth
2 cups beef broth

GARNISH:

chopped chives

YOU KNOW HOW YOU COULD DO THAT?

This is an excellent way to use the zucchini cores leftover from making Zucchini Noodles (p. 168). You can also use all chicken broth instead of the chicken+beef combo.

Find yourself out of chives? When you get over the horror, try topping your soup with thinly-sliced scallions. Consider a drizzle of sesame oil across the top – or place a scoop of Coconut Cauliflower Rice (p. 202) in the bottom of the bowl.

DIRECTIONS

Heat 1/2 tablespoon coconut oil in a large soup pot on medium heat, 2 minutes. Add onions and garlic to the pot. Stir often and cook until soft and golden, but not browned, about 5 minutes.

Add the ginger, coriander, salt, and pepper to the pot. Stir to combine and when the spices are fragrant, toss in the zucchini. Stir to coat the zucchini with fat, about 1 minute.

Add the broth, bring to a boil, cover, and reduce heat to simmer. Let the zucchini cook 45 to 60 minutes until it's very soft.

Purée the zucchini and broth in a blender or food processor. Be careful! Do this in batches and fill the canister only halfway, holding a towel over the lid while you purée. Hot soup expands in the canister and can spurt out if you're not vigilant.

Slurp immediately, or store in a covered container in the fridge. Serve sprinkled with chopped chives.

HOW TO CUT ZUCCHINI WITHOUT MISHAP:

Make sure your knife is sharp. Carefully (1) cut the zuke in half crosswise, then (2) cut those halves in half lengthwise to make half-moon-shaped logs, then place the logs flat side down, and (3) slice into 1/2-inch thick half-moons.

SPRING CHOPPED SALAD

A HAPPY ACCIDENT

SERVES 4

PREP	COOK
15 MIN.	N/A

I'm sure that despite your best intentions, you've had evenings like this: You're hungry. It's time to cook dinner. Maybe you've got burgers or chicken on the grill, and you reach into the fridge for salad fixings to find... you're out of lettuce. And tomatoes. And red bell peppers. What you've got is a bunch of green stuff that, at first glance, doesn't look like it goes together. But time is ticking. Your stomach is complaining. You soldier on. And you accidentally invent a salad that tastes so good, you make it again. On purpose.

INGREDIENTS

- 1 large seedless cucumber, diced
- 2 cups snap peas, chopped
- 4 large scallions, white and green, thinly sliced
- 1 cup fresh parsley leaves, minced (about 1⁄4 cup)
- 2 tablespoons extra-virgin olive oil
- 2 tablespoons lemon juice
- salt and ground black pepper, to taste

NOTES *I hate to disagree with Kermit the Frog, but this salad makes it easy to be green.*

DIRECTIONS

Place the cucumbers, snap peas, scallions, and parsley in a large mixing bowl. Add the oil and lemon juice, then sprinkle with salt and pepper.

Toss with two wooden spoons for about 2 minutes until the vegetables are coated. Taste and adjust seasonings.

YOU KNOW HOW YOU COULD DO THAT?

MAKE IT ASIAN-ISH! *Sub cilantro for the parsley; replace the olive oil with 1 1/2 tablespoons olive oil + 1/2 tablespoon toasted sesame oil and sub rice vinegar for the lemon juice.*

MAKE IT GREEK-ISH! *Add 1 teaspoon dried oregano leaves.*

ZING! *Replace the olive oil and lemon juice with Zingy Ginger Dressing (p. 72).*

TASTES GREAT WITH

Everything! But to be more specific...

STUFFED GRAPE LEAVES, P. 148
SHRIMP SCAMPI, P. 114
SCHEHERAZADE OMELET, P. 154
SB&J BURGER, P. 152
LEMON LAMB TAGINE, P. 142
BEEF STEW PROVENÇAL, P. 122

...and a drizzle of Tahini Dressing (p. 74) is terrific, too.

No bacon? No problem.
Sauté the onion in
coconut oil and move on.

SWEET POTATO SOUP WITH BACON

ADMIT IT: I HAD YOU AT BACON

SERVES 4 *to* 6

PREP 10 MIN. | COOK 30 MIN.

I like my music to be either upbeat or angry, but never middle-of-the-road mellow. I like most of my clothing to be black or, alternately, vibrant colors like orange, neon green, hot pink, or red, but never pastels. And I like my soups to be either big, chunks of meat and vegetables or smooth, veggie-infused purées, but never "throw a bunch of stuff into a pot and simmer 'til mushy." The big, bold flavors of this soup satisfy all of my requirements. Plus, there's bacon.

Heads up! This recipe requires you to do something in advance; plan prep time accordingly.

INGREDIENTS

- 6 slices sugar-free, nitrate-free bacon
- 1 medium onion, finely diced (about 1 cup)
- 1 teaspoon Lebanese Seven-Spice Blend (p. 84)
- 1/2 tablespoon salt
- 1/4 teaspoon ground black pepper
- dash cayenne pepper
- 5 cloves garlic, peeled and smashed
- 2 pounds sweet potatoes, peeled and thinly sliced
- 4 cups chicken broth
- 1 cup water

GARNISH:
chopped chives

Find Whole30-friendly bacon at US Wellness Meats.

DIRECTIONS

Cut the bacon crosswise into 1/4-inch wide pieces. Place the chopped bacon in a large, cold soup pot, turn the heat to medium-high, and fry the bacon until it's crisp, about 3-4 minutes. Remove from the pot and drain on a paper towel. Keep 1 tablespoon of the fat in the pot and discard the rest.

Reheat the fat over medium-high heat, then add the onions, Lebanese Seven-Spice, salt, pepper, and cayenne. Cook, stirring occasionally, until the onions are soft, about 5-7 minutes. Toss in the garlic and stir, cooking until fragrant, about 30 seconds.

Add the sweet potatoes, broth, and water to the pot. Bring to a boil, reduce heat to simmer, cover, and cook until the potatoes are tender, about 10-15 minutes.

Working in batches and being careful, purée the soup in a food processor or blender until it's smooth. Fill the canister only halfway, holding a towel over the lid while you purée. Hot soup expands in the canister and can spurt out if you're not vigilant. Return to the pot, taste, and adjust seasonings. Ladle into bowls, then sprinkle with a little bacon and chives. Both the bacon and soup hold up well in the fridge for a few days.

TASTY IDEAS

I eat mine for breakfast but you might want to try a few of these ideas to make it a meal:

ADD EGGS: *Serve in a shallow bowl and top with fried eggs.*
MAKE IT DINNER: *Top with cooked ground beef, shredded chicken, or pulled pork.*
SPICE IT UP: *Drizzle with a little melted ghee and extra Lebanese Seven-Spice Blend, p. 84.*
FEEL THE MAGIC: *Sprinkle the top with Magic Dust, p. 76.*

YOU KNOW HOW YOU COULD DO THAT?

Many spicy-sweet combos pair well with sweet potatoes. Try these replacements for the Lebanese Seven-Spice Blend: Sunrise Spice (p. 78), Jerk Seasoning (p. 82), Chinese five-spice, or Ras el Hanout (commercial blend or use the recipe from Well Fed, *p. 47).*

Like it fiery? Keep the ribs and seeds in the jalapeño when you mince it.

THAI PINK GRAPEFRUIT SALAD

ALMOST TOO PRETTY TO EAT... ALMOST

SERVES 4

PREP: 10 MIN.

MELD: 10 MIN.

Grapefruit gets such a raw deal! Relegated to breakfast, sliced in half, plopped on a plate, and stabbed with a serrated spoon. Unfair! This pink, juicy powerhouse deserves better and so do you. Instead, peel it with love, then toss it with equally bold flavors – fragrant mint, briny dried shrimp, fiery jalapeño, and sweet coconut – to wake up and shake up your meal, any time of day.

INGREDIENTS

- 1/2 cup unsweetened coconut flakes
- 2 tablespoons cashews, chopped
- 2 large pink grapefruit (about 2 pounds)
- 1/3 cup fresh mint leaves, coarsely chopped
- 1/2 shallot, minced (about 1 1/2 tablespoons)
- 1 tablespoon dried shrimp, minced
- 1/2 jalapeño, seeds removed, minced (about 1 tablespoon)
- juice of 1 lime (about 2 tablespoons)
- 1 tablespoon fish sauce or coconut aminos
- juice of 1/2 orange (about 2 tablespoons)

DIRECTIONS

Heat a non-stick pan over medium-high heat. When the pan is hot, toss in the coconut flakes and cashews. Stir frequently and cook until they're lightly toasted, about 3-5 minutes. Remove from the pan to cool.

Over a large bowl to catch the juice, peel the grapefruit and liberate the fruit from the membranes. Section the grapefruit and peel off the dividing membranes so you're left with just the pink jewels. Cut the grapefruit sections into 1-inch pieces and place in the bowl with their juice.

In small bowl, whisk mint, shallot, shrimp, jalapeño, lime juice, fish sauce, and orange juice. Add the grapefruit and gently fold with a rubber scraper to combine. Sprinkle in the coconut and cashews, then gently fold again. Allow the flavors to meld for about 10 minutes before eating.

This tastes best room temperature, and it holds up in the fridge for 3-4 days.

TASTES GREAT WITH

THAI GREEN CURRY BURGERS/BALLS/BANGERS, P. 90
THAI BASIL BEEF, P. 112
SB&J BURGER, P. 152
THAI OMELET, P. 154
COCONUT CAULIFLOWER RICE, P. 202

Dried shrimp can be found in the Hispanic or Asian section of most grocery stores.

Learn my envy-producing, grapefruit peeling technique at ***www.theclothesmakethegirl.com/wellfed2***

YOU KNOW HOW YOU COULD DO THAT?

SIMPLE, SCRUMPTIOUS MEAL IDEA: *Season chicken thighs with garlic and salt, then grill. Pile on top of Coconut Cauliflower Rice (p. 202), and serve Thai Pink Grapefruit Salad alongside the pile so each bite is hot, cool, sweet, chewy, spicy, and creamy.*

MAKE THAI BOATS! *Fill a romaine lettuce leaf with a teaspoon each of toasted shredded coconut, minced fresh ginger, minced lime (including the rind), dried shrimp, minced red onion, minced jalapeño, and minced mango. Easy, exotic finger food!.*

GARLIC-CREAMED SPINACH

IN WHICH WE UPDATE THE STEAKHOUSE CLASSIC

SERVES 2

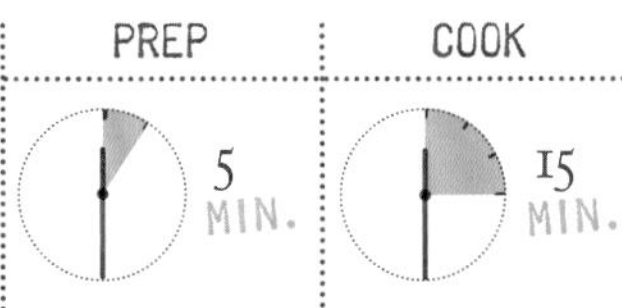

I've eaten the creamed spinach at steakhouses in San Francisco, Las Vegas, and Austin, and it is undeniably delectable. But it should be called "Green-flecked Cream Sauce" because the spinach was practically an afterthought. To make the original, the recipe calls for an entire stick of butter, white flour, and 2 cups (!) of cream. My recipe retains the creamy silkiness, but puts the spinach in a starring role, replacing the dairy-gluten sauce with good-for-you olive oil mayo.

Heads up! This recipe requires you to do something in advance; plan prep time accordingly.

INGREDIENTS

1/4 cup Garlic Mayo (p. 54)
1 (16 ounce) bag frozen chopped spinach
salt and ground black pepper, to taste

NOTES

DIRECTIONS

This can be eaten hot (silkier) or at room temperature (creamier) and tastes just as good made with frozen spinach as with fresh.

Hot: Cook the spinach according to the package directions, drain, and squeeze out excess moisture. Sauté in a non-stick skillet until dry and hot. Remove from the heat and stir in the Garlic Mayo. The mayo may "melt" into the spinach, but the herb-garlic flavors and smooth texture of the mayo will linger. Taste and season with salt and pepper, then eat immediately.

Room temperature: Defrost the spinach in the fridge, then squeeze out as much water as possible. Allow the spinach to warm to room temperature, stir in the Garlic Mayo, taste, and season with salt and pepper. Dig in!

TASTES GREAT WITH

THYME-BRAISED SHORT RIBS, P. 100
PERFECT STEAK, P. 134
CHINESE FIVE-SPICE PORK RIBS, P. 128
ITALIAN PORK ROAST, P. 132

PRO TIP! *Here's the scoop on how to remove excess water from the spinach: Place the spinach in a colander or wire sieve and press out the water with the bottom of a bowl that fits inside the colander, then squeeze individual handfuls of spinach to wring out the remaining water. You should have about 1 to 1 1/2 cups of spinach when you're finished squeezing.*

SPAGHETTI SQUASH FRITTERS

TAKE THAT, PANCAKES!

PAGE 216

SERVES 4

MAKES	PREP	COOK
about 10 fritters	20 MIN.	20 MIN.

Sure, you can make pancakes from almond butter or coconut flour, but they're still treats. And that makes me stabby. I WANT A PANCAKE I CAN EAT EVERY DAY. These are more savory than sweet, but they're tender and fluffy, and turn brown in the pan, and have those toasty, crispy bits on the edges, and they're loaded with vegetables. They're everyday pancakes. Take that.

Heads up! This recipe requires you to do something in advance; plan prep time accordingly.

INGREDIENTS

- 1/2 onion, very finely minced (about 1/2 cup)
- 1/2 cup almond flour
- 3 large eggs
- 1/4 teaspoon baking soda
- 1/2 teaspoon cream of tartar
- 1/2 teaspoon salt
- 1/2 teaspoon ground black pepper
- 4 cups Roasted Spaghetti Squash (p.168)
- 1-2 tablespoons coconut oil

DIRECTIONS

In a large bowl, mix onion, almond flour, eggs, baking soda, cream of tartar, salt, and pepper with a whisk until combined. Squeeze excess moisture from the squash with a clean dish towel or paper towels, then add the squash to the bowl and mix well. Allow the batter to rest 10 minutes. (How about a mini workout while you wait? 10 rounds of :30 air squats + :30 rest.)

Place 1/2 tablespoon coconut oil in a large, non-stick skillet and heat over medium-high until the oil is melted and shimmers. Swivel the pan to coat the bottom, then drop 1/4-cup servings of batter into the pan, making sure they don't touch. Cook until browned on the bottom and starting to set, about 3-4 minutes. Flip gently and cook the other side until browned, an additional 2-3 minutes

Cook in batches, adding more coconut oil to the pan, as necessary. Serve hot.

YOU KNOW HOW YOU COULD DO THAT?

- *Replace spaghetti squash with Zucchini Noodles, p. 168*
- *Cook the fritters in Better Butter, p. 60*

NOTES

Wanna sound more precocious than usual? Refer to your spaghetti squash by its species name, "Cucurbita pepo."

TASTY IDEAS

NEXT TO EGGS AND CHORIZO, P. 90
ALONGSIDE A PERFECT STEAK, P. 134
NEXT TO CHINESE FIVE-SPICE PORK RIBS, P. 128
AS A BED FOR MULLIGATAWNY STEW, P. 150
UNDER A PILE OF CINCINNATI CHILI, P. 104

FRUITS

PEAR AND BACON BITES

A STUDY IN CONTRASTS

SERVES 2 *to* 4

PREP | COOK

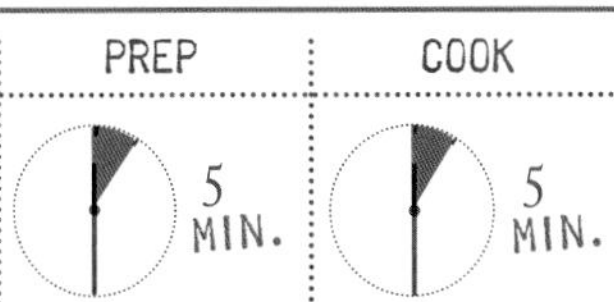

5 MIN. | 5 MIN.

This recipe might sound crazy, if by "crazy," you mean "crazy-good." There's alchemy in the play of contrasts: sweet and salty, cool and hot, crisp and chewy. Each little tidbit is a burst of flavor on your tongue. Whether you're throwing a party or celebrating a random Thursday night, these are super quick to make and guaranteed crowd pleasers. Now who's crazy?!

INGREDIENTS

- 4 slices sugar-free, nitrate-free bacon
- 2 just-ripe pears
- paprika
- ground cinnamon
- salt

Find Whole30-friendly bacon at US Wellness Meats.

NOTES

In the Odyssey, Homer called pears a "gift from the Gods."

DIRECTIONS

Preheat oven to 375F. Cover a large, rimmed baking sheet with aluminum foil.

Cut bacon strips into 1-inch pieces and place on the baking sheet. Bake for 15 minutes, or until just crisp. Using a slotted spoon, transfer the bacon to a plate lined with paper towels to drain excess fat.

Cut each pear into 1/2-inch slices, then into 1-inch pieces. Lay them out on a cutting board and sprinkle VERY lightly with paprika, cinnamon, and salt. So pretty!

Top each piece of pear with a square of bacon and spear with a toothpick. Pop into your mouth. Enjoy.

YOU KNOW HOW YOU COULD DO THAT?

SKIP THE BACON. *Pears spiced with paprika, cinnamon, and salt are a great anytime treat.*

Replace the cinnamon with cardamom – or swap apples for the pears.

Yes, this is a
real strawberry.

SUNNY DAY STRAWBERRIES

THE TREAT YOU SO RICHLY DESERVE

SERVES *you*

PREP	COOK
1 MIN.	N/A

This isn't really much of a recipe at all. It's a taste sensation I discovered one day when I really, really wanted a treat and really, really didn't want to eat something junky. I grabbed a strawberry from the fridge, smeared it with sunflower seed butter, and chomped it immediately. It was just what I needed: juicy and sweet, nutty and creamy, and bite-sized. Craving controlled, no painful aftermath.

INGREDIENTS

1 perfect fresh strawberry

1 teaspoon sunflower seed butter (no sugar added)

GARNISH:

toasted, unsweetened shredded coconut

DIRECTIONS

Hull the strawberry. Spoon the nut butter inside the berry. Sprinkle with coconut shreds. Chew slowly and savor the flavors on your tongue.

YOU KNOW HOW YOU COULD DO THAT?

Replace the strawberry with a slice of apple, a stick of celery, or a few banana coins.

NOTES ***This is also yummy with almond, cashew, or pecan butter. Go nuts!***

BANANA PECAN ICE CREAM

TREAT

LIKE AN ACTION-ADVENTURE MOVIE FOR YOUR MOUTH

SERVES 4

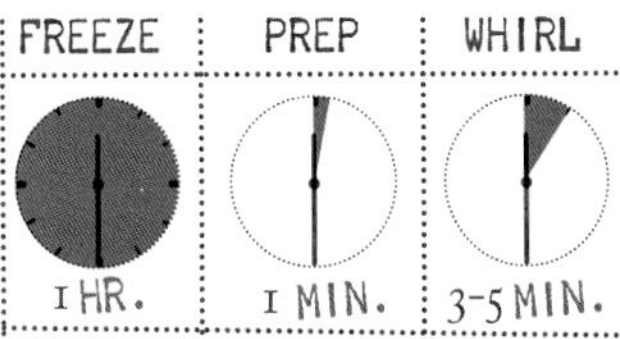

Ways in which bananas are badass: (1) They can cheer you up: they're the only fruit to contain tryptophan, an amino acid that produces seratonin, which makes you feel happy. (2) They're nutritious: a good source of Vitamin C, B6, and potassium. (3) They convey secret messages: Scratch a note on a banana skin with a toothpick, and within an hour, it'll turn dark brown and be readable. (4) They can be transformed into ice cream. ***Bananas: the Samuel L. Jackson of the fruit world.***

Heads up! This recipe requires you to do something in advance; plan prep time accordingly.

INGREDIENTS

- 2 ripe bananas, peeled and frozen
- 1/4 cup coconut milk
- 1 teaspoon vanilla extract
- 2 tablespoons pecans
- pinch salt

NOTE: THIS RECIPE IS NOT APPROVED FOR EATING DURING THE WHOLE30 — BUT IT'S A GREAT WAY TO INDULGE A LITTLE AFTER!

DIRECTIONS

IMPORTANT FIRST STEP: Peel the bananas, cut into 1-inch chunks, and place on a baking sheet in the freezer until frozen solid, about 1 hour. (Or, ya know, just keep a ziplock baggie of banana chunks in the freezer for dessert emergencies.)

Place the frozen bananas in the bowl of a food processor. Whirl until they reach a creamy consistency, about 3-5 minutes. Add the coconut milk, vanilla, pecans, and salt to the processor, and spin until combined. Depending on the size of your processor, you might need to scrape down the sides a few times to help the bananas along their journey from frozen fruit to ICE CREAM.

Scoop into serving bowls and lick it up!

NOTES

In 2001, Britain recorded 300 incidents of injuries related to bananas. The majority of these involved people slipping on banana peels.

YOU KNOW HOW YOU COULD DO THAT?

MORE FRUIT! *Add a handful of frozen berries: Strawberries and raspberries are sweet.*

MORE YUM! *Make it decadent by drizzling with a teaspoon or two of warmed sunflower seed or almond butter.*

SPICED FRUIT STICKS

FOOD ON STICKS JUST TASTES BETTER

SERVES 4 *to* 6

PREP	COOK
15 MIN.	N/A

I've never liked cantaloupe. The texture always seems off – either too hard and flavorless, or too mushy and sickeningly sweet. Blame our conventional produce production cycle, but I've never understood the appeal. Then I tried a perfectly-ripe, organic cantaloupe, and everything changed. It was the very embodiment of the taste of summer, but something was still missing. I gave the lazy-Susan in my spice cabinet a spin and landed on cardamom, then paprika. I fervently hoped it would taste as good on the cantaloupe as it looked. It did.

INGREDIENTS

perfectly ripe cantaloupe or honeydew melon, chilled
fresh mint leaves
pinch cardamom
pinch paprika
pinch coarse sea salt

GARNISH:
a few raspberries (optional)

DIRECTIONS

Cut the melon into 1-inch chunks or balls and thread onto bamboo skewers, adding a mint leaf after every few chunks.

Sprinkle with the spices – a light hand will serve you well. Add a raspberry for a punch of color. Pop the fruit into your mouth and let the sensations roll around your tongue: cool, sweet, spicy, salty, crunchy, tender.

Warning: Spice just the amount of melon you want to eat immediately. Like summer itself, spiced cantaloupe is a fleeting pleasure.

NOTES

Wash the outside of your melon thoroughly before cutting. You can keep cut cantaloupe in the fridge for a maximum of three days.

YOU KNOW HOW YOU COULD DO THAT?

MAKE IT SAVORY! *Add slices of prosciutto to the skewers to turn dessert into a sweet-savory appetizer.*

Stuff to Put on Eggs (p. 47)
Eggs are not AIP compliant.

Paleo Flavor Boosters (p. 49)

1. Good Finishing Salt
Good to go.

2. Tomato Paste
Tomatoes are not AIP compliant.

3. Citrus Juice
Good to go, except for chili powder and Chinese five-spice powder.

4. Oils or Homemade Mayo
Oils are good to go; Olive Oil Mayo is not AIP compliant.

5. Crushed Garlic
Good to go.

6. Chopped Chives
Good to go.

7. Fresh Herbs
Good to go.

8. Coconut Aminos
Good to go.

9. Toasted Coconut
Good to go.

10. Toasted, Chopped Nuts
Nuts are not AIP compliant.

Turn it up to 11: Combos
These are AIP approved combos:
3+5, 3+7, 4+6, 5+6, 5+7

Sauces & Seasonings

Olive Oil Mayo & Variations (p. 53)
Cannot be made AIP compliant.

BBQ Sauce (p. 56)
Cannot be made AIP compliant.

Almost Amba (p. 58)
Omit chile peppers and paprika. Add 3 tablespoons freshly-grated ginger. Note that this amba will be slightly sweeter than the original. Includes seed spices: mustard, cumin.

Better Butter (p. 60)
Cannot be made AIP compliant.

Hoisin Sauce (p. 62)
Cannot be made AIP compliant.

Kickass Ketchup (p. 64)
Cannot be made AIP compliant.

Go-To Vinaigrette (p. 66)
Omit Kickass Ketchup, paprika, and hot sauce. Includes seed spice: dry mustard.

Lizard Sauce (p. 68)
Cannot be made AIP compliant.

Romesco Sauce (p. 70)
Cannot be made AIP compliant.

Zingy Ginger Dressing (p. 72)
Good to go.

Tahini Dressing (p. 74)
Cannot be made AIP compliant.

Magic Dust (p. 76)
Cannot be made AIP compliant.

Sunrise Spice (p. 78)
Omit paprika. Includes seed spices: allspice, nutmeg.

Merguez Sausage Seasoning (p. 80)
Cannot be made AIP compliant.

Jerk Seasoning (p. 82)
Omit cayenne pepper. Add 1 teaspoon powdered ginger. Includes seed spices: allspice, nutmeg.

Lebanese Seven-Spice Blend (p. 84)
Good to go. Includes seed spices: allspice, cloves, coriander, nutmeg.

Protein

Burgers Balls Bangers (p. 89)

Turkish Doner Kebab
Omit cayenne pepper.

Romanian
Omit paprika.

Turkey and Cranberry
Good to go.

Classic Pork
Good to go. Includes seed spices: cloves, nutmeg. (Tastes fine without.)

Greek
Good to go. Includes seed spice: fennel. (Tastes fine without.)

Chorizo
Cannot be made AIP compliant.

AIP ADAPTATIONS

Lebanese
Omit pine nuts. See Lebanese Seven-Spice Blend modifications.

Merguez Sausage
Cannot be made AIP compliant.

Thai Green Curry
Cannot be made AIP compliant.

Japanese Gyoza
Omit sesame oil and crushed red pepper flakes.

Moroccan Chicken and Apricot
Omit almonds.

Bahn Mi
Omit hot sauce.

Moorish
Cannot be made AIP compliant.

Italian
Omit tomato paste and red pepper flakes.

Cuban
Omit tomato paste and almonds. Use green olives that are not stuffed with pimientos.

Old School Italian Meat Sauce (p. 94)
Cannot be made AIP compliant.

Piña Colada Chicken (p. 96)
Omit bell peppers; see Jerk Seasoning modifications.

Reuben Rollups (p. 98)
Cannot be made AIP compliant.

Thyme-Braised Short Ribs (p. 100)
Omit tomato paste.

Buffalo Chicken Salad (p. 102)
Cannot be made AIP compliant.

Cincinnati Chili (p. 104)
Cannot be made AIP compliant.

Crispy Chicken Livers (p. 106)
Omit paprika and cayenne pepper. Includes seed spices: cloves, cumin.
You Know How You Could Do That:
BBQish: cannot be made AIP compliant.
Middle Eastern: see Lebanese Seven-Spice Blend modifications; omit Tahini Dressing.
Chinese: omit Chinese five-spice powder and replace with 1/2 teaspoon ground cinnamon and 1/2 teaspoon powdered ginger; omit Hoisin Sauce.
Jamaican: see Jerk Seasoning modifications.
Classic Fried Chicken: good to go.

Sunrise Scramble (p. 108)
Cannot be made AIP compliant.

Taj Mahal Chicken (p. 110)
Cannot be made AIP compliant.

Thai Basil Beef (p. 112)
Omit red bell pepper and serrano chile.

Shrimp Scampi (p. 114)
Omit Aleppo pepper. Replace ghee with additional olive oil.
You Know How You Could Do That:
Tex-Mex: omit chili powder.
Sunny: good to go.
Asian: omit crushed red pepper flakes.
African: cannot be made AIP compliant.
Tropical: see Jerk Seasoning modifications.

BBQ Beef "Waffle" Sandwich (p. 116)
Cannot be made AIP compliant.

Deli Tuna Salad (p. 118)
Omit Olive Oil Mayo and cayenne pepper; add 2 tablespoons olive oil.

Fiesta Pork Chops (p. 120)
Omit chili powder and green chiles Includes seed spice: cumin. Replace ghee with coconut oil.

Beef Stew Provencal (p. 122)
Replace ghee with coconut oil. Omit tomatoes; replace with additional 1/2 cup beef broth.

Chicken Nanking (p. 124)
Omit Kickass Ketchup and cayenne.

Deconstructed Gyro (p. 126)
Omit Aleppo pepper/crushed red pepper flakes and tomatoes. Contains seed spice: cumin. Skip the Gyro/Kebab dressing; toss with extra-virgin olive oil, lemon juice, and dried oregano leaves.
You Know How You Could Do That:
Tahini Dressing and Gyro/Kebab Sauce cannot be made AIP compliant. See Almost Amba modifications.
Moroccan: cannot be made AIP compliant.

Chinese Five-Spice Pork Ribs (p. 128)
Omit jalapeño and tomato paste. Replace Chinese five-spice powder with

1/2 teaspoon ground cinnamon and 1 teaspoon powdered ginger.
You Know How You Could Do That:
BBQ: cannot be made AIP compliant.
Middle Eastern: see Lebanese Seven-Spice Blend modifications.
Jamaican: see Jerk Seasoning modifications.
Spicy-Sweet: see Sunrise Spice modifications.
Moroccan: cannot be made AIP compliant.

Faux Pho (p. 130)
Omit eggs; see Chinese Five-Spice Pork Ribs modifications. Omit ghee.
You Know How You Could Do That:
Omit Thai curry paste.

Italian Pork Roast (p. 132)
Omit crushed red pepper flakes. Includes seed spice: fennel seed. (Tastes fine without.)
You Know How You Could Do That:
BBQ: cannot be made AIP compliant.
Middle Eastern: see Lebanese Seven-Spice Blend modifications.
Jamaican: see Jerk Seasoning modifications.
Spicy-Sweet: see Sunrise Spice modifications.
Moroccan: cannot be made AIP compliant.

Perfect Steak (p. 134)
Replace ghee with coconut oil. To "Make it fancy" use olive oil and omit pistachios.

Semi Sabich (p. 136)
Cannot be made AIP compliant.

Oven Fried Salmon Cakes (p.138)
Cannot be made AIP compliant.

Tropical Chopped Salad (p. 140)
See Jerk Seasoning modifications. Omit bell pepper.

Lemon Lamb Tagine (p. 142)
Omit paprika and Aleppo pepper. Use green olives that are not stuffed with pimientos. Includes seed spice: cumin. (Tastes fine without.)

Moo Shu Pork (p. 144)
Meat & Marinade: Omit sesame oil.
Stir-Fry: Omit eggs. Serve without Hoisin Sauce.

Plantain Nachos (p. 146)
Omit chili powder, cayenne, and tomato paste; skip jalapeño and tomato as garnish. Includes seed spices: coriander, cumin.

Stuffed Grape Leaves (p. 148)
Omit pine nuts and egg yolks; see Lebanese Seven-Spice Blend modifications.

Mulligatawny Stew (p. 150)
Omit curry powder, chili powder, and cayenne pepper; add 1 tablespoon powdered ginger and 1 teaspoon ground turmeric.

SB&J Burger (p. 152)
Cannot be made AIP compliant.

Scheherazade Omelet (p. 154)
Cannot be made AIP compliant.

Tod Mun Chicken Cakes (p. 156)
Chicken Cakes: omit jalapeño, red curry paste, and eggs; add 1 tablespoon freshly-grated ginger.
Cucumber Relish: omit cashews.

Pan Fried Sardines (p. 158)
Omit Aleppo pepper and paprika; add 1/8 teaspoon powdered ginger. Includes seed spice: cumin. (Tastes fine without.)
You Know How You Could Do That:
Spanish: cannot be made AIP compliant.
Middle Eastern: see Lebanese Seven-Spice Blend modifications.
Jamaican: see Jerk Seasoning modifications; omit Lizard Sauce.
Classic Seafood: cannot be made AIP compliant.
Better: cannot be made AIP compliant.

West African Chicken Stew (p. 160)
Cannot be made AIP compliant.

Vietnamese Chicken Salad (p. 162)
Omit bell pepper, cashews, and Olive Oil Mayo.

Veggies & Salads
Steam-Sautéed Veggies (p. 166)
Good to go, except for nightshades.

Basic Cauliflower Rice (p. 167)
Good to go.

Mashed Cauliflower (p. 167)
Good to go.

Roasted Spaghetti Squash (p. 168)
Good to go.

Zucchini Noodles (p. 168)
Good to go.

Simple Lemon Spinach (p. 170)
Omit pine nuts. *You Know How You Could Do That:* Tahini Dressing and eggs are not AIP compliant.

AIP ADAPTATIONS

Tabbouleh (p. 172)
Omit tomatoes. See Lebanese Seven-Spice Blend modifications. Replace ghee with coconut oil.

Balsamic Grilled Butternut (p. 174)
Good to go.

Casablanca Carrots (p. 176)
Omit paprika and cayenne pepper. Includes seed spice: cumin. (Tastes fine without.)

Classic Coleslaw (p. 178)
Omit Olive Oil Mayo and replace with 1/3 cup extra-virgin olive oil.

Asian Slaw (p. 178)
Omit Olive Oil Mayo and replace with 1/3 cup extra-virgin olive oil. Omit red bell pepper.

Golden Cauliflower Soup (p. 180)
Good to go.

Mustard Garlic Brussels Sprouts (p. 182)
Replace ghee with coconut oil. Includes seed spice: mustard.

Pan Fried Plantains (p. 184)
Good to go. Contains seed spice: cumin. (Tastes fine without.)
You Know How You Could Do That:
See Jerk Seasoning, Sunrise Spice, and Lebanese Seven-Spice Blend modifications.

Belly Dance Beet Salad (p. 186)
Omit pistachios. Includes seed spices: coriander, cumin. (Tastes fine without.)

Citrus Cauliflower Rice (p. 188)
Omit Aleppo pepper/crushed red pepper flakes.
You Know How You Could Do That:
Better Butter is not AIP compliant.

Roasted Cabbage Roses (p. 190)
Omit paprika. Replace ghee with coconut oil.

Sesame Cucumber Noodles (p. 192)
Cannot be made AIP compliant.

Pizza Veggies (p. 194)
Cannot be made AIP compliant.

Herb Salad (p. 196)
Omit walnuts.

Crisp Sweet Collards (p. 198)
Omit pecans.

Sweet And Salty Broccoli Salad (p. 200)
Cannot be made AIP compliant.

Coconut Cauliflower Rice (p. 202)
Good to go. Includes seed spice: cardamom. (Tastes fine without.)
You Know How You Could Do That:
omit jalapeños.

Green Beans With Sizzled Garlic (p. 204)
Good to go. Includes seed spice: cumin. (Tastes fine without.)

Silky Gingered Zucchini Soup (p. 206)
Good to go. Includes seed spice: coriander. (Tastes fine without.)

Spring Chopped Salad (p. 208)
Good to go.
You Know How You Could Do That: omit sesame oil.

Sweet Potato Soup with Bacon (p. 210)
Omit cayenne. Check bacon ingredients. See Lebanese Seven-Spice Blend modifications.

Thai Pink Grapefruit Salad (p. 212)
Omit cashews and jalapeño.

Garlic Creamed Spinach (p. 214)
Cannot be made AIP compliant.

Spaghetti Squash Fritters (p. 216)
Cannot be made AIP compliant.

Fruits

Pear And Bacon Bites (p. 220)
Omit paprika; check bacon ingredients.

Sunny Day Strawberries (p. 222)
Omit sunflower seed butter and replace with coconut butter.

Banana Pecan Ice Cream (p. 224)
Omit pecans. *You Know How You Could Do That:* Nut buter is not AIP compliant.

Spiced Fruit Sticks (p. 226)
Omit paprika. Includes seed spice: cardamom.

GET A COPY OF THE WELL FED 2 EBOOK FOR $1

Thank you for buying this copy of *Well Fed 2!*

As a sign of our gratitude – and in celebration of the awesomeness of digital goodies – we're offering you a copy of the eBook (PDF) version of *Well Fed 2* for just $1.00... and then we're donating that dollar to the **Global Alliance for Clean Cookstoves**, a public-private partnership led by the United Nations Foundation to save lives, improve livelihoods, empower women, and protect the environment by creating a thriving global market for clean and efficient household cooking solutions. Their goal is for 100 million households to adopt clean cookstoves and fuels by 2020.

Almost three billion people in the developing world cook their food and heat their homes with traditional cookstoves or open fires. Smoke exposure from these cooking and heating methods is responsible for four million premature deaths every year. Women and children – cooking the food and tending to the home – are the most affected by the smoke exposure. The Alliance works with hundreds of public, private, and nonprofit partners to help overcome the market barriers that currently impede the production, deployment, and use of clean cookstoves and fuels in developing countries.

For more details about the charity and to snag your PDF, visit www.theclothesmakethegirl.com/well-fed-clean-cookstoves.

Just add the PDF to your shopping cart and enter the code CLEANCOOKSTOVES (during checkout). You'll get a digital copy of the book and a deserving organization will receive funds to support their mission.

Don't hesitate! This offer expires December 31, 2015.

Photo courtesy of United Nations Foundation and Talia Frenkel

METRIC CONVERSIONS

Hey, international friends! These charts should include everything you need to convert my American amounts for your metric kitchen gadgets. When in doubt, you can always turn to Google. Just enter something like this into the Google search field: "2 pounds in kilograms." Google will serve up the answer faster than you can say "Mmmmm.... Sunbutter!"

VOLUME

1/4 teaspoon	*1 milliliter*
1/2 teaspoon	*2.5 milliliters*
3/4 teaspoon	*4 millileters*
1 teaspoon	*5 millileters*
1 1/4 teaspoons	*6 milliliters*
1 1/2 teaspoons (1/2 tablespoon)	*7.5 milliters*
2 teaspoons	*10 milliliters*
1/2 tablespoon	*7.5 milliliters*
1 tablespoon (1/2 fluid ounce)	*15 milliliters*
2 tablespoons (1 fluid ounce)	*30 milliliters*
1/4 cup	*60 milliliters*
1/3 cup	*80 milliliters*
1/2 cup (4 fluid ounces)	*120 milliliters*
2/3 cup	*160 milliliters*
3/4 cup	*180 milliliters*
1 cup (8 fluid ounces)	*240 milliliters*
1 1/4 cups	*300 milliliters*
1 1/2 cups	*360 milliliters*
1 2/3 cups	*400 milliliters*
2 cups (1 pint)	*460 milliliters*
3 cups	*700 milliliters*
4 cups (1 quart)	*.95 liter (950 milliliters)*
4 quarts (1 gallon)	*3.8 liters*

LENGTH

1/8 inch	*3 millimeters*
1/4 inch	*6 millimeters*
1/2 inch	*1 1/4 centimeters*
1 inch	*2 1/2 centimeters*
2 inches	*5 centimeters*
3 inches	*7 1/2 centimeters*
4 inches	*10 centimeters*
5 inches	*13 centimeters*
6 inches	*15 centimeters*
12 inches (1 foot)	*30 centimeters*

WEIGHT

1 ounce	*28 grams*
1 1/2 ounces	*42.5 grams*
2 ounces	*57 grams*
3 ounces	*85 grams*
4 ounces (1/4 pound)	*113 grams*
5 ounces	*142 grams*
6 ounces	*170 grams*
7 ounces	*197 grams*
8 ounces (1/2 pound)	*227 grams*
16 ounces (1 pound)	*454 grams*
32 ounces (2 pounds)	*907 grams*
35 1/4 ounces (2.2 pounds)	*1 kilogram*

OVEN TEMPERATURES

FAHRENHEIT	CELSIUS	BRITISH GAS
200	*95*	*0*
225	*110*	*1/4*
250	*120*	*1/2*
275	*135*	*1*
300	*150*	*2*
325	*165*	*3*
350	*175*	*4*
375	*190*	*5*
400	*200*	*6*
425	*220*	*7*
450	*230*	*8*
475	*245*	*9*
500	*260*	*10*

CONVERSION FORMULAS

CONVERT	MULTIPLY
ounces to grams	*ounces by 28.35*
pounds to kilograms	*pounds by .454*
teaspoons to milliliters	*teaspoons by 4.93*
tablespoons to milliliters	*tablespoons by 14.79*
fluid ounces to milliliters	*fluid ounces by 29.57*
cups to milliliters	*cups by 236.59*
cups to liters	*cups by .236*
inches to centimeters	*inches by 2.54*

RECIPE CREDITS

Unless otherwise noted, my recipes are originals that I made up from my very own noggin, or they're a mashup-up of multiple versions of a traditional recipe that can't be traced back to an original cook. Or, honestly, I straight-up stole them from my mom. (*Hi, Mom!*)

Here are the sources for the adapted recipes in this book:

Sauces and Seasonings

BBQ Sauce: *Cook's Illustrated*
Better Butter: *Natural Food Feasts*
Lizard Sauce: www.thekitchn.com
Magic Dust: *Natural Food Feasts*
Zingy Ginger Dressing: www.topsecretrecipes.com

Protein

Beef Stew Provençal: *McCall's Cooking School*
Chicken Nanking: House of Nanking; San Francisco, California
Fiesta Pork Chops: *The Monday to Friday Cookbook*
Lemon Lamb Tagine: *Cook's Illustrated*
Mulligatawny Stew: *McCall's Cooking School*
Old School Italian Meat Sauce: *Cook's Illustrated*
Oven-Fried Salmon Cakes: Dallas and Melissa Hartwig
Perfect Steak: *Cook's Illustrated* and *Los Angeles Times*
Plantain Nachos: *Cook's Illustrated*
SB&J Burger: 26 Beach Restaurant; Venice, California
Scheherazade Omelet: *The Washington Post*
Taj Mahal Chicken: www.food52.com
Thyme-Braised Short Ribs: *The New York Times*
Tod Mun Chicken Cakes: 3hungrytummies.blogspot.com

Veggies & Salads

Sweet Potato Soup: *Cook's Illustrated*

MELISSA JOULWAN

***Well Fed* Author**

Melissa Joulwan is the author of the cookbook *Well Fed: Paleo Recipes For People Who Love To Eat, Living Paleo for Dummies*, and the blog *The Clothes Make The Girl*, where she writes every day about her triumphs and failures in the gym, in the kitchen, in life.

After a lifetime of yo-yo dieting and food as the enemy, Melissa found the paleo diet in 2009 and has been happily, healthily following it ever since. That year, she also underwent a thyroidectomy. In the aftermath of the surgery and recovery, she became particularly interested in how diet affects hormones, body composition, mood, and motivation. These days, Melissa's workouts are just as likely to include yoga and meditation as lifting heavy things and trying to stay ahead of her stopwatch.

In 2012, her blog won the Homie Award from The Kitchn.com for "Best Healthy Cooking Blog," and two recipes from *Well Fed* were honored by the *Paleo Magazine* Awards (Chocolate Chili and Peach Almond Crisp). She contributed the recipes for the "Meal Map" in the *New York Times* bestselling book *It Starts With Food.* In 2012 and 2013, she participated in a food bloggers' panel and was a featured chef at the PaleoFX Conference. She was also a keynote speaker at "Do It Better: A Practical Guide to Paleo" (Estes Park, CO; 2012). A Community Ambassador for Experience Life magazine, Melissa has also been a featured chef for U.S. Wellness Meats and Lava Lake Lamb, as well as an instructor at Whole Foods Culinary Center in Austin, Texas.

She lives in Austin with her husband Dave and their cat Smudge, but she daydreams of moving to Prague as soon as possible. Her favorite *Well Fed 2* recipe is Zingy Ginger Dressing, although the SB&J Burger runs a close second.

DAVID HUMPHREYS

***Well Fed* Photographer & Illustrator**

David Humphreys is mostly a photographer, illustrator, and business manager these days.

Since shooting the recipes in *Well Fed*, he's contributed to *The New York Times* best seller *It Starts With Food*, and trained at the Austin School of Photography and the Center for Cartoon Studies in White River Junction, Vermont. He's been to Croatia and Slovenia with his wife and two friends. He's also seen his Amazon wish list balloon to 1,234 items. The best book he read this year is *Cartooning: Philosophy and Practice by Ivan Brunetti.*

He still considers himself quite lucky to be living with celebrity chef and first-rate person Melissa Joulwan, and the best cat in the entire world, Smudge.

His favorite *Well Fed 2* recipe is Chinese Five-Spice Pork Ribs – or maybe West African Chicken Stew.

SMUDGE

***Well Fed* Mascot & CEO**

Smudge was foisted upon the authors in 2009 by a white witch. Small and unassuming, she seemed to be a benevolent cat, so she was allowed to stay. By 2011, she was appointed CEO of Smudge Publishing, LLC – she is better than some and worse than others – although she displayed an unerring apathy to food photography and copyediting.

She is best known for sneak attacks from behind dining room chairs, the patented "Barrel Roll of Joy," and her soft belly, widely recognized as the mushiest spot on Earth. Smudge's favorite *Well Fed 2* recipe is Pan-Fried Sardines.

WALKER FENZ

Well Fed Copyeditor & Proofreader

A multi-certified CrossFit Trainer and athlete at Fit & Finish in Austin, Texas, Walker is a former gymnast who makes pull ups and handstands look as easy as walking. She's been a contributor to the Reebok CrossFit Games web site and *WOD Talk* magazine.

When she's not lifting and lowering barbells, Walker is most likely stuffing her face with real food: pre-workout, post-workout, and in between. The only thing she likes more than eating recipes is editing them. Walker was on the first *Well Fed team* and is profoundly responsible for the consistency of spelling, phrasing, and hyphenation; form is just as important in writing as in Olympic lifting.

Walker's favorite *Well Fed 2* recipes are the Burgers, Balls & Bangers. (Balls!)

ALISON FINNEY

Well Fed Copyeditor

Alison Finney is a writer, copyeditor, and content lover. Her work has appeared in *Texas Monthly*, *Austin Culture Map*, *Texas Tour and Meeting Guide*, and other Texas publications.

Ali grew up in the Texas Panhandle, where there were shootouts in the street every day at high noon and all food was served "plain and dry," to her liking. Eventually, she made her way to Austin, and currently, New York City. She's now a copywriter at a fancy-schmancy New York agency.

The original *Well Fed* introduced Ali's taste buds to the merit of green vegetables and spices, and her favorite *Well Fed 2* recipe is the Spring Chopped Salad. (*Editor's note:* That's a lie. It's actually the Banana Pecan Ice Cream.)

KATHLEEN SHANNON, BRAID CREATIVE

Well Fed Creative Director

Kathleen Shannon is the cofounder and creative director of *Braid Creative & Consulting*, branding and visioning for creative entrepreneurs.

Her personal blog, AndKathleen.com, is where her work, life and adventure overlap as a working creative, a dream job creator, a risk taker, a good food eater and a booty shaker.

Kathleen thrives in the overlap between personal and professional. She built her business with her sister, where they share their brand and business know-how with creatives around the world at BraidCreative.com. She loves being able to work with other creative experts, like Melissa and Dave, helping them share their creative genius with the world, too.

Kathleen's favorite *Well Fed 2* recipe is Oven-Fried Salmon Cakes.

KRISTIN TATE, BRAID CREATIVE

Well Fed Graphic Designer

Kristin Tate is a graphic designer who loves what she does and is grateful she gets to do it for a living. Kristin works with *Braid Creative & Consulting* and Kathleen Shannon's team, to help other creatives, designers, developers, authors, and artists shine through their design.

Kristin has an affinity for all things quirky, and all things catty, including her hairless cat Zissou, which she sometimes shares online (the perfect place for cat pictures!) at KristinTate.blogspot.com. Kristin was born and raised in the midwest but is packing it up and moving to Brooklyn, NY and should be living there snuggly by the time *Well Fed 2* hits the streets and kitchens everywhere.

Kristin's favorite *Well Fed 2* recipe is the Banana Pecan Ice Cream (even though, sadly, it is not Whole30 approved).

STEFANIE DISTEFANO

***Well Fed* Potter & Mosaic Artist**

Stefanie is a potter, mosaic artist, and perhaps, the very best kind of witch. Everything she touches in her pink-infused studio, known as Flamingo Ranch (www.flamingoranch.com), shimmers, glitters, shines, and glows. Her mosaics transform the mundane to the magical, and her handcrafted pottery graces the pages of *Well Fed 2*, as well as hundreds of stylish tabletops around the world.

She was mentored by Isaiah Zagar, the greatest mosaic artist on the East coast and like her mentor, she is absolutely committed to and immersed in her art. You can see Stef's made-with-love pottery and snippets of Flamingo Ranch on these pages: 112, 142, and 186.

Stef's favorite *Well Fed 2* recipe is the Romesco Sauce, calling it "the best thing Melissa has ever made."

HAVE FUN IN THE ♥ KITCHEN

WELL FED
THE ORIGINAL

Hungry for more luscious paleo recipes you can eat every day? Take a bite of *Well Fed: Paleo Recipes For People Who Love To Eat*. Published in 2011, the original *Well Fed* is packed with 115+ recipes that are free of grains, legumes, soy, sugar, dairy, and alcohol – and all but one are Whole30 approved. (We're looking at you, Peach Almond Crisp!)

In addition to the recipes, you'll learn how to do a Weekly Cookup and make Hot Plates that will keep you and your family happily fed, without you spending all of your free time in the kitchen.

Find *Well Fed: Paleo Recipes For People Who Love To Eat* at booksellers online and offline, or at *The Clothes Make The Girl* (www.theclothesmakethegirl.com/store).

SOME OF THE RECIPES YOU'LL FIND INSIDE

Chocolate Chili
(winner of the Paleo Magazine Award for Best Savory Recipe)

Pad Thai

The Best Chicken You Will Ever Eat

Sunshine Sauce

Ranch Dressing

Meatza Pie

Scotch Eggs

Rogan Josh

Shepherd's Pie

Bora Bora Fireballs

Coconut-Almond Green Beans

Cumin-Roasted Carrots

Cocoa-Toasted Cauliflower

Jicama Home Fries

Velvety Butternut Squash

Peach Almond Crisp
(winner of the Paleo Magazine Award for Best Treat Recipe)

PEOPLE ARE TALKING ABOUT WELL FED (MAYBE EVEN WITH THEIR MOUTHS FULL!)

"I am a bad cook. However, I used your recipe for the Creamy Spice Market Kale and it tasted like something that someone else made. That is one of the highest compliments that I can write. GREAT flavor!"

"Not only my best paleo cookbook, this is my best cookbook period!"

"I ended up reading the whole thing, cover to cover. It is JUST. THAT. GOOD."

"If the pictures, beautiful design, and wonderfully warm and witty voice don't capture you, the endless amount of recipe inspiration the author provides will."

"It's one thing to write a cookbook for foodies. It's another thing to write a cookbook that can appeal to both experienced cooks AND novices. I highly recommend this cookbook. It's a life changer."

INDEX

INDEX

J

K

L

M

N

O

P

R

S